PERSEVERANCE
Life Lessons on Leadership and Teamwork

by Marc Trestman
with Ross Bernstein

PERSEVERANCE
Life Lessons on Leadership and Teamwork

by Marc Trestman
with Ross Bernstein

Published by Bernstein Books, L.L.C.
Eagan, MN 55122
www.bernsteinbooks.com

ISBN: 0-9787809-3-0

Photos courtesy of: the Trestman family, University of Minnesota, University of Miami, Minnesota Vikings, Cleveland Browns, Detroit Lions, Tampa Bay Buccaneers, San Francisco 49ers, Oakland Raiders, Arizona Cardinals, North Carolina State University, Montreal Alouettes and Joe Theismann.
(Cover photo courtesy of Reuters.)

*Proceeds from the sale of this book
will benefit the Marc & Cindy Trestman Foundation.
Thank you for your support!

WWW.COACHMARCTRESTMAN.COM

For Cindy, Sarahanne & Chloe

THE MARC & CINDY TRESTMAN FOUNDATION

I am humbled and honored to announce that proceeds from the sale of this book will benefit the Marc and Cindy Trestman Foundation, which will assist the National Alzheimer's Research Foundation. My wife's mother, Julie, died from this insidious disease five years ago and we are trying to do our part in order to help find a cure. It is a cause that we both wholeheartedly believe in. If you would like to learn more about the Foundation or if you would like to make a donation to our newly created non-profit entity, please visit www.marcandcindytrestmanfoundation.com for further details. Thank you for your support, we both really appreciate it.

— *Marc & Cindy Trestman* —

For information or to make a donation, please visit:

www.marcandcindytrestmanfoundation.com

TABLE OF CONTENTS

I first met Marc when I was a still a pimply-faced teenager one summer back in the mid '80s. I was an aspiring gun-slinger, hoping to learn the ropes from the QB guru himself at his quarterback camp in Minneapolis. I remember my two big brothers razzing me about going and about wanting to be a "prima donna" quarterback. They reminded me about how cruel genetics could be, and that since they were both slugs, I too would soon be slug-like as well — when my body "filled out." They knew that I would eventually wind up on the offensive line, with all of the other slugs. That wasn't going to deter me though because in my eyes, I was a quarterback.

In fact, in my backyard growing up, I WAS Vikings quarterback Fran Tarkenton. I absolutely worshipped that guy. I am not sure if I ever took

Yours truly, looking rather "slug-like…"

off his No. 10 jersey long enough for mom to actually wash it. I wore that ratty thing so much it actually turned from purple to brown. You see, like Marc, I too grew up loving the Vikings. They were the bond that connected us to our fathers and still bring us much joy even to this day, despite their 50 years of gridiron futility.

Anyway, I went on to play in high school and even earned all-conference honors as a guard/slug for the mighty Fairmont Cardinals. After coming to terms with the fact that I wasn't good enough to play in college, however, I instead focused on turning my passion for sports into the next best thing — a career writing about them. Proudly, I have since written nearly 50 sports books and am truly having a ball, meeting and writing about many of the athletes and coaches who I looked up to as a kid.

One of my favorite projects was a coffee table book I wrote a few years back entitled "Legends and Legacies," which chronicled Minnesota's greatest coaches. It was while I was working on this book where Marc and I would later reconnect. He was serving as the offensive coordinator of the Oakland Raiders at the time when I called him up out of the blue. It was during training camp and he was extremely busy, yet he took an hour out of his day to speak with me over the phone to help me out. I really appreciated that. As you might imagine, I meet a lot of jerks in my line of work, but I could tell right away that he was a really good guy.

A few years went by and I got a call one day from Marc. He told me that he was living in Raleigh, North Carolina, and that he had just been fired as the offensive coordinator of the North Carolina State Wolfpack. He explained to me that he had a couple of years of "paid vacation" left on his contract and that he was in the process of "rediscovering himself." He had recently gotten into doing some motivational speaking and wanted to know if I might be interested in working with him on writing a book.

I thought about it for a few seconds and simply replied, "Absolutely." I didn't even have to think about it, I just knew. You see, I get asked to write about a dozen celebrity athlete biographies every year, and am luckily in a position where I can pick and choose the ones which particularly interest me. This one was a no-brainer; I was "all in." I knew Marc's story and I knew what an incredible person he is. I was extremely flattered that he would confide in me and was really excited to be able to help tell his amazing story. And so, from those humble beginnings, so began what would ultimately turn into a two year odyssey of what I like to refer to as "finding Marc."

When I told my dad that I was writing a book about Marc Trestman, he said very matter of factly, "Oh, Jerry's son... the coach. Sure, we know the Trestmans, great people. Jerry was the musician who played at your Aunt Cookie and Uncle Harold's wedding back in 1953." It is funny to think about how life comes full circle sometimes. Marc is a big believer in karma, and something was telling me at that moment that I had made the right choice and that this was going to be one hell of an adventure.

Marc and I immediately jumped in and got started. He told me that he had already written down a few notes and wanted to know if I could take a look at them. I said great, e-mail them over to me and I would go through it right away. Needless to say, I was expecting to get a two to three page outline. What I got instead, however, was my first clue as to what kind of person Marc Trestman is. Let's just say the guy is thorough. Real thorough. So thorough, in fact, that it took me nearly two weeks to get through his "few notes."

Incredibly, that ginormous document, what I now commonly refer to as his "Jerry McGuire Memo," was only the beginning. There would be many, many more "ideas," "thoughts," and "dissertations" to come. Reading about his life story was riveting though and I found myself not being able to put it all down. The adventure he has lived around the game of football has been nothing short of remarkable.

I was fascinated to learn that so far there have been eight stops in the NFL, two in the NCAA and one in the CFL. I had no idea that he had been an offensive coordinator with four NFL teams and that he had led each of those teams to the playoffs in just his first season behind the bench. The fact that his oldest daughter had lived in eight cities by the time she was 13 spoke volumes to me about this man's relentless determination and perseverance. I wanted to learn more.

The problem was that amidst the sea of information he had sent me, I eventually came to the conclusion that there were in reality two books there, not one. So, I told him that I was interested in the human story. The one about his life lessons dealing with leadership, motivation and team building, as it applies to business. The other one, about coaching and the dynamics of what it takes to become a world class quarterback, was going to have to be for someone else. We agreed.

With that, I shoved all of the information that he had sent me aside and started fresh, from scratch. I began recording our conversations over the telephone and after 30+ hours of tape, I came up for air. I told him that I needed a while to disseminate it all before reconvening again to try to make sense of it. In the meantime, we both went our own separate ways — Marc to Canada, to coach the Montreal Alouettes; and me to finish some other books that were on various deadlines. We huddled back up several months later and finally, after two long years, were able to bang out a finished product that we are both really proud of.

Marc has seen the best and worst of times as it relates to winning and losing in this game. He has spent the last three decades living and breathing the game of football alongside countless Hall of Fame players and coaches. What he has learned and observed along the way is the basis for what readers will take away from this book. It is a travelogue of experiences that will hopefully capture your heart and fill you with raw emotion. In it, Marc passionately shows how to turn everyday negative experiences into positive ones by using football themes and principles which transfer to success in everyday personal and business life.

By the time it was all said and done we had created more than a new book, we had created a wonderful new friendship. All of the meetings, phone calls, e-mails and texts — it was all a part of the process that helped to bring us together, both figuratively and literally. There were times when I felt like Marc's shrink, listening to every intimate detail of his life story. Sometimes I laughed, other times I cried. It was powerful stuff and it really had a profound effect on my own perspective on life.

To think about what he has been through over the years, yet the way he keeps coming back time and again, more determined than ever — it was so inspiring to me. And it wasn't just about his amazing perseverance or persistence either, it was about how he has led his life with such class. He has so much respect for others and for the game of football. Interviewing the other players and coaches for the book just reinforced it too, because they all spoke so highly of him. I admire the guy more than he will ever know, I really do.

As a person, Marc is so thoughtful, so brilliant and so genuine. He is an amazing listener. He is also a wonderful husband and father, always putting his family first, regardless of the situation. He is an unbelievable motivational speaker too, with so much passion and courage. I have seen him in action a couple of times and he is really dynamic. As a coach, his work ethic is simply second to none. In addition, he is and always has been a student of the game, constantly trying to better himself by whatever means necessary.

Case in point: I called him one day and he was about to have coffee with former Pittsburgh Steelers Head Coach Bill Cowher. They both live in Raleigh, he had called him because he wanted to know if Bill, who led the Steelers to the Super Bowl in 2006, could give him any advice about how to follow up a good season. You see, Marc had just led his Alouettes to the Grey Cup Finals and he was looking for new ways to motivate his players to not only get back to the title game, but to win it. It must have been pretty good advice, because sure enough, Marc led the Als to the Grey Cup championship that next season.

That's Marc, always learning... always trying to stay one step ahead of the other guys. Those are the kinds of things that have made him such a winner, both on and off the field. He is an amazing person and I am extremely proud to be able to say that not only am I his co-author, I am also his friend. As you will read, this guy truly is the definition of perseverance. Enjoy!

PERSEVERANCE

perse-ver-ance [pur-suh-veer-uhns]

-noun-

Definition: steady persistence in a course of action, a purpose, a state, etc., especially in spite of difficulties, obstacles, or discouragement.

INTRODUCTION
By Marc Trestman

During the course of a football game, halftime is an opportunity to briefly "re-assess" your game plan. Have we seen what we expected or planned to see? If so, we stick with the plan with maybe a few minor adjustments that can be simply communicated and understood. But, with many game plans, things happen in the first half where changes are necessary because things don't always go as planned. Sometimes, you can make an adjustment that can have a profound effect on the game's result.

Welcome to my own personal "halftime." In 2006, at 51 years young, I was out of work after being fired with two years remaining on a four year contract as the offensive coordinator at North Carolina State University, in Raleigh, N.C. After overcoming considerable anger and a lack of self-confidence, I began to see this extremely disappointing and professionally devastating time in my life as my greatest opportunity.

Football became my obvious metaphor as it does for many, and I began to equate this as being "halftime" in my life. As I reflected on my professional life I realized how much time I had spent trying to make first downs and score touchdowns. My focus had now changed into trying to be more about people and serving others. In my next job, my primary focus was going to be about trying to find the hidden value in people. I was going to be a "facilitator" for their personal and professional growth, and get them to see that when you decide to become part of a team that everyone involved (and I mean "everyone") has an unconscious and very human desire to be a part of something bigger than themselves. They say a lot of us begin to feel this way as we pass into our 50's. As mortality becomes more of an issue, perspective on life changes and a person's focus can begin to change dramatically. It certainly had with me.

With this in mind I decided one of the things I wanted to do was write a book where I could share what I have termed "LIFE LESSONS" from almost 30 years of playing and coaching what I passionately believe is the greatest game ever created. Even as I write this, I am concerned that this book will be perceived as more self promotion than a sincere attempt to serve others, but that is a risk I am certainly willing to take if one interested reader can collect a nugget to improve the quality of his or her life.

So, I have begun to make some "half-time" adjustments. As my relatively new friend and mentor Gary Stevenson said, "How many guys get two years 'paid' to figure out what they want to do with the rest of their life?" One thing for sure, I was tired of worrying about where everybody was in their career and how much "they" had accomplished. I was also going to stop worrying about my own success (and all that means) and start serving others. And as I began to serve people, I was going to really try to get to know them. When I asked them how they were doing, I was really going to mean it and I would be "really" mindful of what they had to say.

Over the last 30 years I have worked for 17 different head coaches in 10 different cities, lived in 11 different houses and moved my now two teenage daughters countless times in and out of numerous schools. My wife Cindy has been stressed to the "max" during these times and in most cases executing the moves across the country by herself. Cindy has embraced each move as an opportunity to make our house a home within weeks of our arrival and give our girls every opportunity to get acclimated socially and educationally into a new environment. It is not easy to find new doctors, new schools, and new friends in very short periods of time, but somehow she has done it and I am forever reminded by her actions and amazed at her strength and loyalty.

This book was written because I simply feel compelled to share these lessons I have learned through a career that has taken me on a journey which has allowed me to grow both professionally and spiritually in ways I never imagined. It is an opportunity to also thank the many coaches, players, and others who have shaped my character and allowed me to follow a totally unexpected path. It is a path that I feel very fortunate and honored to continue to be a part of.

Aside from that, I love the challenge of this game that in many ways is so complex and in other ways yet so simple. When I am coaching I really don't think about winning or losing games, I just want to do everything I can to help my players be the best that they can be. I know when I stay focused, good things will undoubtedly happen.

Football is without question the greatest game ever created. I love it, I really do. I never for a minute ever thought of coaching as a possible profession early in my life and for the most part that was because I simply wasn't paying attention. Without me knowing it as a young boy, it was my destiny and it remains my true passion to this day.

On a metaphysical level, I believe we are drawn to football because it is a microcosm of what we would like our world to be, working together for the common good. Football brings young people from different ethnic, social and economic backgrounds together to achieve a common goal like no other game. In order to achieve success though, the players and coaches as well as everyone in the organization must unselfishly relinquish their personal needs for the betterment of the team. They must ultimately learn to put the team ahead of themselves. When that happens, incredible things can occur — things many would have never imagined possible. I have seen this phenomenon many times over in my career, and it never ceases to amaze and inspire me.

This game has allowed me to have enjoyed a lot of relative success over the past three decades, but I have also had to overcome a lot of adversity. As such, this book is an opportunity to show my appreciation to those people who I have crossed paths with and who have helped me along the way. I have learned so many life lessons on this amazing journey, both on and off the field, and I feel very privileged to be able to now share them with others.

I am coming out of the tunnel for the second half of my professional life and I am fired up! I have gotten off to what coaches call a "fast start" as a first time head coach for the Montreal Alouettes of the Canadian Football League. Like many others, a head coaching position had eluded me for many reasons for many years, but now I am living a bittersweet opportunity north of the border. It's professional football, but very different from the NFL. In Canada the field is wider and longer; they play with 12 players (versus 11) per side; and there are only three downs (versus four). And if that weren't enough, the primary language in Montreal is French!

After being an assistant coach and offensive coordinator for so many years, however, this was the challenge I was looking for. How I got this job will be discussed later, but the incredible part of the story is Alouettes owner Bob Wetenhall, who has allowed me to return to Raleigh for the six months of the off-season to be with Cindy and the girls. As a result, the girls have been able to continue to attend the same high school in Raleigh as I had hoped and promised them. Also, he has provided me with the resources to bring my family back and forth to Montreal during the course of the season so we can remain a family during that time. This is just amazing.

Thirty months ago I was angry and disillusioned, but today I am excited for my third season in Montreal after coaching the Alouettes to the Grey Cup (the CFL's Super Bowl equivalent) and being named as the Coach of the Year by the CFL's Player's Association. What an honor.

Whether you are at the beginning, end, or at halftime like me — and you love the game of football — there is something here for you. I feel that I am in a place that a lot of you can relate to right now. You love what you are doing and are happy and comfortable, but you are not exactly where you planned to be. I have not accomplished professionally what Bill Cowher or Tony Dungy have in their careers. These Super Bowl champion coaches are great guys and contemporaries of mine, and have all since retired. Yes, I have many goals left to achieve.

Heck, I have more energy and passion now than I did 20 years ago. And I know why, because I am not in the football business. I am in the "people business." When I get up in the morning my focus is NOT on me, but rather on teaching and serving those around me. And boy does that feel good! I really feel as though I am just getting started, and is there any rule out there that says this cannot be the case?

As a coach in the NFL, CFL and NCAA, I have made my fair share of mistakes over the years. I am proud to say, however, that I have never made a single decision that was not in the best interests of my team, or of the players who I have coached. I am proud to say that I am as passionate about the game of football today as I was when I was eight years old. I still love to script and call plays. I still love to go to practice. I still love to go to meetings to set up game plans. I still love to win.

I think that there are some universal laws that are out of our control. It goes along with our hard work and our passion, but I really believe that we are drawn to certain things in life. For me, this is it. I was born to coach. I would have loved to have made it as a player, believe me, but that just wasn't in the cards. I always say though that if my body could have done what my mind saw, I would have played for 15 years in the league and been a perennial Pro Bowler. But I digress.

In the game of football, every season becomes a journey through unknown territory, where you expect the unexpected on a daily basis. It is a marathon through uncharted territory of certain adversity and success. I have been hired in some miraculous ways and fired in ways that can best be described as "emotionally turbulent." The adventure has been most unique though and through this book I hope I can relate some important concepts that I have learned through working for and with some of the best minds and players to ever coach and play the game.

All in all, this book has given me an unbelievable opportunity to give back to the game which has given me so much. It has also given me an opportunity to leave a legacy, both professionally for my peers as well as personally for my children. Hopefully my message of sacrifice, persistence and perseverance will resonate with others who, like myself, have a passion and love for what they do in life. Thank you for the opportunity to let me into your mind and into your heart. Now let's get started with the "second half!"

Bud Grant and I having lunch in 2009...

ACKNOWLEDGEMENTS

I would like to acknowledge several people who have truly made a difference in my life. First and foremost, I would like to thank my wife Cindy, who has been there by my side throughout this journey and has given me the strength to continue to pursue my dream of being the best in the world at what I do. We have lived in Cleveland, Minneapolis, Boca Raton, San Francisco, Detroit, Phoenix, Oakland, Miami, Raleigh, and even part time now in Montreal. Amazing. To my two beautiful daughters, Sarahanne and Chloe, who have sacrificed so much. I am so proud of them. And to my mom and dad who showed me the importance of family and hard work, which burns deep within me to this day. Thank you all from the bottom of my heart.

Professionally, I would like to thank several coaches who I greatly admire and whom I have learned so much from over the years. To Howard Schnellenberger, who saw something in me and took a chance on me back when I was a law school student at the University of Miami. To my mentor and hero, Bud Grant, who watched me play high school football in suburban Minneapolis against his son Mike, and 10 years later hired me onto his Vikings staff without so much as even a job interview. Bud has taught me so much, and most of it goes far beyond the X's and O's.

To Jerry Burns, who allowed me to flourish as a very young professional coach. To Bobby Ross, for showing me the importance of great preparation and detail, and that you can be a kind and generous person along with being a successful head coach. To Marty Schottenheimer, whose success has always been based on sound fundamentals as well as on processing information from the people who surrounded him.

To Jimmy Johnson, who, in addition to giving me the freedom to coach, took the time to convince me not to go to the USFL, but rather to stay and wait for my NFL opportunity. His loyalty to his coaches has been something I have always admired from a distance. To my friend George Seifert, who rescued me from a career in the bond business and gave me my dream job, entrusting me with the keys to the best offense in football.

To Jon Gruden, who kept his promise of hiring me when I was out of work in 2001, and to Bill Callahan, who had the faith and confidence to hire me as his offensive coordinator with the Raiders in 2002. I also want to thank Mr. Al Davis for providing me the opportunity to showcase my talents and to be a part of something that was bigger than myself. To Chuck Amato, who brought me to Raleigh to raise my daughters and coach some ball. It didn't work out the way we had hoped, but I will always be grateful. To Sean Payton, thanks for thinking of me and letting me be a part of your team in New Orleans, it means a lot. To Jim Popp, who brought me to Montreal and finally gave me the chance to coach my own team. Thank you so much.

To all of the players who I have had the privilege of coaching over the years, thanks for listening and thanks for caring. Each one of you has taught me more than I could ever give back in return. Specifically, to Bernie Kosar, whose great play as a red shirt freshman catapulted my career to the NFL and whose friendship has been lifelong. Bernie is the truest example of a leader and "field general" I have ever been around. To Vinny Testaverde, who I knew would be destined for greatness because of his hard working and humble approach to the game. I am so proud of not only what he accomplished on the field, but for the class in how he handled himself. I am only sorry we have not stayed closer over the years.

To Jerry Rice, the greatest of them all, my thanks for never missing a day of practice and for your amazing work ethic. To Steve Young, who showed me that greatness can be wrapped in genuine class and humility. You are a brilliant man, and as courageous as I have ever been around. Thank you for always being there for me. To Brent Jones, who has become a treasured friend long after our time together in San Francisco. To Joe Theismann, who has been an incredible friend and advisor to me for over 30 years. Our friendship goes way beyond football and our passionate discussions about the game have been so enlightening for as long as I can remember.

To Scott Mitchell, a brilliant man, and a quarterback who never got the credit for his work ethic, passion for the game, and pinpoint passing. He is coaching now at his old high school in Salt Lake City and all I can say is that those kids at Springville High are very lucky. Scott will teach them in ways they never thought possible. To Rich Gannon, when, for one season, no quarterback and his coach could have been in more perfect harmony. I was so proud of what you accomplished as the NFL's MVP. Nobody knows how hard you worked or how much you demanded of yourself except me and your wonderful wife, Shelly. To Tony Dungy, my old college teammate, who showed me that you can indeed win a Super Bowl and still remain the same humble and thoughtful person you always were.

To Anthony Calvillo, who many of you do not know. You are truly one of the greatest quarterbacks to ever play the game of football. You are the quarterback of the CFL's Montreal Alouettes, the 2009 Grey Cup champions. You are a humble and incredibly hard working leader. You transcend a locker room and work unselfishly daily for the betterment of your team. It has been a privilege to coach you over the last two years, where you have been the league's MVP. You would be the first to tell us that the reason for your success is because of the hard work and endeavors of others. You are truly a champion.

In addition, I also want to thank the tremendous group of assistant coaches and players on the 2009 Alouettes football team who worked together to become a part of something that was bigger than themselves. Further, I want to acknowledge the hard work of Patrick Johnson, an Elon University law student who helped me a great deal during the editorial process; and Noah Sidel, who helped me acquire many of the photos in the book. I couldn't have done it without you guys.

Last, but certainly not least, to Ross Bernstein, my author and sensei — thank you for your guidance and for your patience. I am so grateful to you for your encouragement in putting this book together. Your passion inspires me. You told me that there was a great book inside my head nearly two years ago and to be honest, I wasn't sure if I believed you. Thank you for proving me wrong. I value your opinions and am proud to call you my friend. I am looking forward to seeing you out on the motivational speaking circuit.

I first met Marc when I was with the Vikings back in the early '90s. I have a lot of respect for him, he is a great guy and a great coach. He went above and beyond in terms of helping me with my development and I will always be grateful for that. He used to make me come up to his office where he would sit me down and work with me. He really cared about me not only as a player, but as a person, and I appreciated that so much. I was just a young guy at that point and he really helped me become a more well rounded player.

He would show me film and ask me questions and just teach me about how to manage a game. You talk about attention to detail, he was on top of everything. He was concerned about my development; about what I said to the media; how I behaved on the field; what my demeanor was like; and everything else that he felt it took to become a great professional quarterback. He had a huge impact on my career.

Then, to be able to work with him again in Oakland, 10 years later, was really a treat. He had learned so much by then by being around so many great quarterbacks, and had so much credibility. It was amazing. Our relationship sort of came full circle. I remember he would always sit down with me and talk to me about the game plan. He would listen to me and ask me a lot of questions that would in turn give me more confidence. He would ask me what I liked, what I didn't like, what I felt comfortable with, and what we should put in or take out. He would include me in the process and design a plan that would be built around my strengths.

Marc wasn't afraid to try new things and he wouldn't get his feelings hurt either if you didn't like a certain situation that he drew up for you. Very few play callers were like that. I mean I have had coordinators literally talk me into things, because it was all about them. Not Marc, he has no ego. He is so unselfish, a team guy, first and foremost. It was all about the players to him, and that was one of the secrets to his success in my opinion.

The situation we went through up in Oakland was so tough too. I have always said that it wasn't a hard place to play, it was an impossible place to play. Marc lived it. He dealt with so much adversity yet was able to overcome it. He was one of the big reasons why we made it to the Super Bowl in 2002, without a doubt. I give him a lot of credit, he worked some ungodly hours and really put in the time to go the extra mile. I had a great season, personally, and Marc was a huge reason for that.

Marc is such a bright guy and is extremely intelligent when it comes to understanding the game of football. He understands offenses like nobody I have ever seen. The way he can break things down and formulate game plans is amazing. He is one of the premier signal callers in the business and is great at adjusting on the fly too. He is just the kind of person who is always learning. He doesn't miss many opportunities to learn from situations.

Look at what he did up in Montreal. He went up there and learned a different game with different rules and in six months took the team to the Grey Cup Finals. That is amazing to me. And, in typical Marc fashion he did it very quietly. Of course their quarterback had one of his best seasons ever too. That is where everything starts and stops with Marc, the quarterback. He knows that once that guy is playing well and implementing his system, then everything else will fall into place. He has always been successful in terms of offensive productivity and with the development of his quarterbacks. In fact, I would say that he was the best in the business at

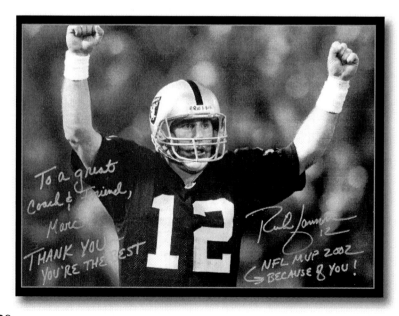

doing that.

I am just so happy and excited for him that he finally got to be a head coach and do things the way he always wanted to. Everywhere he has always been he has always had to work with an owner, a general manager, a head coach, and deal with all of the politics. I am thrilled that he is now able to put more of his own thumbprint on a football team. I am really proud of him. Then to see the way he led that team to the Grey Cup championship in just his second season behind the bench, truly incredible. There is no doubt in my mind that when his opportunity comes in the NFL, he is going to make the most of it and prove a lot of people wrong. I will be there too, rooting for him.

FOREWORD
By Bernie Kosar

I initially met Marc when I was a true freshman at the University of Miami and he was a senior in law school there, serving as a volunteer assistant coach. We hit it off immediately. I learned so much from him, he was the first great coach I ever had. I used to spend an hour a day with him in practice, just listening to him as he taught me about why and where all 22 players were on the football field at any one given time. It was amazing.

We later reconnected in Cleveland, where he came in as our quarterbacks coach and was later promoted to be our offensive coordinator. Those were great times. We had some really good teams in those days and Marc was leading the charge. When he joined our coaching staff it was like a dream come true for me. I was totally spoiled having him work with me. Having him watch over my every move was a godsend. It was like he was out there with me on every play.

I think that Marc's best quality was his ability to get the most out of guys, regardless of their talent. I think back to when our Browns went to the AFC Championship Game in 1989, we used to laugh that we were the "smoke and mirrors" offense. No disrespect to any of my teammates, but we did a lot that year with far less talent than in some other years.

Even later in his career, when he was with Oakland, look what Marc did with Rich Gannon and Jerry Rice. Those guys were pushing 40 and on the downsides of their careers when he came in and they wound up setting all sorts of offensive records en route to going to the Super Bowl. Guys that age don't typically dominate the way they did, and a lot of the credit for that has to go to Marc, who was able to design specific plays around their strengths.

Marc has such a love and a passion for football. He has an intense, intense loyalty to his teams too. He sees football like a chess match. He is so smart and such an intellectual guy. He has an open mind and is really a student of the game, always willing to learn and try new things out on the field. He would study tendencies, protections and coverages, while always trying to figure out new ways to stretch and attack defenses. The guy was an offensive mastermind. His attention to detail and his work ethic was second to none too. He would spend hours and hours watching and breaking down video. He was just always prepared and always ready to go.

Another thing that sets Marc apart from most coaches is his ability to adjust and adapt. Case in point: you could get a monkey to tell you what to do on Monday, after the game is over and he has watched the game film 50 times. It takes a true tactician, however, to be able to tell you at halftime about how to change up your play calling and make adjustments. Marc was the best in the business at doing that. He saved me so many times on stuff like that. I had so much faith in him. I absolutely trusted him because I respected his football intelligence.

Marc trusted me too, and as a result he would let me do my own thing out there. As a quarterback, I really appreciated that. He would make me study so hard and he would prepare me so well, that on game day he had all the confidence in the world in me to do my job. Marc made the game

slower for me. He showed me how to read defenses and how to key in on the safeties, so that I could read the field. He taught me how to be better, which in turn made the team better. He gave me the tools to take my game to the next level. That was his true gift.

Marc is such a humble guy, he really is. You know, most coaches go to the Senior Bowl every year down in Mobile, Alabama, to fraternize and make friends, so that they can get hired for jobs. Marc is not that type of guy. That is not is scene. He isn't one to go around "Eddie Haskelling," as I like to say — to kiss butt and suck up in order to get something in return. He is great with people, but he is not big on politics. That may have cost him over his career, because he didn't want to play that game, but I respect the hell out of him for how he has chosen to go about his business.

To see him go up to Canada to finally get his shot at being a head coach is the ultimate testament of his perseverance to me. To watch him take that team, a non-playoff team, and lead them to the Grey Cup Finals in just his first season, that was amazing. Then, to see him win it all the very next season, that is almost unfathomable to me. I mean the guy didn't even know the rules of the game before heading up there. That is the kind of person he is though, so smart, such a competitor, so passionate and always up for a challenge. He just hates to lose and seemingly refuses to fail. His God-given intellect has allowed him to try things that most coaches would never do. He has so much confidence in himself, yet he is so humble. It is an incredible combination.

I am so proud to call Marc my friend, I think the world of him. He is like a big brother to me. I am even the godfather to his oldest daughter, Sarahanne, which means a great deal to me too. I just have a ton of respect for him as a coach and as a person. He is one of the smartest, nicest guys I have ever known. Truly.

I just hope so badly that somebody takes a chance on Marc down the road as a head coach in the NFL. It is totally unfair that he hasn't gotten his shot because the guy absolutely deserves it. He has paid his dues and come so close. He has had so much success everywhere he has been, yet he keeps getting the short end of the stick. Whatever team finally does pull the trigger and hires him though, they are not going to be disappointed. They are going to get a tremendous leader and winner. I can't wait.

FOREWORD
By Joe Theismann

Marc Trestman is an incredible person. I don't know if there is a nicer guy out there than Trest. He might just be the most sincere individual in the world. He has tremendous dedication. He is a great teacher. He is so loyal. He is a great communicator. As a coach he is so bright. I mean in football circles he has a reputation as an offensive genius.

Aside from all of that though, I think the secret to Marc's success is perseverance. He is just that type of a person. He never quits. He has always believed he could do it, regardless of the situation. No matter how the deck was stacked against him, he has always dug in and gotten through it. I really respect that about him. That takes a very special person, to be able to have gone through some of the things that he has gone through, and not get deflated. Football is such a tough game. I mean everybody is lining up to beat you up, both on and off the field. He has taken his share of lumps over the years, but he keeps coming back stronger and stronger. I really admire him for that.

All you need to do is look at his body of work to see how successful a coach he is. Look at what he did with guys like Steve Young and Jerry Rice when he was the offensive coordinator in San Francisco. Look at what he did with Rich Gannon when he was the coordinator with Oakland. Look at what he did with Jake Plummer in Arizona when he was the coordinator in Arizona. It is amazing to think about what he was able to do coming into those situations.

If Marc wants to be a head coach in the National Football League someday, there is no doubt in my mind that it will happen. For whatever the reason, there just hasn't been an owner who has been infatuated with him as of yet, but give it time. Our business is so finicky. It has become a league of "It's not what you know, but who you know" in terms of getting a head coaching position. He has certainly proven himself though. Hell, I would put his credentials up against any coach in the NFL.

I am just so tickled that he finally got the opportunity to become a head coach up in Montreal. It is really the only thing that was missing on his resumé. I remember when he called me when he was putting his staff together up there. Just listening to him, the excitement, it was as if he had been preparing for that moment all his life. There is no doubt in my mind that he is going to continue to have tremendous success up there.

Do you want to know what kind of person Marc Trestman is? Bill Walsh once asked Marc to write a book with him. Bill Walsh! He was one of the greatest coaches in the history of professional football. That speaks volumes about what kind of a coach Marc is. That is all you need to know. Sometimes all you need to look at is who people have been associated with. It tells you about their character; about the quality of the person; and the class of the individual.

Another word need not be said about this man's ability to contribute to society in every way — as a person, as a father, as a husband, as a football coach, and as a builder of men. I think of Marc and I think of class. He is one of my very best friends. I love the guy, I really do. I just couldn't be prouder of what he has accomplished, both on and off the field.

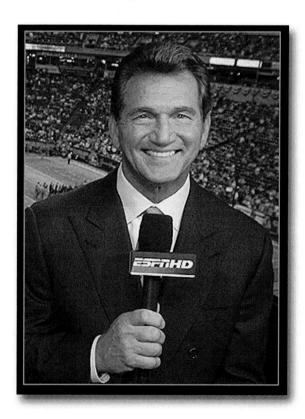

MARC TRESTMAN'S BODY OF WORK

Head Coach, Montreal Alouettes (2007-Present)

Consultant, New Orleans Saints (2007)

Offensive Coordinator/QB Coach, N.C. State University (2005-06)

Assistant Head Coach/QB Coach, Miami Dolphins (2004)

Offensive Coordinator/QB Coach, Oakland Raiders (2002-03)

Senior Assistant/QB Coach, Oakland Raiders (2001)

Offensive Coordinator/QB Coach, Arizona Cardinals (1998-2000)

QB Coach, Detroit Lions (1997)

Offensive Coordinator/QB Coach, San Francisco 49ers (1995-96)

QB Coach, Minnesota Vikings (1990-91)

Offensive Coordinator/QB Coach, Cleveland Browns (1989)

QB Coach, Cleveland Browns (1988)

QB Coach, Tampa Bay Buccaneers (1987)

Running Backs Coach, Minnesota Vikings (1985-86)

QB Coach, University of Miami, Florida (1983-84)

Volunteer Assistant Coach, University of Miami, Florida (1981-82)

CH. 1) LEARNING THE VALUES OF HARD WORK FROM AN EARLY AGE WHILE DISCOVERING MY PASSION

The best leaders are those who care about those they lead. They lead by example, work hard, and are respectful because they recognize they are in "the people business." Leaders recognize that the people business is about making those they lead content both in work and life. Without family, close relationships, and people you enjoy being around, all the work in the world just isn't worth it. Leaders realize this and work to create understanding environments in which subordinates feel accountable to the outcomes of what they are working on. Respected leaders spawn increased productivity from those around them because followers feel respected and thus a mutual obligation to perform is achieved.

My name is Marc Marlyn Trestman and this is my story. I was born in Minneapolis, Minn., on January 15, 1956, to the parents of Jerry and Sharon Trestman. I have one sister, Cari, who is a year younger than I am, and we grew up in a tiny duplex near Cedar Lake in Minneapolis. When I was about five years old we moved to a very modest home in St. Louis Park, a Twin Cities suburb. Having a yard was amazing, I practically lived out there. As a kid all I can remember doing was playing sports; that was my life. I would go to school, come home and play ball. It didn't matter what the season was, I was outside playing with my buddies. I liked baseball and basketball, but I loved football — that was my passion. It was a great childhood.

I was brought up in an environment where I was able to learn the values of hard work in a pretty unique way. My father owned a bar/restaurant called Danny's, which was on the corner of 14th and Chicago, on the edge of downtown Minneapolis, just a few blocks from where the Metrodome (home of the Vikings) stands today. He worked six days a week, leaving early in the morning and coming home late at night — what we commonly refer to today as "coach's hours."

My father was a very good manager and was extremely disciplined. He was caring and loyal too, as evidenced by the fact that he had several waitresses and other employees who worked for him for more than 25 years. Years later as a head coach, I realized that my dad wasn't just in the food and beverage business, he was in the "people business." I learned early on that when you treat people with respect and dignity, they repay you with hard work. Dad definitely had it figured out, and on a personal side he enjoyed this part of his job as well. He never had a lot of money, but he always found a way to help his employees who needed a couple of extra bucks.

As a kid, I loved hanging out with him, but it wasn't always easy. I had to either wait until the weekends, or set my alarm to wake up at 2 a.m. when he got home from the restaurant. We would have peanut butter and butter on toast together down in the kitchen, where we would talk about sports and life.

Eventually I begged him to let me work at the restaurant. Reluctantly, he agreed, but I knew he wanted to spend time with me as well. I would wash dishes, run errands and do whatever I could to help out. I certainly didn't get any preferential treatment for being the boss' kid either. I just did what I was told and soaked it all in. I learned a lot just watching and listening, seeing what it took to run a business from the ground up.

That time with him was invaluable. I learned so many life lessons from the respectful way he treated customers and employees. It took me many years to truly appreciate all of that wisdom, but I look back on those days fondly. I am certain that the foundation of my blue collar work ethic was fostered during that time. My friends delivered newspapers and ran lemonade stands; I worked in a bar with my dad.

My dad really worked hard and did whatever he could to provide for our family. He was a modest man, and even though he never went to college, he was very, very smart. He was actually a musician by trade and decided to get into the restaurant business after he had settled down and had kids, ultimately wanting to get off the road.

As a musician, my dad was really good. He played the local wedding, graduation, and bar mitzvah circuit in the Minneapolis, St. Paul area. Dad was not raised in a conventional family either. In fact, his brother raised him while they were on the road traveling as musicians. He was on the road at the age of 11 and had performed in 48 states before he was 15. He grew up pretty quickly. He had to go to work; that was just the hand he was dealt. He made the most of it though and he made a very good life for my mom, my sister and himself. In addition to the restaurant, he and his brother also owned a "mom and pop" music store they started back in the 1960s. They sold instruments and did very well until they eventually sold out in 2008.

My dad worked very hard, no question, but he also made sure to spend time with his family. That was by far the most important thing in his life. I remember living for the weekends, and especially for Sundays during football season in the fall. Sunday was our day, the day he and I would watch our beloved Minnesota Vikings. Saturday nights, those were for mom, but Sunday afternoons, those were my days with dad. I have great memories of those days. Even though we didn't have a lot of discretionary income in our family, my dad made it a priority to get season tickets at old Metropolitan Stadium.

My dad always made time for the Vikings. It was his escape. It was so important to him that it was almost like work, because we planned our outings and watched the games intently. It was fun to be there, but they served a higher purpose for both of us. My dad was invested; he loved to follow the team and wanted so badly for them to win. For me, I was always watching and learning. I could never just watch and enjoy the game; I had to see what the quarterback was doing; what the receivers were doing; and how the defense was reacting accordingly. I didn't realize it at the time, but I was coaching. I guess that is just my nature; it all started back when I was a kid.

Home games were the best because we would go early and watch the pre-game warm-ups. We would sit there, in the second row along the first base dugout, and analyze each and every play. I watched everything that was going on in great detail, just soaking it all in like a sponge. I couldn't wait until the players would come running out of the tunnel and onto the field, it was the most exciting feeling for me. I just loved it.

It didn't matter how cold it was either. I can still remember not being able to feel my toes during some of those games, but I would never dare say anything for fear of having to go inside and warm up. Mom would pack one thermos with coffee and brandy for dad and another with hot chocolate for me. We would then put our legs in an insulated sleeping bag together and try to stay as warm as possible. I used to love the car ride home when dad would blast the heater and we would finally be able to unthaw our frozen toes.

Then, if the team was on the road, we would hunker down in the den and watch the games on TV. That was our "war room," complete with plenty of chips and sodas. The Vikings had some great teams back in those days too, so it was a lot of fun to watch them and to share that passion with my dad. I was so in awe of watching the team's legendary coach, Bud Grant, patrol the sidelines. It could be 20 degrees below zero, and he would be out there talking on his headset and studying his clipboard like it was 70 degrees and sunny. No gloves for the players or heaters on the sideline either. No way. He had this stoic aura about him that was just amazing.

The Vikings had some great players in those days too, guys like Mick Tingelhoff, Paul Krause, Ron Yary, Alan Page, Bill Brown, Dave Osborn, Roy Winston, Jeff Seimon, Ahmad Rashad, Joe Kapp, Bobby Bryant and Karl Kassulke, among others. All of the Vikings were my heroes, but I especially liked watching Fran Tarkenton. No. 10 was my guy. I was completely enamored with quarterbacks. The way he could scramble around to buy time and the way he could make things happen out there just amazed me.

I also liked Pittsburgh Steelers quarterback Terry Bradshaw, who I thought was really tough. Roman Gabriel, Bart Starr, Len Dawson, Roger Staubach, Joe Kapp and Archie Manning were good too, as was Joe Namath — who I especially liked because of his swagger. I will never forget the time when the New York Jets came to town. My dad took me to the game three hours early, just so I could watch "Broadway Joe" warm up.

I was so interested in things like that, even at a very young age. There was a real passion there and I really can't explain it. I mean nobody in my family was very athletic. I don't know where it came from, but it was there and luckily my father saw that and encouraged it. I am a sort of quarterback historian to this very day and can remember the smallest details about them dating all the way back to when I was eight years old. I remember what numbers they wore, their big plays and even their stats. I was really into it, even as a little kid.

In August, dad and I would take the 90-minute drive to Mankato, a small college town in the southern part of the state, to watch the team at training camp. It was a thrill to see the players up close and to meet them after practice, where you could get their autographs. We would spend the day at camp and then talk about the team's strategy for the upcoming season the whole way home. We would have it all figured out, who should play where and which guys should start. It was the glue that bonded us together. It was wonderful. From there we couldn't wait for the season to start.

Fran Tarkenton

My mom was 20 years old when I was born. She was devoted to me and my commitment and love for sports. She is also a strong and mentally tough woman who has an extremely positive outlook on life. She has tons of friends and is extremely loyal and caring. She has overcome health issues her entire life and refuses to start each day without a positive attitude. She is street smart and opinionated, and extremely loyal to her family and friends.

My mom and dad didn't go to college, but both were committed to providing me with an environment where I could succeed. My mom instilled in me the concept that you never give up, and that there is nothing wrong with dreaming big. She was also the mother in the neighborhood who, when it was 20 below zero, would go around the neighborhood to pick up all of my friends and take us to school. She is a wonderful person and I am so appreciative of everything that she did for me.

I started playing football when I was eight years old. To say I enjoyed it would be the understatement of the century. At that time, we only had 13 guys on our neighborhood team, so we used to call ourselves the "dirty dozen plus one." We didn't have enough guys to practice against each other, but we loved playing together and being outside until it got dark.

My coach was Paul Schwartz, a Vince Lombardi look-alike who played the tough guy role but had the heart of a teddy bear. He was a growler and a screamer and if we messed up he would whack us on the behinds with his shoe. His assistant was Vic Lewis. Vic was a neighborhood guy who was seriously wounded in Vietnam and ended up spending his life coaching kids in St. Louis Park.

I will never forget the day Vic encouraged Coach Schwartz to move me to quarterback, it changed my life forever. As I reflect on this time, it is clear that both men coached to positively impact our lives and reinforce the importance of hard work and the team concept from a very early age. These principles have certainly been part of my life on a daily basis for more than 40 years.

I became consumed with football. I have vivid memories of laying awake at night and drawing up plays on a note pad. I can still remember the plays I diagramed and then tried to execute with my three best friends from the neighborhood. We would play two-on-two against each other all day long in my yard. It was awesome.

I even had a playbook I made out of an old notebook that I would bring with me to refer to during huddles. If it was a short throwing route it was a "30," if it was a medium route it was a "60" and if it was a long one it was a "90." It's crazy to think that I still remember that stuff all these years later. Little did I know this manifest destiny would eventually start me on a spiritual journey I am still on today.

I liked school, but I didn't love it. I look back and realize that by working hard in school I was developing positive habits that helped me in all facets of my life. I got good grades all through high school and even college, but my passion was never academics, it was always athletics. My parents never told me to stay inside and study or anything like that, I just did it so I would have time to play sports. I knew it was important to them for me to get good grades though, so I always made it a priority. Nothing really ever came easy to me, so I had to study a lot in order to be successful. I was sort of a grinder, or a grunt, when it came to school.

Paul Krause

I was never really great in anything I did, but because I worked hard I was able to achieve success in almost everything I tried my hand in. I was focused and diligent and applied the disciplined work ethic I learned from my father towards school, sports, and whatever else I was doing. It is something that served me well back then and continues to do so to this very day.

I played football, basketball, and baseball through junior high school and into high school at St. Louis Park. I remember as a freshman, promising my dad I was going to work out as hard as I could during the summers so I would be able to earn a scholarship. My dad bought into it and got behind me. I worked exceptionally hard conditioning, lifting weights, and getting into shape. I worked at the bar on the weekends bussing tables to earn extra money and to show my dad that I was responsible. I can remember the waitresses tipping me really well, not because I was the owner's kid, but because I worked hard.

Eventually my father's love of music rubbed off on me and as a result I wound up performing in a band with four of my neighborhood pals. I

Jim Marshall

played guitar and we performed at sweet-16 parties and bar mitzvahs. It was a lot of fun. We charged $25 dollars a night, which meant five bucks a piece for each of us — pretty good money in those days. By the time high school rolled around though, I was too busy with sports and regrettably I had to give up music. I spent the next four summers working out during the day and then working periodically at Danny's in the evenings. I was on a mission. I was never the best athlete on my teams, but I was determined to outwork everybody.

During the summers I played American Legion baseball. We had a great team. In fact, we made it all the way to the state championship game during my senior year, which was a real thrill for me. Playing Legion ball was also a test of sorts for me. You see, because it was during the summer, there were no teachers or coaches from the school involved. As a result, you would occasionally see kids drinking and smoking pot. Luckily, that stuff scared me to death and I stayed as far away from it as I could.

Looking back, I led a pretty boring high school existence and didn't have much of a social life. I never dated or went with my friends to parties; I

Check out these short-shorts, Yikes!

just focused on sports. I was reclusive, probably to a fault. It was just all about sports for me. That was what I wanted more than anything. It was my purpose and it truly drove me.

I had been a quarterback in junior high school, but then switched over to play cornerback. I started as a junior in high school at cornerback, while also serving as the team's back-up quarterback. Then, as a senior, I started both ways as the quarterback as well as in the defensive backfield. I also started in basketball and baseball, but football was my favorite sport and the one I focused on the most.

My varsity coach was Bob Roy and he was a great guy. He taught me a lot about hard work and preparation as well as about being a team player. The most endearing quality about Bob was we knew he really cared about his players and that was something I took with me as a solid life lesson.

I remember being enamored with coaches from a very early age. Some were better than others, but I tried to learn something different from each of them — regardless of the sport. My favorite, of course, was Vikings

Batter up!

head coach Bud Grant, who I just worshipped. I will never forget playing against his son, Mike Grant, during a high school game. Seeing Bud up in the stands watching our game was surreal to me.

As a senior we finished the football season at 5-4, nothing special. We swept the Edina schools, which was huge, but then fell apart towards the end of the season. We were really competitive, but just couldn't come together down the stretch. I was extremely disappointed. On a personal level, I received All-State honors, but would have gladly given them back in exchange for a conference title.

I did get recruited by a handful of colleges that season, however, and even received scholarship offers from Colorado State, Montana State, North Dakota and Minnesota. In addition, I was also recruited by Harvard and Yale, who both contacted me early on in the process. I wasn't very familiar with the Ivy League at the time though, and my parents didn't understand the prestige of an Ivy League education.

I also visited Notre Dame, but they didn't offer me a scholarship. I was

Here I am playing high school football

fortunate to meet Joe Theismann while I was there though. Joe was a star quarterback for the Irish a few years earlier and was kind enough to share some of his wisdom with me one day over lunch. Little did I know at the time, it was the beginning of an incredible friendship that has now lasted more than 35 years.

Being recruited was pretty special, but the University of Minnesota had always been my top choice. I always wanted to wear the maroon and gold for the Gophers and that was what I ultimately decided to do, accept a full-ride scholarship in the spring of 1974. I wanted to stay close to home so my parents could come to my games and it was just a good fit for me. The "U" was a decent school too, so I knew I was going to be getting a good education for life after football.

Their head coach, Cal Stoll, was well respected and I had built a good relationship with his top assistant, Tom Moore, who had recruited me. Tom was one of the brightest offensive minds in the game back then and remains so to this day, as the longtime offensive coordinator with the Indianapolis Colts. I looked forward to learning as much as I possibly could from both of them; I was just thrilled to have been given such an amazing opportunity.

Signing my letter of intent with Coach Cal Stoll

CH. 2) TAKING MY GAME TO THE NEXT LEVEL AT THE UNIVERSITY OF MINNESOTA

Within any organization a person's decisions affect many and are most effective when made selflessly with the "team" taking precedent. Everybody has to recognize their role, understand what they do well, and feel important to the results. Leaders are good at making those they lead feel important and at creating an environment conducive to productive results. Different management styles spur different responses, so understanding your own style as well as others' will enhance success. Success comes in many forms but failure often stems from a lack of passion. Leaders further recognize the stress and toughness of the job can strip one's passion and therefore make time for rest and relaxation in order to clear the mind and refresh.

I was excited to be playing Division I football, it was a dream come true. I had made good on my promise to my dad by receiving a scholarship and that felt pretty good. I had been selected to play in the first High School All-Star game in the summer of '74 and played very well, which put me over the top I think. From there I worked extremely hard that summer getting into shape and preparing for my freshman year. I had tremendous confidence in my ability and believed I could come to training camp and compete for a job. I knew the odds were against me going in though. I remember meeting with Coach Stoll before the season and talking about his expectations for me. He told me it was up to me to determine my own destiny and that I would have to pay my dues.

I wasn't quite sure what he meant at the time, but soon figured it out when

I met the team's starting quarterback, Tony Dungy. Yes, the same Tony Dungy who, after going on to play professionally, would become one of the greatest NFL coaches of all time. Few people remember Tony as a college football player, but I can personally attest to the fact that he was one of the best during that era.

I moved out of my home and onto campus where I lived in a dormitory, Sanford Hall, alongside the Gopher football and hockey players. Training camp was extremely demanding, we practiced three times a day the first week with most of the practices on our stadium's artificial turf. August in Minnesota is hot, muggy, and buggy. One local columnist used to refer to Minneapolis as part of the "five county mosquito control district." The turf was sometimes 20 to 30 degrees hotter than the outside temperature and during those days we were only allowed one cup of "Gatorade" with ice cubes in it, half way through practice. In today's football that would be seen as harassment and unhealthy. Water is available today at all times during practice. Back then we would suck on every piece of ice to the bitter end. When players dehydrated, IV's were never given. Today it is a common practice.

During the evening practice, we went behind the Bierman Complex, the athletic facility that housed the football offices, and worked out for an hour. These practices were much more about surviving the swarms of mosquitoes surrounding the fields around dusk. It was crazy practicing

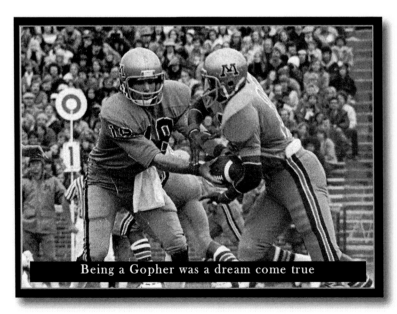

Being a Gopher was a dream come true

from morning until night and it became much more about being able to focus and having "mental toughness" than it did about football.

I remember after a Saturday scrimmage, I went home which was about 15 minutes away, sat with my dad on the front steps of our house, and told him I wanted to quit. I was broken, tired, worn out from training camp, and felt like I just wasn't good enough. Dad recognized the fatigue and what 10 days of three-a-day work-outs was all about. He wouldn't allow me to quit. This was a test, and Coach Stoll and his staff were trying to find out who had the strongest will to succeed. That was all I needed to hear, however, as I got back into my car and headed back to Sanford Hall.

The lessons I learned from those days have never been forgotten. The practices and 18 hour days took their toll on not only the players but also the coaches. But the harsh conditions on those hot August days and nights helped our entire team and staff build the backbone necessary to handle not only the adversity that is always part of a football season, but the success as well.

As I look back on these days and the guys that were on those Gopher teams, it is amazing to see how so many went on to become so successful in their business lives. The toughness, being able to work unselfishly with others, and the ability to communicate in a stressful environment are qualities necessary to succeed in any vocation. Coach Stoll certainly prepared us for our futures while getting us in shape and ready to play.

As a coach today, I can honestly say that as much as I work to prepare my players for the season and the games, I always remind them that the demands we place on them and the work they are doing now will serve them well when their playing days are over, and these principles if used properly will allow them to achieve even more when their careers are over. I truly believe that.

I also constantly assess the morale and stamina of our coaches. It is clear to me that successful businesses today who really get it, take into consideration the importance of rest, relaxation, and family involvement when it comes to employees being productive. Coaches I have worked for often demonstrated and stressed that we were going to work hard, but we're also going to take the time to decompress periodically, and our families would come first. I have been blessed with head coaches who have allowed me to leave the office to take Cindy to the doctor, or attend one of my daughter's recitals at school. When the staff is rested, productivity goes up. When the wives are happy, coaches can remain focused. In the early 70's coaches worked ungodly hours that affected their work productivity and demeanor. Today, most head coaches are much more aware of the necessity for a coach to recharge his batteries.

I did pretty well at our pre-season training camp and even though I was a true freshman, I honestly felt like I had done well enough to win the starting job. Most quarterbacks believe they are the best on the team and I was certainly no different. Tony got most of the starts, but I got my feet wet with some playing time in a backup and cleanup role. I played in about five games that season, mostly in clean-up, but did get the start against Northwestern University — a close game that we won 21-13. My parents never missed a game and my grandmother even came to see me play too, which was pretty special.

Being a backup to Tony Dungy was very enlightening for me. His football intelligence, work ethic, presence and quiet yet confident demeanor were

Tony Dungy

43

instrumental in my understanding of the game. He was a very good college quarterback. We were roommates on the road and became friends. He was so calm and carried himself with such class. He was also what I refer to now as a "gym rat." A gym rat from my (now) coaching perspective is a player who is always around the football office. He is watching video, working out by himself and with teammates, or just being interactive with those in the office. Tony was always around. In fact, legend has it that Coach Stoll gave Tony his own key to the football office because he would come over even earlier than the coaches.

Tony was the first player in my life to illustrate what it really took to even have a chance to be great at the quarterback position. His relationship with our offensive coordinator, Tom Moore, was also my first education in the relationship a quarterback must have with his position coach to be successful. (Tom would later serve as Tony's longtime coordinator when Tony was the head coach of the Indianapolis Colts.) A quarterback and his coach must be really "tied at the hip" for a quarterback to play at the highest level. Tony and Tom practically lived together during their years together at the U of M. Tom was a very demanding coach, and there isn't any doubt after coaching quarterbacks for over 25 years myself, that a quarterback cannot reach his potential without a coach who will stimulate him daily, encourage his love for the game, and demand the highest standard of excellence.

No doubt about it, Tony Dungy was a gym rat. He was extremely passionate about the game of football, and his unique personality and quiet confidence transcended the entire football community in Minnesota. This is still part of the formula I use today in evaluating the most complex and dynamic position in all of sports.

The lowlight of the season came in week four, when another quarterback, Steve Olson, got the start and we got beat by Nebraska, 54-0. After the game Coach Stoll threw a fit like I have never seen. He yelled and screamed at us and began throwing chairs all over the locker room. This was disturbing to me in many ways. I don't believe Coach Stoll was acting. I believe he was genuinely upset, but to respond to defeat in this manner appeared more self-serving than in the team's best interest.

What I have learned over the years, and this really has stuck with me now that I am a head coach, is everyone handles defeat differently and that is one of the intriguing elements in sports. I have been on planes after bitter defeats and there will be guys playing cards and laughing as if we had won the game. Others are so devastated they become angry and often say things to others and even the media they truly regret.

I now understand the way people handle defeat has much to do with how they were raised. This again goes to the beauty and diversity of our sport. What I consider most important now is that I don't judge a player's commitment to the team by his demeanor after games, as long he shows common respect for those around him. I simply lay out the ground rules that if we are together after a game, let's give everyone the opportunity to handle the situation as they see fit, just make sure your behavior is one of common sense that doesn't distract or disrespect others.

Tony Dungy and I recently sat down in a quiet corner of the Westin Hotel in Indianapolis between workouts at the Indianapolis College Scouting Combine. It had been nearly 30 years since we had more than a five minute conversation. It also felt like we hadn't missed a day talking with each other. We were now family men. I felt awful for Tony after having lost his son in a tragedy the year before. Two ball coaches, one just coming off a Super Bowl victory, thinking about retiring and soon to be in the NFL Hall of Fame, and the other out of work trying to rediscover himself and find a new direction. It was wonderful to catch up with my old friend.

As my freshman season went on, I eventually moved down the depth chart and ended up as the team's third-stringer. It was frustrating, but I made the best of it. I just tried to take it all in and learn as much as I could about all aspects of the game. I stayed as involved as I could, without distracting from the quarterback's or team's preparation. When I was on the sidelines, I paid close attention to game situations and watched how Coach Stoll and his assistants handled themselves. Not really knowing it at the time, I was becoming a student of the game and wanted to become as well rounded of a football player as possible.

While football was an emotional roller coaster ride my freshman year, school was going well. I was a political science major and I enjoyed getting lost each day with the other 50,000 students on one of the nation's largest campuses. During the winter, I worked for my dad on the weekends and I even had a girlfriend. But my social life was limited. I went to some team parties and even to some night spots around town, but fortunately I never got into drinking or doing drugs.

I am thankful that my personal makeup was such that I really never tested myself in these areas. It was best for me. But, over my years as an assistant in the NFL and college, and now as a head coach, I have learned not to be judgmental of others. Kids are going to try things and take chances. The challenge is to make them conscious of how each and every one as member of the team is interconnected, and what each does as a player is what we figuratively do as a team.

On my first Grey Cup team our team mantra became EVERYTHING MATTERS. The point was that whether it's football or social, the choices you have, and the decisions you make, on or off the field, can have consequences that affect all of us. This I believe is true in all businesses, and NOT just in the business of football.

In the spring before my sophomore season, I worked hard to become the team's starting quarterback. The staff gave me a legitimate chance to compete and for the most part I stepped up and took a hard run at it. Going

Dropping back to launch a bomb

into the fall, I had hoped I could make a final run at the job after having a competitive and productive spring game. But something happened to my arm in the early fall that left me devastated. I simply could not throw the ball. For some reason, I lost my ability to throw with any velocity. It was unbelievable. The doctors looked at it and injected me with cortisone (an anti inflammatory), but my arm never responded. For the first time in my life as an athlete, I faced adversity and the realization that my football career might be over.

The coaching staff decided to red-shirt me for my sophomore season, and sit me out, in order to save a year of eligibility. When I finally rehabbed my arm and got healthy again, I found myself way down the depth chart behind a number of good quarterbacks on the team. As such, I ultimately decided to switch positions and try my hand as a defensive back. I had played defensive back in high school, was physical and not afraid of contact, and really wanted to get some playing time on defense or special teams and contribute to the team. I just wanted to play.

For whatever the reason though, Coach Stoll didn't see me in his plans. I didn't have a great relationship with Coach Stoll. As a young man, I was very judgmental of the way he coached the team. I saw him as more of a salesman, and someone who really didn't understand what I now term as the "science of the game." I did not believe he really cared about his players, nor got the most out of the talent we had at the time.

Yet, other guys on the team worshipped Coach Stoll and played hard for him. Over the years as I have talked to former teammates, such as Tony Dungy and Desi Williamson (one of our country's great motivational speakers), and from those conversations I have changed the way I see Coach Stoll. As a head coach and longtime assistant coach, I understand now that there are so many different types of management styles. People, depending on their individual makeup and backgrounds, respond in different ways to various leadership approaches. One size does not fit all as the saying goes. I just never got it at that time when it came to Coach Stoll.

But what I did find impressive was his ability to recruit and hire the best coaches, such as Tom Moore, Roger French (our line coach), or Dick Moseley and Norm Parker (both defensive coaches). I also respect the fact that he did not come into the program and just fire everybody either. I agree with this approach. Do the research, gather information, and assess an employee's value before kicking that person out the door. Also, remember these people have families and lives at home.

No decision should ever be made without it being what is best for the team and organization. But, how do you know what is best without really finding out an employee's true value? This makes sense to me and is the way I have initiated my term in Montreal. Coach Stoll did the same by keeping one of the best assistant coaches to ever coach at Minnesota in defensive end coach Butch Nash. At the time, other than Coach Nash, our staff was made up of hard working up and coming coaches, many of whom have gone onto very successful coaching careers in college and in the NFL.

I now realize Coach Stoll's management style was to hire good people and simply let them coach. He believed his job was to motivate the team with words, not specific words, but stories and abstract illustrations. I just didn't get it at the time, but today I understand why his words meant so much to Tony and Desi, as well as many other guys who crossed his path. For me, I didn't need to be motivated and inherently really never have needed those words. I had already developed a strong work ethic at a young age from my dad, as well as a relentless inner strength from my mom. My character was relatively strong, I just wanted to learn football. Now I realize that's why Coach Stoll hired Tom Moore and others, because they were teachers and were skilled in the language of football.

Throughout my career I have studied the management styles of all the head coaches who I have worked for. In addition, I have learned a great deal from others by reading their books. I find that the most important thing is to be brutally honest with yourself first and know what you do best, then hire accordingly. But for me, as for many others, there are some prerequisites:

I am looking for high character and integrity. None of us are perfect, nobody is, but coaches represent all of us and how they conduct themselves on and off the field reflects on me as well as the entire organization.

They have to be a great teacher. It is critically important that they are verbal, quick minded, and enjoy the science of the game. Great coaches come in all different packages, but these individuals must transcend many different kinds of people. Beyond that, they must work quickly at practice and concisely be able to teach and stimulate their players in a classroom setting.

They must be emotionally intelligent. Football is an emotional game played and coached by people extremely passionate about the game. An assistant coach, like his players, must learn to be resilient and pragmatic during the inevitable adversity that comes through the course of a game and season. They must also show consistency and humility during the good times as well as the bad. I have always tried to take an even-keeled approach during the highs and lows of a season because it really is all about the journey. You never find out who you are as a team until the season is complete.

Coaches must pay attention to detail. They will be unable to manifest this in their players unless they show them they are doing it themselves. Having attention to detail is an unreachable standard, but it allows us to keep searching for better ways to accomplish our ultimate team goals for success.

As a player, I responded best by being direct and by having someone use very specific terms. That wasn't Coach Stoll. My perception of him was much different from others he coached. I have much more respect for him today than I did nearly 30 years ago. The experience has been a life-long lesson to look much deeper when drawing conclusions about others.

Finally, after my junior year in 1978, I decided to take a leap of faith and transfer to Moorhead State University. No, this was not the same Morehead that NFL great Phil Simms attended in Kentucky — this was a small Division II school way up in the northwest corner of the state, adjacent to Fargo, N.D. I only had one year of eligibility left and just simply wanted to play football. So, after some serious soul-searching, I packed up and headed north. My family and friends supported my decision and wanted me to be happy, which was a big relief. I remember driving up there that January. It was so bitter cold. I will never forget getting off the freeway at the Moorhead exit. My car just came to a screeching halt. It was an old Ford Grenada and the gas line had frozen up. It was shot. Thankfully I was on the exit ramp with a gas station just ahead, or I literally could have frozen to death.

At that moment, I asked myself what the heck I was doing. I seriously wondered if I had gone crazy. I simply loved the game of football and was so passionate about it that I refused to give up. I was going to play foot-ball, even if it meant leaving friends, family and a girlfriend behind. I was willing to deal with all of that along with the personal humiliation of not making it at my state university as a Division I football player. It took more guts then I realized at the time, and as a result I believe it is very much part of my personal makeup today.

At Moorhead I gained a totally different outlook on football and life. Most of the players had jobs and were not on scholarship. These guys were just like me; they loved the game, knew they weren't going to the pros, but wanted to be part of a team and a game they loved. It was very simple, and they worked hard at it, they really did. This gave me a totally different perspective. It was very refreshing.

Ross Fortier was our head coach and I learned a lot from him. He knew football, particularly the passing game, and his teams were consistently pretty good over the years. A retired Brigadier General in the Army Re-serve, he had a strong yet quiet demeanor, and he had a real passion for the game. He carried himself with great confidence and was extremely

Ross Fortier

even keeled in his approach. In fact, he was the first coach to show me screaming and yelling was not necessarily a prerequisite to getting your point across on the practice field. That was not his way and it worked.

In the fall of 1978, I could not even earn a starting job at a Division II school and was significantly beat out by a sophomore by the name of Mark Reed, who coincidently went on to get drafted and play a backup role in the NFL for a few years. Mark was a genuinely good player with a solid arm and very good running skills. But fate struck two days before our first game against rival University of North Dakota when Mark hit his throwing hand on an oncoming defender's helmet and was sidelined for the first few weeks of the season. My play, during those first few weeks was sub par, but the lesson I learned from that day has been so important in my development and understanding of the business of football.

You see, the most important person in a football organization is the quarterback. He will never tell you that, and in most cases nobody will ever admit it outwardly, but a quarterback is the guy who flies the plane... it does not run on autopilot. With that in mind, his safety in practice is critically important to everyone in the organization. Each year in training camp as a quarterback coach and now as a head coach, I always remind everyone to **STAY AWAY FROM THE QUARTERBACK.** I show a video of what not to do and what to do when a player gets too close to the QB. I take this very seriously, it is just that important.

Players and coaches must be totally unselfish in this area. Defensive coaches must be sincere proponents of this by demonstrating and explaining what is and is not acceptable. This is so important to a team's health and welfare. A team's quarterback gives the entire organization hope. In whatever business, when there is hope, there is a chance for success.

My roommate at Moorhead State was a kid by the name of Pat Richie. Pat was an offensive lineman on the team and we hit it off right away. We became good friends and remain so to this day. Ironically, Pat's dad was one of Bud Grant's best friends and we used to love to talk about our mutual love — the Vikings. Pat was also a very spiritual person and would later go on to become an ordained minister. In fact, he was able to combine his love of theology and his love of sports and make a career out of it, later going on to serve as the longtime team chaplain of the San Francisco 49ers. Pat was so good at what he did and provided such an important service to the players and coaches, that the organization even awarded him three rings for his contributions to the team's success after Super Bowls XXIII, XXIV, and XXIX. It was totally unprecedented. As you can imagine, we had some riveting conversations about God and about life while lying in our beds at night. His Catholic and my Jewish roots made for some interesting dialogue around bedtime, that was for sure. It helped me grow spiritually and in my understanding of the importance of spirituality and religion in many of my players' lives over the years. Today, Pat owns a teamwork and leadership consulting firm that works with Fortune 500 companies and travels the world as a motivational speaker.

Transferring to Moorhead proved to be a good decision. It was truly a unique life experience. I again had to deal with the personal adversity of little or no playing time, but in some ways I can honestly say I didn't have as much fun at any other point in my college career. My Moorhead experience only lasted about nine months. I then headed back to the University of Minnesota in the spring of 1979 to finish the two classes I needed to secure my bachelor's degree.

Coming back to the University of Minnesota was bittersweet though. On one hand I was thrilled to be finishing up my undergraduate work, and proud to be the first in my family to get a college degree, but on the other I was apprehensive about my future. I went to college to build a resumé to play quarterback in the National Football League. That was the only goal I had, and I never deviated from it even in Moorhead. Now there was the hard reality of not knowing what I was going to do with the rest of my life. I think back to a line my grandfather used to say, "We plan and God laughs." But what I was to learn in the next few years, however, was that a plan exists — whether we make one or not.

CH. 3) A CAREER IN LAW IS PUT ON HOLD FOR A SHOT WITH THE PURPLE

When a passionate vision is combined with a proactive daily attempt to succeed, the vision will manifest itself into a reality. To make these visions a reality, great leaders have a variety people around them with diverse backgrounds and experiences. If you get the chance to "coach on the other side," take it because much can be learned just by observing other aspects or perspectives of what you do on a daily basis. For example, if you are a defense attorney, be a prosecutor; if you are a writer, read a book; if you are a boss, be the employee. Before you can win, you need to learn how not to lose and seeing things from all angles gives you this ability. If you fail, don't dwell on it, channel the energy, and refocus on the vision or goal and how to accomplish it. Worrying about what failure will bring only saps you of the energy you need to get better today.

With football behind me it was now time to enter the real world. So, after a good heart to heart with my parents, I decided to apply to some law schools. Being a lifelong, task-oriented, type-A personality, and someone who wasn't afraid of demanding work and enjoyed a good argument, I had always figured I would make a good attorney. I got accepted to a couple of good programs but ultimately settled on Loyola, in Los Angeles. After spending the last winter in Moorhead, I was really excited about the possibility of going to class in shorts and a t-shirt.

In June of 1979, I packed up my 1974 Oldsmobile Cutlass Supreme, kissed my mom and dad good-bye and drove to L.A. I am sure that they were extremely happy I had put my football goals behind me and was off to build a career that would allow me to flourish professionally and economically. My dad found a way to pay for a very expensive Law School education which didn't get me on the school's Law Review (the journal for elite law students), or sitting on the Federal or Supreme Court, but what it did do was continue to build my relentless work ethic, an astute attention to details, and my competitive desire to be the best at whatever I tried to do at the time.

It was California or bust. No sooner than a few days after I got out of there and started to settle in, I got a call from one of the scouts from the Minnesota Vikings, Frank Gilliam. Frank had been tipped off about me from one of the executives with the Vikings, Jeff Diamond, who asked him to please give me a tryout with the team as a defensive back.

You see, Jeff's brother was one of my best friends from grade school and his dad was my dentist, so he knew me. Incidentally, Jeff would go on to become the president and general manager of the Vikings, and later serve in the same capacity with the Tennessee Titans — even earning NFL Executive of the Year honors in 1999.

When I got that phone call I was so excited. There was some air left in my childhood dream to play in the NFL! I was really going to get this chance and to do it for my team, the Minnesota Vikings, and their great future Hall of Fame coach Bud Grant, what a thrill. I was going to get the tryout as a defensive back. Tony Dungy had made this transition, why couldn't I do it? In my mind I was confident that if I could run well enough, then I could get myself into training camp. I knew I could learn anything and I was physically very strong at the time. I was convinced toughness and being physical would be a given. Not wanting to pass up what could have been the opportunity of a lifetime, I packed up my car in late June and drove all the way back to the Twin Cities to continue preparing for my tryout. I had never stopped training and it took me very little time to get in the kind of condition I needed to be in for a successful tryout.

Unbelievably, on the day of the tryout, I had barely gotten out of bed, when my back completely went out on me. I mean I was literally paralyzed. Seriously, it was so bad I spent four days in traction at the local hospital. I cannot even express in words how in a split second my dream was taken away. My opportunity finally presented itself and then I got injured. I obviously missed the workout, but to my surprise, Frank agreed to reschedule it once I got healthy. It was a huge relief.

Two weeks later, I had my tryout and I did well enough that Frank Gilliam signed me to a free agent contract. I was beyond excited; I was now a Minnesota Viking. Law school was going to have to wait. A few weeks later, I headed down to the team's training camp in Mankato, about an hour and a half southwest of Minneapolis. I had made that drive many times before with my dad when I was a kid. This time I was alone, a local kid, going to play for his hometown team, not just watching them. Yes, dreams do come true!

Writing this book has allowed me to reflect and grow in so many ways. How did this happen? I mean really, so many young kids grow up watching their NFL heroes and dreaming they would one day be wearing their team's colors. Very few get a tryout, fewer get drafted, and even fewer make the team and get to play for extended careers. So how did this happen?

I realized developing lifelong relationships really mattered and the quality of those relationships mattered even more. My sincere and genuine relationship with Jeff Diamond and Pat Richie created an opportunity years later. Jeff was like a brother to me; he was family. He stepped to the plate, put his reputation on the line and sold Frank Gilliam that I was worth an hour of his time for the betterment of the team. My friendship with Pat, unbeknownst to me, came into play. Pat had become a very close friend while at Moorhead and I was sure his dad was influential in convincing his close friend, Bud Grant, that this local kid had enough talent that he would never embarrass himself in training camp.

Then there was Bud, my boyhood coaching idol and Minnesota icon. Over my high school years I had competed in football and basketball against his son, Mike. How many times did I look into the stands and see Bud watching his son and I compete against each other? I believe Bud remembered those matchups between his son and I and when the time came six years later it helped him with his decision to give me this incredible opportunity. I really do. Mike is today arguably the most successful prep head coach in Minnesota history, already winning six Minnesota State Class AAAAA football titles. At Eden Prairie High

School. Like his father, Mike is already a legend at a very young age. Is anybody surprised? I don't think so.

In retrospect, we just don't know who is watching or why we have crossed paths with certain people. I now live as purposefully as I can in a unique state of awareness where I have a vision of where I want to go, yet my focus is solely on the moment. I share that with my players daily, to a point I have them measure their effort level during the course of the day and especially during practice. It is amazing how this results in improvement in all facets of play and individual growth. This is a habit not easily sustainable but worth the effort. When you work in the moment, you save energy necessary to play the game at the end of the week. Again, worrying about what will happen only saps you of the energy you need to get better today.

The strong relationships I built and effort I gave during competitive times were the criteria that really gave me this opportunity. Building strong relationships doesn't just happen. You have to take the time to get to know people, share time, and develop genuine dialogue — which is essential. I

Bud Grant

also owe a great deal to Frank Gilliam, who gave me a second chance. To this day when I get calls from agents or players, I use my best and good faith effort to help the player get his opportunity. It has stuck with me that every kid wants just one chance to show he can do it. I am going to be that guy who returns the phone calls, texts, or emails to get the young man a look. You just never know. I was that kid some 30 years ago. Frank and Bud gave me a second chance opportunity and as a result, their legacy lives on through my coaches and players. Now that I am a head coach, I do the same thing. Everyone who comes to camp will get a chance to compete and make the team.

Bud also treated his players like men during training camp and I try to do the same. For instance, we have no hazing by veterans, no rookie shows, or no singing at dinner. These old school traditions only take away from a young man's primary focus and that is to make the team. It also hurts the team because in these environments a good player can get lost in the milieu of others. Finally, every player gets treated with the utmost respect and dignity. This is common sense business practice, isn't it? As a leader, aren't we responsible for an environment that will allow an individual to be the best he can be?

I wanted to get to training camp as quickly as possible, but it was Bud's philosophy to go in as late as possible. Bud had a staff that had been together for a very long time and a smart team which knew the systems of football that had been implemented for over a decade. His philosophy was to get the fundamentals and techniques re-taught as quickly as possible and get to the season without getting anyone hurt. When I was coaching with the San Francisco 49ers, our great head coach George Seifert would always say, "Guys, my number one job as your head coach is your individual safety during practice so we can get you to the games." That was clearly Bud's attitude as well. "Let's get these guys to the season healthy and in one piece,' he would say. "That will give us a chance!" As a head coach I too now live by this philosophy.

Upon arrival in Mankato, I was directed to the locker room to be issued my equipment. It was one of the biggest thrills of my life to put on that beautiful purple jersey for the first time once. I remember just standing there and staring at myself, "No. 41... Marc Trestman," like some sort of out of body experience. It was truly surreal. Shouldn't this jersey have been retired? It was former Viking Dave Osborn's number, a tough guy running back that had played for Bud on some of his best teams. Now it belonged to me.

Determined to make the most of my situation, I worked hard, kept my mouth shut and just tried to learn as much as I could. Bud Grant was the master of observation on the practice field. He didn't miss a thing. He constantly evaluated his players. Most people don't know that Bud was never an assistant coach, anywhere. He went right from being a player with the Philadelphia Eagles to being a head coach for the Winnipeg Blue-Bombers of the Canadian Football League. He was a master tactician, yet I never saw Bud draw an "X" or an "O." Rather, he would hire great assistant coaches who could work cooperatively together and who could tolerate each other's differences on a daily basis during the chaos of a season filled with countless ups and downs. This is much of the same criteria I used to hire my initial staff in Montreal and will continue to do so in the years ahead. Isn't this a reasonable requirement for any hire in business as well as football? As with everything Bud did, it was just good common sense.

The look of determination...

Training camp started well for me. I was picking up the defense quickly and felt in my mind that I was physically and athletically capable of playing the weak or free safety position in the NFL. I believed I had an advantage because my background was offense, and I had a sense for pass pattern development during the course of a play. I also knew that although we didn't do any tackling during practice (once again for player safety), that hitting someone wouldn't be an issue. I just felt very confident in my abilities.

As I look back on those first few weeks of training camp, the real purpose behind this opportunity (which I did not know or understand at the time) was to better understand defensive structures for when I later became a quarterback coach and offensive coordinator. My time on defense with the Vikings along with the coaching that I received, allowed me to clearly understand the mentality of most defensive coordinators and better articulate their concepts and philosophies to my own players. I have always felt that I have had an edge as a coach because of my time on defense. I always recommend to young coaches that if they get the opportunity to coach on the other side of the ball that they should do it. The insight I gained has certainly been powerful for me as a head coach in being able to address these principles with my players and coaches.

As training camp continued to progress, I had more of a feeling of belonging. Chuck Foreman, the great double threat running-back of the Vikes, took me under his wing. He was friends with some family friends of mine and he helped my confidence grow along the way. He was truly confident I would be there to the end and ultimately have a chance to make the final roster. You see, free safety Paul Krause, the NFL's all-time interceptions leader and future Hall of Famer, had just retired from the team and as a result I was one of just two free safeties in camp. With Chuck's support, I was genuinely confident that I was going to make the team as not only a reserve safety, but also in a special team's role as well.

I will never forget our first pre-season game; I was the first rookie to get into the game. That meant a lot to me because it was a strong signal from Bud that he trusted me and wanted to see me compete. That, or he just wanted to get the better guys off the field so they wouldn't get hurt. Either way, I was out there playing for the Minnesota Vikings. Amazing. In any event, Bud liked smart players, and what coach doesn't? Bud put a premium on a player's football intelligence. This is a criteria coaches use at all levels because good coaches know that before you can win you have to learn how not to lose. This means doing things on the field that you can control and that do not get you beat.

This is harder than it seems on the surface. When a player has football intelligence, he has not only the ability to learn football, but also inherent decision making abilities to do the right things during the highly competitive, emotional roller coaster, and violence of a football game. It is during these times players jump offside, tackle when a player is out of bounds, or fail to communicate an important call, amongst other things. Whether in business or the business of football, you want people who can keep their heads and think clearly during the chaos and pressures of the day.

Running out onto the field for my first pre-season game was such a memorable moment for me. I knew where my dad was sitting and I immediately made eye contact with him. I will never forget the look on his face when he saw me wearing my Vikings uniform for the first time. He got really emotional and so did I. All I could think about was how the two of us spent our Sundays together when I was a kid, watching and being totally

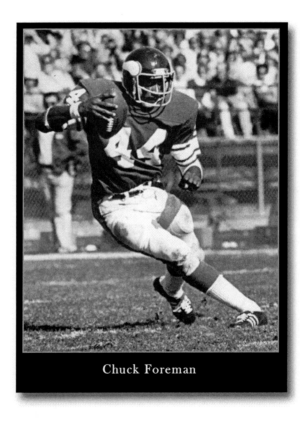

Chuck Foreman

consumed with the team. He was a pretty modest guy, but I am sure that it was one of the proudest moments in his life. Now that I am a father myself, I understand once again how proud he must have been and how thankful he must have been to those who gave his son the opportunity to fulfill a lifelong dream.

This brings to question, does a person's passion and emotional attachment to a vision equate to it becoming reality? The science today says yes. Certainly there have been tremendous accomplishments born more out of luck than a passionate vision, but in most cases I am confident the latter is the norm. I am a huge believer that when a passionate and emotional vision or goal is combined with a proactive daily attempt to achieve, these attempts will manifest themselves into that vision. All of us have read stories about those types of people and there are far too many to illustrate in this book. This is the universal law of attraction and the more I assess life at so many levels, the more I believe. This has always been an important part of my coaching philosophy as well. I have my players write their specific goals down on paper. The key is having tangible written evidence that through daily work and focus, that vision will eventually manifest itself into reality. Without passion and a sincere love for the game at its most basic level, however, it will not and cannot happen.

I remember flying with the team to Seattle for our first preseason game. I bought a new beige suit just for the occasion and wore it proudly. I was a member of the Minnesota Vikings, but then my dream came to a screaming halt when, being the culinary novice that I was, I stuck my knife straight into a piece of chicken kiev — which then exploded all over my new suit. It was awful; the guys just looked at me like a rookie plague or something. I was so embarrassed. I took a lot of kidding from the guys, and in this instance I just had to laugh right along with them.

You cannot be part of a football team without having a thick skin. Everyone at sometime is going to get criticized, make a mistake, or be made fun of for some personal flaw, however small it may be. To have a championship environment the guys must have a closeness that enables them to have a sense of humor without someone going off in anger. A sense of humor is extremely important during times of adversity as well. When you are working through a losing streak or an injury spell that hurts your team, a sense of humor, not silliness, is so important. It is the sign of a team that knows who they are, that embraces the adversity as an opportunity to show its backbone, and it keeps guys from not tightening up and putting undo pressure on themselves.

I first recognized this as a member of the 49ers coaching staff in 1995. I was on a team with a very confident swagger. George Seifert reiterated this when he spoke to the staff before the start of each season, a reflection of (his predecessor) Bill Walsh's coaching philosophy. Bud never talked about it like George did in our preseason meeting, but it was evident that his players and coaches had that philosophy too.

I played periodically during the remaining pre-season games. I thought at the time the coaches were pleased with my development. Chuck Foreman continued to encourage me and my confidence continued to grow. Just as I thought things were going well, an incident happened that changed everything. During a pre-season game in San Diego, I hit Chargers running back Johnny Rodgers by our sideline really hard. Afterward, I jumped up and immediately started trash-talking the guy, saying words that I had never said aloud.

I had never been in this state as a quarterback, but now here I was, truly part of the violent game of professional football. For whatever the reason, I got carried away and let my emotions get the better of me. This was a moment that has really helped me understand a player's mentality under the stress of a game. In fact, it has become a point of emphasis in everything we do to promote team discipline and respect, not only for our players, but for our opponents as well.

Back to that ugly incident on the sideline, I will never forget looking up at that very moment and seeing Bud just staring at me. Was it approval or disapproval? Needless to say, I didn't play in our next pre-season game, which just so happened to also be our last. Not playing in that game was a big deal too, because it was an indication as to whether or not a player was going to make the final roster. You see, teams didn't want to risk having a player get injured and then having to put him on the injured reserve list, because that meant having to pay his salary — which they obviously didn't want to do. So, they kept me on the sidelines, out of harm's way. I knew the end was near.

The next week Paul Krause, the team's great veteran free safety, decided to come out of retirement and rejoin the team. Bud called me into his office to give me the news. Interestingly, his tone and demeanor was extremely positive. He knew me well enough to know I had other avenues to pursue in life besides football and that I was going to be all right. He also knew that my lifelong dream had just come to a tragic end and that it was time for me to move on. I have never forgotten that day in Bud's office. He knew how I felt and understood what guys like me were going through. We had worked our whole life for that moment and were now being told it just wasn't going to happen. I have been in both situations now and I can tell you that it's tough as a player and it's tough as a coach.

This moment has dramatically helped in my career as an assistant and now as a head coach. I always embrace the opportunity to spend time with a player who has been cut. This is not an easy time for the coach or the player. These are never personal decisions but business decisions that everyone feels is in the team's best interest. I will spend as much time with a player as I can because often this is a life defining moment for the person. I will also be as honest as I can, telling the player if I think he has a chance to play in the league and to not give up, or if it is best for him to move on. I will ask him what he will do from here, see if there is a way I can help him, let him know he can reach me at anytime, and wish him well. Cut day is a very difficult day for the player, but coaches everywhere will tell you cutting a player is the toughest part of the job. Leaders must make decisions in the best interests of the team, even when it's tough.

Handing the jersey over to the equipment manager was one of the toughest things I had ever done. I was devastated. With that, I decided to put plan B into action and return to law school. The problem was that Loyola had already started their fall semester, and the only other law school that hadn't started where I had been accepted was the University of Miami. So, I packed up the old Cutlass and headed to south Florida. I didn't get too emotional about it, I just moved right on to the next thing.

As I look back, this began a pattern for the next 20 years of having success and then dealing with adversity. I just inherently had the inner strength and unconscious belief in myself that I wasn't going to hang around and dwell on it. I was going to channel all of the energy from football and move on and focus on becoming a world class litigator. That was my new mission.

I drove 24 hours straight before falling asleep in a hotel parking lot outside of Atlanta. After waking, I continued the last 12 hour leg and headed straight to South Beach. What an amazing place. In my eyes spending the winter in south Florida was going to be a fantastic consolation prize in exchange for having my dream of playing in the NFL shattered. I have always tried to find a positive in a negative, and this time it was law school at UM.

Miami had the reputation of being a very good law school. I was anxious yet tentative to get started. There was no time to decompress after a month of training camp. Going from the physical world of football to the demanding academic environment of being a first year law student was dramatic. It didn't take me very long to feel like a fish out of water. I walked onto campus wearing a t-shirt, shorts, a baseball cap and flip flops, while other students were dressed in coats and ties carrying briefcases. Where was I and what was I doing here?

I stayed true to myself during the early weeks of law school. I had no free time and was immersed in Property, Contracts, Constitutional Law, and a subject called Torts. Classes and the professors were extremely intimidating. It was evident I was around some very smart people, and although I got very good grades in college, I had never participated in any intellectual or argumentative dialogue. I was completely out my element.

My theory of school was to find a quiet area of the library and grind it out hour by hour. This is what I did as an undergrad and it worked. I figured why change now? Although I did make it through law school, I did so at a cost. I left law school with very few relationships that have helped me over the years, enhanced my life, or enabled me to be a more successful person on many levels.

I look back at my class at UM and am amazed at just how successful so many of them have become. A number are trustees of the University; many are very wealthy; some are incredibly philanthropic; and most are influential on many levels, both locally in south Florida as well as on a national scale. Over the years I get frequent emails from classmates who have followed my career. They are both proud of my accomplishments and supportive when things haven't gone as well. They are good people, brilliant, and very, very successful in their own careers. I regret not having taken the time to reach out and get to know those people. In retrospect, I was so reclusive. My wife Cindy knows better than anyone, it wasn't them, it was me. I just stayed to myself, uninterested in anyone else and so focused on my immediate goals. Boy, have I learned the hard way by the quality of life I lost and the friends I have missed out on. I have promised myself that in the "second half" that will not happen again!

Cindy has been a major influence in changing me, because she knew that my stand-offish personality was a cover-up for the person I am and can become. Over the years, she has referred to me as reclusive, anti-social, and socially dysfunctional. In fact this was a precursor to my philosophy as a coach. I would go in my office, close the door, and grind my way to finding first downs and touchdowns. I achieved relative success by doing this and have the stats to back it up. Again, it came at a price.

Today, I have made a massive shift in my demeanor. I make it a point to reach out to almost everyone who enters my space during the normal course of a day. If I think it is time to introduce myself to someone, I do it. I ask their name and make it a point to remember it or ask again if I missed it. If I feel like asking them how they are doing, I know I really mean it. When you do this, amazing things can happen, and when the moment is right they usually do too. It took me over 40 years to truly understand people are meant to engage each other. In so doing, lifelong friendships can develop, with opportunities and happiness to boot. It's almost a guarantee.

I am the best example that you can teach a relatively old dog new tricks. I even have a new motto, "Lifelong relationships can begin at 50." I have already found this to be true. I am grateful to my new friends, and even more appreciative of my few lifetime friends who have stuck by me. They have supported me in both success and hardship.

By the time I completed my first few weeks of law school, I had already became a conditioned animal. Wake up at 5:30 a.m., eat, get to the library by 6 a.m., study for Property at 8 a.m. and move through the day leaving the library at the stroke of midnight. I did this everyday, Monday through Friday. I would also work all day Saturday and Sunday until 6 p.m. This was the only way I could do it. My only other constant was lifting weights, playing basketball, or running for an hour almost every day. I always tried to stay in shape and exercise was a way to clear my head. I do the same today and highly recommend it. Every once in a while I would even take off to nearby Key Biscayne to get some beach time. Getting away is also something you have to do from time to time to keep your sanity, I recommend doing it as often as possible as well.

I was internally driven to get through the first year of law school, the most challenging undertaking of my relatively short life. It consumed me, and eventually I came to the conclusion that I was not meant to practice law. I never considered quitting though, that was out of the question. I was going to get my law degree and finish what I started. Even to this day, Cindy and I have a motto with our girls, Sarahanne and Chloe: "The Trestmans Never Quit." We are imperfect and have a long way to go, but we are constantly working to keep our family promise to one another.

Although I was a bit of a recluse, there is a common saying that goes: "Every once in a while even a blind squirrel finds an acorn." That acorn for me was making friends with a few classmates during my first year. I remember sitting at lunch one day at a restaurant located a few yards from the law school when a girl I recognized from Contracts walked by and asked if anyone had taken one of the few empty seats available. I said no, and invited her to sit down. Her name was Dina Cellini and we started a conversation together. She talked about the usual stuff but then really caught my attention when she told me that her fiancee played football in the NFL with the then St. Louis Cardinals. Ironically, later that January I ran into him in the law school library elevator. It didn't take a rocket scientist to see he was a football player. A conversation ensued, one thing led to another, and today Sean Clancy is the godfather of my daughter Chloe. Amazing.

Obviously Sean and I hit it off, and I was invited by he and Dina for some great Italian cooking at their apartment. We all became friends and sometimes I would even fall asleep on their couch afterwards. Before long Sean and I began working out together. Sean was getting ready for his second year in the NFL and I was just trying to stay in shape. It was great to be able to work out with someone who I could relate to and who could push me to be better.

One other friend I made in law school was a guy by the name of David Simon. On the first day of classes, the auditorium was packed with very nervous first year students. At the podium was the school's renowned Dean, Soya Menscicoff. Dean Menscicoff was in the process of teaching us the elementary law school discipline of briefing a case. The auditorium was so full that day that folding chairs had to be placed in the aisle. Laptops were not the technology, just pens and yellow legal pads.

I was sitting in an auditorium chair on the aisle, and this tall, loud talking, first year student was looking over my shoulder and copying everything I was doing. I took a mental note to stay away from him and did so until I coincidentally ran into him early in the semester. He of course began the discussion by relentlessly asking me a thousand questions. He was from New Jersey and was intrigued by my quiet demeanor and Midwestern accent.

To make a long story short, this guy with an outgoing and inquisitive personality, became the glue that really allowed me to stay somewhat sane over the next two years of law school. David made the school's prestigious Law Review at the end of the year and has gone onto incredible professional success with his own Park Avenue securities company in New York City. I was even the best man at his wedding. He and his wife Linda are close friends, and to this day he prods at me to keep my balance and focus on what is truly important. He is wealthy, healthy, has three beautiful children and has deep pockets for his charities. I am just happy to say that I still I enjoy the phone calls, and thankfully I don't need the pep talks as much as I once did.

You see, I had written off my now good friend David from the beginning. I had been presumptuous to think that we had nothing in common. I hadn't spent much time around anybody but jocks, and I was just not comfortable in my new environment. I thought, "Why would I want to hang with him?" What a life lesson learned about first impressions and second chances. Before we write people off and pull a "young Marc Trestman" by deciding they are not for you, do some real research. Get to know what goes on inside with people. It can truly change your life.

I continued to work out with Sean and through his encouragement I began to get the itch to give football one more shot, as long as it didn't interfere with law school. I figured that if I caught a break and made a team, then I would just cross that bridge when it came. On the other hand, if I tried out and got cut, then I would certainly be able to make it back to Coral Gables for year two of law school. I just felt like I had to give it one more shot.

With that, I finished my first year of law school and headed back to Minnesota. Over the last semester, I had put in periodic calls to Jeff Diamond and Coach Grant to see if I could get another opportunity to try out. They were honest with me from the start and told me that a lot would depend on the draft and on how the free agent market sorted itself out. I appreciated their frankness, and sure enough, I got the call in late June. Incredibly, I would have another shot at my dream. I remember making that drive to Mankato in the late summer of 1980 feeling more prepared, confident, and focused than ever before. I was in great shape and felt like that time off had really recharged my batteries. I felt invigorated and ready to take on the world.

I arrived at camp feeling like a seasoned vet and immediately went to get my equipment fitted. After getting my helmet and shoulder pads the equipment guy handed me my jersey. It was No. 44. Are you kidding me? I didn't deserve this. No way. Sadly, Chuck Foreman had left the team that off-season to join the New England Patriots and I had been given his number. I felt completely unworthy, but took it as a good omen nonetheless. I was determined to do everything in my power to make the opening day roster.

This time when camp started I wasn't coming in as a wide-eyed rookie. I had already been through it once before and that experience was extremely beneficial to me. I knew most of the players, coaches, defensive

Standing on the sideline was never any fun...

terminology, and what Bud and his staff expected of me. Things were going smoothly, until one day during practice when I dove for a loose ball and badly tore my calf muscle. At first I thought I just got kicked in the calf, but it would prove to be much worse. From there on out every step was brutally painful. I tried to practice, but it only made it worse; I was in incredible pain. There was no way I could efficiently or competitively practice, yet I refused to sit out. No way. In fact I did everything I could to hide the injury. As much pain as I was in, I was on a mission to make the team.

I really tried to hang in there for a few weeks, but eventually the calf got the best of me. No amount of ice or aspirin could help me, I just couldn't perform. I couldn't cut or accelerate and I was getting consistently beaten in practice. In retrospect, if I only would have sat out for a few weeks and let it heal, I probably would have mended up and been just fine. Instead, I re-injured it again and eventually was cut for the second time after the third pre-season game.

I was heartbroken about getting released. I was realistic though and came to the conclusion that I had given professional football my best shot, it was truly time to move on. I didn't really know what the future had in store for me other than I was going to finish the next two years of law school. Maybe I would change my mind and decide to become the great litigator I intended to be a year earlier? There was a plan out there, I could feel it. Figuring out what it was, however, was going to be the challenge.

CH. 4) SAYING GOOD BYE TO THE PURPLE AND HELLO TO THE ORANGE

Even though strong leaders often are in the position to tell others what needs to be done, they are rarely outworked. A proven leader learns that sometimes success is even more difficult to handle than adversity. Both can be overcome, however, with a steady and even keeled approach toward following a united vision. Leaders are not complacent and work hard to better those around them even in times of success because they understand adversity is always right around the corner. Not accepting complacency is a major factor in who steps up to lead. All leaders were at some time followers who were eventually given an opportunity. Passion, confidence, and a clear and concise vision often are the difference between who steps up to lead and who falls back. Leaders find ways to use prior experiences and relationships going forward so as to not make the same mistakes twice and ultimately achieve their goals.

On the evening of January 2, 1984, I walked into an empty University of Miami coaches locker room at the Orange Bowl in Miami and fell to my knees in tears of elation and joy. Despite being 21-point underdogs, the University of Miami had just defeated the undefeated University of Nebraska for the NCAA National Championship, 31-30, in what many believe to this day was one of college football's greatest games. Nobody could have imagined what had just happened because it was so mystical and incomprehensible.

The Most Valuable Player of the game was a gangly but brilliant, six-foot-five inch red-shirt freshman by the name of Bernie Kosar, who had just passed for over 300 yards in the Hurricanes victory. His quarterback coach and teacher, meanwhile, was a 26-year-old rookie who had only recently graduated from law school and had just passed the Florida Bar Exam. Eight months earlier he was wondering whether or not he would be gainfully employed. How was this possible?

It was the fall of 1981 and I was anxious to get back to Miami to begin my second year of law school. I was living on a couch in a spare room of this random lady's house near campus for $100 a month. At the time it seemed like not a big deal, but when my dad came to visit me for the first time and saw how I was living, I could see it really bothered him. He had promised me if I would take on the challenge of law school, he would find a way to pay for it. That included reasonable living conditions. In his mind, this was not reasonable for his son who he knew was working his tail off to become something special. Dad wrote me a check on the spot, insisting I find a nicer place to live. So, I gathered my belongings and moved into a nearby apartment complex. In retrospect, it was a huge relief to get into the new place. It provided me an environment to better focus on my work, and certainly a space where I could kick my feet up and simply relax. I was so grateful that my dad was able to provide me with the resources to have a better quality of life. It meant a great deal to me.

The second year of law school was much different than the first. The first year was really a hazing period. Professors taught by the Socratic method and put each student on the spot over the course of the year by asking hypothetical questions from case studies. Under this style of teaching, students would then have to stand up and give answers based on the existing laws while their peers listened and developed arguments for or against. At the time, I had never felt so much pressure to perform. For each hour of class, it took at least three hours of preparation, and there were no shortcuts for me. Listening to these students was amazing and the dialogue in class was impressive. There were obviously a lot of very brilliant young people who I was not only competing with but learning from on a daily basis — many of whom were the sons and daughters of some of our nation's most prominent and influential people.

I remember sitting in class sometimes feeling like a nervous wreck, just hoping to avoid the professor's gaze. Getting called on as a first year law student prepared me so well for the job I have had all these years though, that is for sure. It was long hours where personal discipline was at a premium. The preparation had to be detailed and meticulously organized. Your answers had to be given confidently and with clarity of thought — just like a coach's. The pressure of standing and speaking before your peers, opening yourself up to criticism and analysis, has made calling plays in front of millions of people each week relatively easy. Making it through that first year toughened me and gave me life skills that put me far ahead of the game at an early age. Nobody would outwork or out prepare me.

In the second year of law school, the pressure is less and the opportunity to do work outside the classroom is recommended at most schools. Miami was no different. I networked and was introduced to a fine attorney at a local law firm by the name of Joe Martinez, who has since gone on to become a prominent federal court judge in south Florida. Joe hired me and paid me $10 an hour to do part-time research work for him as a clerk. The hours were flexible and I was even able to find the time to do some of my own research at the library for upcoming cases as well. I had very little money at the time, so to be able to have a few bucks in my pocket made a huge difference in my quality of life.

One late afternoon while taking a dinner break from studying for midterms, I decided to barbecue some chicken breasts out back on the patio behind my apartment building. I was sitting there, alongside an empty pool waiting for my chicken to cook, when a young guy in his late 20's casually came by to barbecue on an adjacent grill. Eventually he started up a conversation with me. Little did I know, but this guy was about to change my life forever.

His name was Mike Archer, and he was the defensive backs coach for the University of Miami Football team. We started talking football and hit it off immediately. He was a very outgoing and intelligent person, and I could tell right away that he had a real passion for the game of football. In fact, he would go on to become the head football coach at Louisiana State University, and later serve as the linebackers coach of the Pittsburgh Steelers. (Ironically, today he is the defensive coordinator at North Carolina State in Raleigh, and actually sits in the same office I did when I was coaching there... but we'll get to that later.) Anyway, Mike appeared intrigued and legitimately interested in my background. Well, one thing lead to another and he told me that they had an opening on his Hurricanes staff for a volunteer assistant coach. He asked if I might be interested in applying for it.

This totally caught me off guard. I mean I had never really thought about getting into coaching, other than maybe someday working with my kid's peewee or the high school team. Without hesitation and without even thinking about my time commitments to school and to my clerking position though, I just barked out, "Sure, why not?" I was interested and intrigued. It is somewhat ironic that I met Mike that afternoon because as you probably have inferred thus far, I was not one to make small talk with random people I had just met.

As I was soon to find out, Dad getting me off that couch and writing that check which led to a new apartment and a chance meeting with Mike Archer was no coincidence. My life's path was about to change forever. A few days later I was sitting in Coach Howard Schnellenberger's office. He was a husky man with a very low voice, and sitting behind his desk was very intimidating. He reminded me of legendary Alabama Coach Bear Bryant, who I once saw as a young boy. Coach Schnellenberger's voice was so low with almost an intentional mumble that it forced you to really listen and focus on his words.

The first thing he said to me was, "You want to be an agent, don't you?" He figured that since I was in law school, that I was motivated to meet the players, develop close relationships with them, and then represent them as professional players. He questioned my desire and assumed I wanted to use the opportunity to just make money. I told him that I had no interest in being an agent, but that I loved football and would be willing to help out the team any way that I could. I just spoke from my heart and told him that I wanted to be around the game, because football had always been my passion.

As I was walking out he paused to show me something. It was a stack of over 100 résumés from coaches all over the country who were way more qualified than me, that were applying for this same unpaid assistant coaching position. I took it as a "Thanks, but no thanks, kid," and figured that there was no way I was going to ever hear from Coach Schnellenberger again. So, I went back to school as if nothing had transpired.

Surprisingly, a couple of days later he called and offered me the job. I was completely blown away. I was back in the game, only now I was a football coach. Just like that. Incredible. I believe Coach Schnellenberger ultimately saw my sincerity and that I had earned his trust. He was willing to give me a shot and I was excited for the opportunity.

I was excited to jump in head first, but at the same time leery of what I had just gotten myself into. I would be working for free, with no specific hours and no specific job description, but I could eat my meals at the team's training table which was fortunately only 50 paces from the front door of the law school. What a deal!

Now, at the time, the University of Miami was in the building process after almost dropping their football program only two years earlier. It was nothing like we know of it today, one of the most dynamic and winning programs of the late 20th century. Little did I know, however, that I was about to join a program that was only two years away from winning its first of what would ultimately prove to be five NCAA National Championships.

My first spring with the team was a whirlwind. Between class, clerking and spring practice, I was exhausted. My day started at six in the morning with the team at the morning training table. From there, I went to class until two o'clock in the afternoon. After that I would go to the football office to work as a coach until after dinner, at which point I went to the law library to study. And, I was still clerking for Joe Martinez. Basically I had no life! No girlfriend, no partying, nothing. I was doing an 18-hour shift, completely focused on school, clerking, and coaching. That was it.

I was learning a lot though and just soaked it all in. Coach Schnellenberger was in the process of almost single-handedly willing this lowly program into a national powerhouse. To do so, he had surrounded himself with an outstanding staff which was made up of several future NFL coaches, including: Joe Brodsky, Tom Olivadotti, Hubbard Alexander, Kim Helton, Mike Archer and Gary Stevens. Coach Schnellenberger had earned a lot of credibility in the coaching world prior to coming to Miami. I mean here was a guy who had become an NFL head coach at just 34 years old and had already been with the Rams, Colts and Dolphins. In fact, he was a key fixture on that iconic 1972 Dolphins team that went undefeated — the only team ever to do so. The bottom line was that guys listened to him, they knew he had a plan.

At that time, college football programs had eight full-time and four part-time coaches, along with one volunteer like myself. Coach Schnellenberger had me work with running backs coach Joe Brodsky, who was one of the part-timers. He was a Florida legend, having won state titles as a high school player and head coach, and he was destined to later coach on two National Championship teams at Miami, followed by three Super Bowl teams with Jimmy Johnson and the Dallas Cowboys. Sadly, Joe passed away a few years ago from cancer. He was my surrogate father, an unselfish mentor, and one of the funniest men I have ever been around. He forced me to learn the demands of coaching from the first day I arrived on the staff and I will forever be grateful for what he taught me.

As a part-timer, Joe would arrive at the office just before practice. It was my job to fill him in each day on what transpired in the staff meetings, and give him the schedule for the day. Joe saw something in me and allowed me to do more coaching of the running backs than I was certainly qualified to do. It also gave me a lot of self confidence that he would entrust so much to me. His sincere and humorous support was invaluable. He was a completely unselfish person and tremendous role model for me. I have consciously used Joe's approach in my mentorship roles over the years. Selflessly challenging younger coaches; loosening the reigns so they can grow, learn, and at times fail; and even adding a very dry sense of humor are some of the many lessons I still apply to my own coaching philosophies today.

I also spent a good deal of time learning the game from then part-time quarterbacks coach Earl Morrall, who gave me so much insight to the position. Earl worked with future Hall of Fame quarterback Jim Kelly at the time, and it was a great learning experience to watch those two work together on the field plans. Earl had a unique way of teaching fundamentals. He would say, "Marc, when you are coaching QB's, you have to work out of your rolodex (a file with all the requisite fundamentals necessary to play the position), and pick one or two each day to work on. Any more than that is just too much and will become information overload." What great advice, and it is still part of my philosophy today.

During the season, my coaching duties expanded, and on the weekends I was the advance scout for the next opponent. Needless to say, I was busy. It was baptism by fire too, because I was truly winging it without having had any prior coaching experience. Being a former quarterback and then making the transition to defensive back with the Vikings, however, had enhanced my understanding of the game and allowed me to grow immensely from an overall picture of how both sides of the ball functioned.

Somehow, despite being so busy, I was able to balance the three existing aspects of my life with little stress. I was healthy too. I always found time to take a run and I was eating better than I had ever eaten, courtesy of the Hurricane training table. My boss, Joe Martinez, who was a big Hurricane backer, even cut me some slack and gave me a long leash. I think he enjoyed helping me make a little extra money and I really appreciated that. Little did I know at the time but I was getting a PhD in multitasking, which was a necessity in my future coordinator jobs and now as a head coach.

I was having a great time being around the game and traveling to different college campuses to do the advance scouting. The team did well and I was learning that coaching was a much different lifestyle than that of a player. It was long hours, constant scrutiny in the papers, and all sorts of pressures to succeed. I had made it through my first year of law school though, so coaching seemed like a piece of cake compared to that stress. I saw it like this: I got to like law school, but I loved football. Big difference.

The next fall was even better. I began to spend a great deal of time with a pair of promising freshmen signal callers who we had recruited; Bernie Kosar from Boardman, Ohio, and Vinnie Testaverde, a Long Island kid

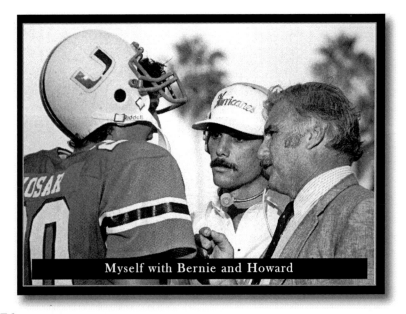

Myself with Bernie and Howard

76

who had spent a year at a Virginia prep school. These young men had so much potential, but nobody was really working with them due to time constraints. I saw that as an opportunity.

Seeing this was the state of affairs, I took my new found passion for coaching and my love for the quarterback position, and seized the opportunity to ask Coach Schnellenberger if I could work with them on a weekly basis since they would be red shirted and not be playing in the 1982 season anyway. After spending hours putting a proposal together on how I could facilitate an environment for them to better learn the game, I scheduled a meeting with him. I was really motivated to do this but I knew I had to be thoroughly prepared and convincing. I mean this man had coached Bob Griese and Joe Namath — both Hall of Fame quarterbacks. So, what was this 25-year-old with no coaching experience going to bring to the table?

My written proposal went something like this:

Coach Schnellenberger,

There is a progression of learning for every position on the football team, but we both agree the proper development of a quarterback that leads to his success on the field is critical to a team and a program's survival. As you well know, the quarterback position is the most complex, dynamic, and cerebral position in all of sport. A quarterback must be able to comfortably handle a massive amount of information and be able to quickly organize and simplify it in order to use his inherent and God-given intangibles to reach a high performance level.

Next spring and into the fall, these young men will be competing to become the successor to Jim Kelly as UM begins a new QB era for the first time in three years. For the quality of quarterback play to continue at the highest level, their preparation must immediately be initiated.

With this in mind, I would like to spend a minimum of two nights a week with Bernie and Vinny while the varsity is in game plan meetings and give them personal coaching in a classroom setting that would accelerate their learning curve for the upcoming spring. I enclosed a complete syllabus of what I would be teaching and the methods I would use to accomplish this task.

To my astonishment, Coach Schnellenberger approved it. Looking back, I see why he gave me the go ahead. My proposal was clear and concise.

My passion was clearly evident and my demeanor was one of confidence, yet at the same time honest and humble. In my mind first and foremost was helping the team, and the quarterback position was my area of so-called expertise. I just let myself go and threw it out there. I believe Coach Schnellenberger was the first to see something in me that I didn't even see in myself. To this day he stays a close friend and mentor, and a truly great leader. He said yes, and sometimes I think he just did it because I would do a good job of babysitting his two young quarterback prodigies.

Today, in meetings, I use the term "game defining moment" or GDM. This might be a goal line or short yardage play that was particularly relevant in the game's result. This meeting was not a GDM, but rather an **LDM, a LIFE DEFINING MOMENT.** The importance of preparation, passion, and luck, as well as a piece of humility, cannot be over estimated. In a football game as in life, you never know which play will really be the GDM. You have to play every play as if it is, because you just never know what will transpire. To me that means thorough and detailed preparation with an all out passion to succeed. On that day during that moment in Coach Schnellenberger's office, I was all of that and more. I was now

Coaching in Miami

"Marc Trestman: Quarterback Coach..." even if it wasn't officially written in the team's media guide. Thank you Howard, a thousand times over.

With no formal coaching background it was basically like teaching "Quarterbacking 101." I covered everything slowly and methodically, using transparencies, chalk boards and plenty of video tape. I would script practices and we would go outside and go through it over and over again. Beyond that, there was just an incredible array of dialogue that challenged the two of them with a multitude of theoretical questions. I needed them to be free and uninhibited with regards to speaking their minds. I wanted them to have confidence out there.

I broke everything down with them too. Each night I would challenge them to read and react on various issues including: blitzing scenarios, drops and reads, protection schemes, blitzes, gap coverages, rushing routes and formations. I would even send them home with tests where they could assess their own development in those areas. I cannot even express how exhilarating it was to be around these two young men and what a tremendous learning experience it was for me.

Being a quarterback takes a great deal of discipline and preparation. As I have said more than once in this book, in my opinion it is the most dynamic and complex position in sports and it takes an intelligence level that is second to none. So, as the quarterback coach, I knew that I needed to be one step ahead of these guys. I needed to find different ways to stimulate them and continually inspire them. This was my challenge then and it is no different today. As a result, I set extremely high standards and pushed myself even harder than I pushed them. I soon figured out that it was not about the quarterback living up to my standards, it was about me being able to live up to my quarterback's standards. That has never changed.

Again, I think my law school background really helped me to prepare for this. Law school included long hours of studying, meticulous note taking, maintaining an intense focus, paying attention to detail, implementing precise time management skills, and possessing an overall determination to succeed. You had to have a lot of mental and physical endurance to work such long hours and under such stress. Luckily, I had those skills and was now putting them to good use.

It took me a while, but I eventually learned that every player learns differently. So, as a coach, you have got to find that way of getting to them — whatever that may be. Some guys have to walk it; some guys have to hear it; some guys have to see it; some guys have to rep it; and some guys have to do all of the above. They are all different, and that is what is so exciting as a coach, to work with these young men and to help them figure those things out. To see them come in raw and undeveloped, and then to see them grow and mature is very rewarding. Throw in discipline and hard work and it is like a light bulb goes off for them. Then, to think that you had a small part in serving in their evolution towards success, that's what is unbelievably rewarding.

I have known from a very young age that quarterbacks are not born, they are developed. And without a coach to train him, and teach him the fundamentals and details in a dignified, organized manner — and at the highest standard — the quarterback can not and will not succeed. No quarterback ever played at a high level without a demanding coach, and no coach ever became a great coach without exceptional and consistent quarterback play. The two are completely intertwined.

As for coaching quarterbacks at 26, I just taught myself as I went along. I used what I had learned from previous coaches — especially Coach Morrall, borrowed from my experiences as a member of two NFL camps, and reinforced what I was able to pull out of our UM offensive playbook. Having played the position at the collegiate level was obviously a huge bonus as well. Nobody really showed me or trained me how to do it though. I just worked through each day and used my passion, my ability to stay on task and be organized, and my empathy for the difficulty of playing this position. I just became a teacher. I was instinctively demanding at times and appropriately nurturing at others. At the end of the day though, to be able to mentor these young men was unbelievable.

I developed my own style which, believe it or not, I still use to this day. In coaching as with any line of work, you really have to be comfortable in your own skin. I have been around so many great quarterbacks and coaches, and I have truly learned something from every one of them. Due to my respect for the world's greatest game and for the people who play and coach it, I am extremely demanding of quarterbacks. However, I try to be reasonable, extremely organized, and empathetic to the difficulty of playing a position that is more difficult mentally and physically than any other. The system might be unorthodox, but it works. In fact, I use the same formula for coaching quarterbacks as I do as a head coach.

Coaching was a lot of work, but there were some great perks too. I will never forget the day Joe Namath came and spoke to the team. That was a real thrill for me because he was one of my idols growing up. I remember reading his book when I was a kid; I wanted to learn as much about him as I could. I dropped back into the pocket like he did and I even wore white shoes in high school just because he did. He was so charismatic as a player, with such swagger, and he carried himself with such confidence. Joe was coached by Howard at Alabama and the talk he gave our team the night before the National Championship game versus Nebraska was memorable and inspiring to all of us.

When I finally graduated from law school it was a huge relief. I had been working so hard for the past two years as a volunteer assistant and was thrilled to be done with classes, studying, and exams. I wasn't sure exactly what I was going to do career-wise, but I knew that I had to take the Bar Exam to officially become a lawyer. I even interviewed with a local firm that specialized in personal injury litigation. At that time in the early 80's, Florida courts were giving out millions of dollars in judgments to plaintiffs and the law firm of Spence, Paine, Massington and Grossman was doing very well.

Paul Levine was a partner in the firm, as well as a Penn State alumni and huge Joe Paterno fan. I met Paul on a plane traveling from Pittsburgh after we had both been at State College to see a game. I was there to scout the Nittany Lions and Paul was there to see his beloved alma mater. I was sitting on the aisle of the plane completing my scouting report when he walked by on his way to the lavatory. He asked what I was doing, and the conversation eventually led to an interview as well as a 30 year friendship. Paul is in Los Angeles today, where he has written numerous books and TV show pilots. Stuart Grossman was another partner who I am also proud to call my friend. He is still a practicing attorney and a life-long supporter of UM athletics. At the time the partners in the firm were all relatively young, but many years later after they finally closed the doors, there were a lot of very wealthy attorneys who left there to all go their separate ways.

While preparing for the Bar Exam, I began to send out job applications to schools all over the country, asking for an opportunity to work as an assistant coach. I would have loved to have stayed in Miami, but there weren't any job openings on the team. At the time, I didn't really know if I would be coaching football another year or practicing law. What I did know was that I had to start making a living and get off my Dad's payroll.

Incredibly, out of over 100 personal letters sent to head coaches all over the country, I got one interview. One. It was with Wally English, who had recently left the Miami Dolphins to take over as the head coach at Tulane University. He was familiar with me from his time in Miami and was willing to give me an interview. I went to his home in Miami to meet with him but ultimately was turned down. I was certainly disappointed, but I reminded myself about Dad's advice to always have a "Plan B." Yes, I had my law degree to fall back on, but in my heart I wanted to coach. That had become my passion.

Then, in the spring of 1983 something amazing happened. The NCAA announced that college football programs could now hire one extra full time assistant coach, going from eight to nine. The volunteer position was now eliminated. Coach Schnellenberger had always promised me that if a position opened up that I would be first in line for consideration. Sure enough, as soon as the rule went into effect I got the call. Luckily, Earl Morrall didn't want to go full time, and our offensive coordinator, Kim Helton, left to join the NFL's Tampa Bay Bucs.

With that, Coach Schnellenberger offered me a position on his staff as the team's quarterbacks coach and I was absolutely thrilled. I would make $19,000 per year, drive a company car, and get to coach the game I had loved since I was barely old enough to stand. This was incomprehensible to me. Once I gained my equilibrium, however, I realized that Jim Kelly, the future NFL Hall of Famer, had set the bar for UM quarterbacks at the highest level. If we were to continue on the path to becoming "Quarterback U," then I had some real work ahead of me.

As an assistant coach I was going to have to do my fair share of recruiting. I drove up and down the Florida coast, from Boca Raton to Vero Beach, hat was my recruiting territory. I would walk into schools during the day and meet the coaches, possibly rub shoulders with a player or two, talk to coaches about their Division I prospects, and then catch some practices in the afternoon.

To be honest, I was somewhat uncomfortable in this part of the college coaching process. I was not a great conversationalist and was inherently over-serious at the time. Beyond that, I just wasn't big on driving around all day. It got to be a grind. Great recruiters are hard to find because it takes a relentless passion and certain level of competitiveness to succeed. In many regards this was not football, this was hard core sales. At the time it just wasn't for me, but I actually came to enjoy the process some 20 years later when I got back into coaching at the collegiate level at N.C. State. Getting out of the office, meeting coaches and exchanging football ideas and concepts, meeting families, and working to properly and unselfishly steer young men in the right direction can be very rewarding. This was a totally new perspective for me that was certainly not present in 1983.

At the time, I wanted it to be about football, not all of the other stuff that came along with it. I was just a little bit older than these kids at 26, and was not that interested in chasing them and convincing them to come to our school. So, without any experience, I just dove in and did it the best I could. I had no plan going in, I really didn't. It's almost funny to look back at now when I think about it.

Anyway, my first year as a full-time member of the staff turned out to be a memorable one. I worked very closely with Gary Stevens, who was the offensive coordinator. He called the plays and I would relay them in to the quarterback from the sideline via hand signals. The chemistry between Gary and I was unbelievable. Oftentimes in the collegiate ranks the offensive coordinator also serves as the quarterback coach. On our staff, however, I handled the quarterback duties while Gary doubled up as the receivers coach.

The thing that was especially unique in my situation was the fact that he really let me coach. As I look back, the trust and confidence he had in me was amazing. While he focused on working with the receivers and with the offense as a whole, he gave me complete control to work with the quarterbacks. Nowadays, that is something that is almost unheard of. I would work with Bernie and Vinnie the entire week and deal with them exclusively. Then Gary, myself, and the quarterbacks would come together in Gary's office late in the week and that is where we would pull the game plan together. The karma was great between us and as a result our quarterbacks played at a highly efficient level.

Our 1983 season would turn out to be one for the ages. Bernie and Vinny battled all pre-season, but Bernie ultimately emerged as the starter. It was a tough call, but we all agreed. Both were outstanding, but we just felt that he was a little bit more prepared at the time. We opened the season in September against rival University of Florida and we got beaten badly, 28-3. We did not execute our game plan and were handily defeated.

The next day, after the game, I was walking down the hallway of the football offices. I was doing everything I could to avoid Coach Schnellenberger, when all of a sudden I ran right into him as he walked toward me. He stopped me and asked me what I thought after looking at the tape. I answered by saying we chose the right guy in making Bernie the No. 1 quarterback and that we would get better over time. He looked at me through his thick mustache and in a reassuring way said, "If that's true, then 'they' are going to think we are geniuses." He then just turned and kept on walking. I breathed out a huge sigh of relief. I guess that was about as much of a vote of confidence as I was going to get.

We got on a roll from there and won our next 11 games in a row, ultimately winning the NCAA National Championship. I remember talking to Coach Schnellenberger, who had been with the Dolphins when they went undefeated and won the Super Bowl back in '72. I asked him how he did it, week in and week out, dealing with success. He held out his hand to make a straight line and he said, "You just have to stay steady." It

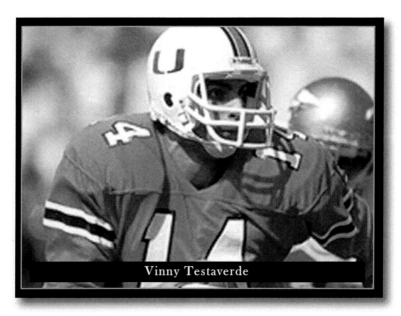

Vinny Testaverde

was great advice. That was what we did too; we stayed focused and never got too high or too low.

I stress an even keeled approach with my players today. Every game and every season has adversity that you must deal with, but often you begin to ride a wave and everything goes well. This happened in my first year of full-time coaching in Miami and it resonated with me this year as head coach of the Montreal Alouettes. I often think that dealing with success is more difficult than dealing with adversity. It takes confidence, humility, common sense, and an even-keeled approach that you — meaning I — are not the reason for the cumulative success that the team is dealing with. Even when everyone is telling you how great you are. The key is that the success is the result of everybody being accountable for their piece of the puzzle, and that truly "we" are all interconnected in "our" success. In fact, our motto in Montreal this season was: "Everything (and everybody) Matters!"

I remember playing Florida State at the end of the season. Bernie got hurt and went down late in the game. We called a time-out and Vinny came right over and said he was ready to go in. He was a red-shirt freshman at that time and if he went in, even for one play, he would lose an entire year of eligibility. It was really a sign of what kind of player he was, so unselfish. He didn't care about the eligibility; he just wanted to help his team win. It turned out that Bernie was okay after the time out and was able to go back in. He didn't want Vinny to lose any eligibility either. They were tight. We ended up winning the game, but I will never forget that moment. It really said a lot about the character of both of them. They were competitors in that they each wanted to start, yet they were teammates and both wanted to do what was best for the team. That is the kind of selflessness you seek daily with your players and it is the most difficult thing to create.

From there we played an unbelievably talented Nebraska team for the National Championship in the Orange Bowl. We were 21 point underdogs going in, but we put together an amazing game plan and executed it perfectly. Plus, it was in Miami, and with home-field advantage and an incredibly fast start, we were able to hold on for a thrilling 31-30 upset victory. We sealed the victory when Husker Coach Tom Osborne refused to go for the tie on the last play of the game and attempted a two point conversion for the win instead. Nebraska was down by one point when our cornerback, Kenny Calhoun, broke up the conversion pass from Husker quarterback Turner Gill to Jeff Smith end the game.

In those days, the tie went to the top ranked team, which they clearly were, and as such they would have been named as the national champions. You have to hand it to them for going for the win, but it certainly cost them big time. That Nebraska squad was as good a team as there has ever been in college football. But the University of Miami, with a focused and confident group of players and coaches, a red-shirt freshman who played much bigger than his age or experience, and a head coach who refused to allow his team to miss this opportunity (combined with a little bit of luck), became a dynasty that is now the standard for every Division I program in America. I had been coaching full-time for eight months and already had a National Championship ring on my finger. There have been many, many outstanding individuals who have coached for decades and never achieved that kind of success. I figured this "coaching thing" was going to be a piece of cake, but boy was I in for a rude awakening.

After winning the title, I figured we would take some time off to celebrate our accomplishment. No way. I think we enjoyed the moment for maybe a few hours, and then it was immediately all about getting back to work. We were already late in the recruiting process. There were no trips to the White House or anything like that in those days either, it was just "OK, you won the title, now go out and do it again." Miami was suddenly a col-

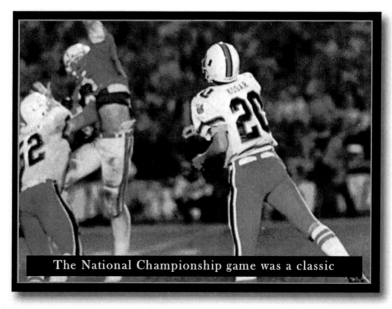

The National Championship game was a classic

lege football powerhouse and Coach Schnellenberger was dead set on keeping it all going.

I was so happy that we had won the title and was determined to do everything that I could to help us win it again that next season. I knew it was going to be tough though because we now had a big target on our backs, everybody was going to be gunning for us because we were No. 1. Then in May, my world turned upside down. I was on the road going to recruit at a local high school when all of a sudden I heard on the radio that Coach Schnellenberger was going to resign. I nearly ran off the road. It was a block-buster story, just huge. He had apparently gotten into an argument with the administration, and relationships were disintegrating quickly.

Not knowing what to do, I literally started to panic. Here I was, out recruiting kids who were obviously not going to sign with us if he was no longer the coach, and I was beside myself. Not to mention the fact that if he quit then I would probably be let go as well. So, I immediately turned around and drove back to campus to try to find out what was going on. Just as I got there I saw him walking out of the Hecht Center. I ran over to him and asked if we could speak. He was extremely cordial and we walked upstairs to his office together. He could see that I was shook up. I told him I heard that he was thinking of leaving UM and that I didn't know whether it was true but I hoped it was not the case. Before long I was practically begging him to stay on as head coach. He said little, but my sense was that he was on his way out. He eventually thanked me for coming by. I think he genuinely appreciated the fact that I would put myself out there and shared my true feelings. He knew that I genuinely believed in him as a great leader.

I later found out that he was headed to the USFL, a start up pro league that was hoping to give the rival NFL a run for its money. I was skeptical of the new league and pleaded with him to wait for an NFL opportunity. He didn't see it that way though and wanted a change of scenery. Coach Schnellenberger was the first person to see something in me that I didn't see in myself, and I will forever be grateful for the opportunity he gave me. Had he stayed, I have no doubt he would have been the Bear Bryant of our day, and won many more National Championships. He was as fine a coach as there was. He knew how to discipline; he was tough and demanding; he was extremely brilliant; he was so passionate; he knew the science of the game; and he literally single-handedly willed our football team to that national title. He taught me so much about what kind of work ethic it takes to be successful. He had this business-like approach to the game and what I learned from him was unbelievable. He refused to fail and stopped at nothing within the rules to make sure he succeeded. He is the reason the "U" has been the powerhouse it has for over 25 years.

It's funny but as I look back, if I would have become an agent, I might have gone on to become the east coast's Leigh Steinberg of that era, given all of the superstars that the Miami program would produce during the '80s and '90s. Howard recruited some amazing talent during those years without a doubt. Ironically, the USFL coaching position fell through for him a short while later and he ended up becoming the head coach at the University of Louisville, where he would also have a great deal of success.

As for me, it took me little time in my new found profession to realize that a fine line separates the good and the bad and that there is always adversity right around the corner. I went from finding ways to celebrate an improbable championship to starting to look for a new job in the course of just weeks. What kind of business had I gotten myself into?

A week later I was sitting in a small Marriott Hotel ballroom next to Miami International airport with the other UM football assistants when Coach Schnellenberger's successor Jimmy Johnson, who had been the head coach at Oklahoma State, walked into the room. He was well groomed and immaculately dressed in a stylish suit. It was an uneasy situation. I was terrified, figuring for sure I was going to get fired on the spot. It was pretty emotional. For starters, several of the full-time coaches were really upset over the fact that they had been passed over to succeed Coach Schnellenberger as the head coach. Jimmy could sense this and it was awkward. Then the athletic director stood up and announced to us that while Jimmy was brought in to be the head coach, the entire staff was going to remain the same. We all just breathed a huge sigh of relief. It was as if the weight of the world had been lifted off of my shoulders.

It was a tough situation for Jimmy and I felt for him. Not so much at the time, but now that I have worked in this profession for so long I can empathize with what he was up against upon his arrival. Yes, it was an amazing opportunity for him, but knowing Jimmy today I know that it was tough for him to come in and not be able to bring any of his assistant coaches from Oklahoma State with him. We all understood the challenges ahead of us though and just made the best of it. There was no time to waste, we had a national title to defend.

With Jimmy as our head coach it was a totally different environment. His personality early on just seemed different to me, almost a polar opposite of Coach Schnellenberger, and it was an extremely difficult transition for me to make. His focus was different, from the way he wanted to recruit to how he engaged the players. He was an extremely enthusiastic guy, very intense, highly emotional, and extremely bright. He also came to the program with a sense of quiet confidence and direction. He had a tough act to follow but he was up for the challenge.

Jimmy did not come in and try to micro-manage everything. His management style was to delegate and let the guys do their jobs, which was great. Plus, he was a defensive coach, so he especially left the offensive coaches alone. I just tried to listen as best as I could and soak in as much as possible. Jimmy's style made me understand that in coaching, as well as in business, you have to be flexible with the people that lead you as well as with the people you work with. In football, with so much variance in personality and culture, we all have to learn how to really listen, cooperate, and most importantly tolerate differences in one another. For me, being a first year coach, not to mention a Midwesterner, it was just different working for Jimmy. Nonetheless, it was an incredibly positive growing experience for me.

Expectations were high as the season opened, obviously, as defending national champs. We went 8-5 and overall had a very good year offensively, but struggled on the defensive side of the ball. Bernie started the season and played brilliantly. In fact he became a Heisman Trophy candidate and finished third in the voting behind winner Doug Flutie, out of Boston College.

Vinny was upset about his lack of playing time. So much so in fact that he came by my office and told me that he was prepared to transfer because he could not play behind Bernie another year. This was a life changing moment for both of us because I really wanted him to stay. So, with the help of his great parents, we changed his mind and he stayed at Miami. I spoke from my heart and told him that he was going to be a great player and that it just wasn't his time. I reassured him though that his time was coming and that I was going to be there with him to make sure he got his shot. I looked him in the eye and said, "Listen to me; you are going to be great, just hang in there." I am proud that he stayed and of his accomplishments as a college and long time NFL player. But as I watch from afar, I am most proud of the class that he has carried himself and the great father and husband he has become. Vinny T — a class act.

Towards the end of the season, I got a big affirmation that I was indeed doing all right as an assistant coach when I got offered the head coaching job at a small university in Alabama. One of our staffers took over as the program's athletics director and he knew me. I was flattered but didn't think it was the best fit for me at the time, so I turned it down. They were just getting their program started and I was leery about getting into a situation like that. In retrospect, it was a huge mistake not to take it. This is where I go back and wonder if I only had a good mentor in my life, maybe I would have taken that job. A good mentor would have slapped some sense into me and said, "You are 27 years old and you are turning down an offer to become a head coach... are you kidding me?"

A short while later I got a call from Lee Corso (now of ESPN fame), who had taken over as the head coach of the Orlando Renegades of the USFL. He asked me if I wanted to come in to interview for his offensive coordinator position. Again, I was blown away. I remember showing up for the meeting and Lee started razzing me about not wearing a coat and tie to the interview. Again, if I had a mentor in my life, someone to fill me in on these things, I would have shown up looking presentable. I didn't come in wearing shorts and a t-shirt; I just had on nice slacks and a dress shirt. It simply didn't cross my mind that I should have worn a suit. Crazy, I know. To this day, whenever I see Lee, he always teases me about that.

Anyway, I got back from my interview with Lee and Jimmy called me into his office. He had Gil Brandt on the phone, the legendary executive of the Cowboys, and he put me on with him. As a favor, Jimmy offered Gil's time to me with regards to some free career advice. Gil was a very powerful NFL figure in those days and his opinion meant a lot. He asked me what I ultimately wanted to do. I thought about it for a second and then said that I wanted to coach in the National Football League one day. His advice to me was simple: "Stay at Miami and keep doing what you are doing." He reassured me that I couldn't be in a better place, under Jimmy, as far as continuing to make a name for myself. I felt good about the conversation and felt good that Jimmy had given me a vote of confidence.

Jimmy Johnson taught me a lot in the short time I was with him. He showed me how important it is to be loyal to your staff, to be a mentor to them, and to do whatever you can to promote them in their career initiatives. He was also very generous in showing his personal thanks to his coaches. Then-future head coaches Norv Turner, Butch Davis, and Dave Wannstedt among others, would certainly tell you that without Jimmy's mentorship, loyalty, and support, they would not have been able to achieve the levels of professional success that they did. I am sure of it. Jimmy and I have not traveled in the same circles over the last 20 years, but his show of loyalty toward me allowed me to be patient and wait for that NFL job that at the time I did not know was right around the corner.

I didn't get the USFL job after all, but I knew that I was on the right track career-wise. I felt that my hard work had been validated in some way, just by being considered for the position. I didn't get overly confident or too sure of myself either. I never looked at myself and thought, "Gee, you're special; or you've got this gift..." or anything like that. I was just happy that I had a good job and was going to follow Gil's advice by staying in Miami and working hard.

Then, near the end of December in 1984, about a week before we were set to play UCLA in the Fiesta Bowl, I got a call out of the blue that would change my life yet again. I answered the phone and it was none other than Bud Grant. He had retired the year before but had just announced that he was going to come out of retirement to reassume his position as head coach of the Minnesota Vikings for the 1985 season.

He said, "Marc, I would like to offer you a job as an assistant coach with the Vikings. Are you interested?" Before he could even finish saying the word "interested," I had already blurted out, "Absolutely!" I didn't even flinch. I was so excited that I could barely contain myself. I said, "When would you like me to come up for an interview?" He said, "There is no interview. The job is yours. Do you want to be an NFL coach?" Bud knew me and knew what I was all about, so there was no need in his eyes for him to fly me up to Minneapolis to ask me a bunch of questions that he already knew the answers to.

I said, "What position would I be coaching?" He said, "I am not even sure yet. We'll find something for you, don't worry about that. Do you want the job or not?" I said, "Yes, but can I finish my obligation to

Miami?" "Sure," he said, "just call me after your bowl game. Good luck." That was it. I just stood there, dumbfounded. It was like a dream come true. I was going to get to be a coach with my childhood team, the Vikings. I was also going to "make the last cut" and be with the team for the entire season. Amazing. Simply amazing.

Well, I coached at UM through the Fiesta Bowl on New Year's Day in Phoenix, where we lost to UCLA, 39-37. Bernie and UCLA quarterback Steve Bono dueled it out and the Bruins ultimately came out on top in what turned out to be a heck of a game. It was indicative of our season though, because while we scored a boat-load of points, we gave up almost just as many on defense. Jimmy was beside himself at times because of it too. I remember blowing a 31-0 halftime lead to Maryland, as well as the infamous 47–45 loss to Boston College, which was immortalized by Doug Flutie's "hail mary" touchdown pass on the game's final play.

I will never forget Bernie coming to my hotel room the morning after the Fiesta Bowl to tell me that he had decided to forego his final two years of eligibility and enter the NFL draft. It was an amazing story but it didn't come as a surprise to me. Bernie graduated with honors two full years ahead of his freshman class with a double major in finance and economics. In addition, he had won a national championship and earned All American accolades to boot. Needless to say, there was nothing more for him to accomplish at the University of Miami. I told him that I was proud of him and that I was looking forward to joining him in the big leagues as well, as I also confided in him that I too was headed to the NFL. We both just laughed and wished each other well. It was a special moment.

As for Vinny, he would now have his long awaited opportunity. The starting quarterback job was now his and he wouldn't disappoint. He would lead the team to a pair of national title games and even won a Heisman Trophy along the way. From there, he would go on to play in the NFL for more than 20 years and establish himself as one of the league's all-time greats. What else can you say about the man? He is incredible.

I have so much respect for Vinnie and Bernie, I really do. Not only are they truly amazing players, they are such classy individuals. It was a real blessing to have been able to work with them at that stage of my career. I owe them a great deal. They both had remarkably different ways of seeing the game. Bernie was more verbal and expressive, with a multi-dimensional perspective. Vinny, meanwhile, had a quiet, very thorough, yet almost ingeniously simple way of seeing the game. Vinny's genius was his ability to take something that was said in a complex fashion and turn it into something so clear and simple. Both persevered and had unbelievably illustrious careers.

Soon after, I told Jimmy of Bud's offer. Knowing of my personal goal of coaching in the NFL, he wished me well. He would have great success down there though, leading the team to a national championship in 1987 and then going on to win three Super Bowls with the Dallas Cowboys after that. What can you say about Jimmy Johnson? He truly is a Hall of Fame coach. You know, one of my regrets is that I didn't stay in touch with him, personally, over the years, because he definitely positively affected me as a coach over my career. His enthusiasm, the way he handled players, his focus on the types of players that he wanted for his specific system — the guy was just a brilliant coach. I have always regretted not letting him know.

As for leaving Miami, it was bittersweet. It was an amazing opportunity for me to begin my coaching career and I was sad in some aspects to say goodbye. On the other hand, I was thrilled to be going home where I could be closer to my friends and family. As for my legacy with the Canes, it would be coming the following year, in the form of Steve Walsh, a stud quarterback who was from my home state of Minnesota.

It was ironic that I was able to convince Steve to come to Miami, given the fact that I never fancied myself as a very good recruiter in those days. I remember volunteering to go up and meet him because I figured it would be a free trip back home to see my family. And, it wasn't like the other coaches on the staff were jumping to the front of the line to fly up to Minnesota in the winter to take a look at the kid either, trust me.

When I met him though, we really connected. I went and saw him play at Cretin High School in St. Paul and I was really impressed. I saw something in him that a lot of other folks obviously didn't. He came down to Miami the next year, in '86, and didn't waste much time in making a name for himself. He followed Bernie's academic path and posted a 23-1 record in his two seasons as the team's starting quarterback. He also set the school record for career touchdown passes, and even led the Hurricanes to a national championship. Not bad for a kid a lot of schools didn't think had what it took to play Division One football. He went on to play in the NFL for 11 seasons after that as well. As of 2010, Steve is beginning a new career as the head football coach at West Palm Beach's Cardinal Newman High School. Boy, are those kids lucky. Steve will undoubtedly do a great job.

By leaving Miami, I gave up the opportunity to go to Dallas with Jimmy, win three Super Bowls, and be one of the dedicated coaches he promoted to a coordinator position or head coach in the NFL. Who knows what would have transpired had I stayed? Instead, I chose to take the "bird in hand," and go with the sure thing back in Minnesota. I was really excited about becoming a coach in the NFL, especially with the team and under the coach that I grew up following. I couldn't wait to see the look on my dad's face the first time he saw me down on the sideline standing proudly next to my new boss, Bud Grant. I knew that I had a whole bunch of hard work in front of me, but I was ready for the challenges that lay ahead. I was anxious to begin the next chapter in my life. I was going home!

"I remember the day Marc came into my office to interview for a volunteer coaching position with the Miami Hurricanes. He was in law school at the time and I could tell that he was a very intelligent young man. He later joined my staff as an assistant and we were thrilled to have him. He had a lot to do with the development of Bernie Kosar and Vinnie Testaverde, two of the best college quarterbacks of all time in my opinion. He knew how to motivate those guys and they thrived under his tutelage. He just had a great understanding of the game and was a really hard worker."

"From a technical standpoint, he is one of the best around in terms of game planning and designing offenses. He has the intensity and the drive to succeed. He has the ability to get those around him to buy into his concepts and philosophies. He is a great coach and a great manager. He is a winner. I am just so happy that he finally got his chance to be a head coach in Montreal. He has worked a long time in preparing himself for this and I have every confidence that he will have a lot of success up there. It is heartwarming to see your former assistants move on and into head coaching roles of their own, so I am certainly very proud of what he has accomplished." — *Howard Schnellenberger, Longtime NCAA & NFL Head Coach*

CH. 5) LIFE LESSONS WITH BUD BACK IN MINNESOTA

Leaders are facilitators. They put people in the positions they need to be in, in order to succeed. Leaders don't always have all the answers. Good leaders are open and straightforward about their lack of knowledge in particular areas, which is okay because they delegate and let those they lead do their jobs in a supportive environment. Leaders hire good people they can trust and then let them do their job. Leaders can lead without drawing attention. Leaders are always learning and asking questions from other leaders to improve themselves and gain knowledge so as to be able to provide answers and feedback.

Although most sane people would not enjoy packing up their belongings into a car and moving from sunny Miami to freezing Minneapolis in mid-January, I was thrilled. I later found out that I was coming in as the team's new running backs coach and I couldn't have been more excited. My backfield consisted of Darrin Nelson out of Stanford, Ted Brown, a prolific running back out of North Carolina State, and Alfred Anderson and Allen Rice, both from Baylor. They were all extremely talented, smart, and classy guys with very good character.

The Minnesota staff was full of extremely experienced professional football coaches. It was a fantastic learning situation for a young coach like myself to be coming into. I was going to be working alongside offensive line coach John Michaels and offensive coordinator Jerry Burns. Both coaches had been with the organization for almost 20 years and were just legends in my mind. I had watched these coaches for what seemed like my whole life and was so excited to be working with them, especially after getting to know them as a player in training camp. We also had defensive coordinator Floyd Peters, defensive line coach Paul Wiggin, who was a former head coach with the Chiefs, and Floyd Reese, a brilliant young defensive coach who has since gone on to work in the front offices with the Tennessee Titans and New England Patriots.

With a group of veteran coaches already in place, Bud wanted a couple of young coaches on his staff. So, in addition to myself, he also brought in a guy by the name of Pete Carroll to serve as the defensive backfield coach. Pete is now the head coach for the Seattle Seahawks, after being the head coach at USC for nine years, where he won a couple of NCAA National Championships and established himself as one of brightest minds in college football.

Even though Pete was a defensive coach, it didn't take long to see why Bud hired him. He was and remains extremely articulate, highly charismatic, and passionate about the game. This would not be the first time Pete and I would cross paths on the same staff. The two of us quickly became Bud's boys. Bud took the time to work with us, taught us the pri-

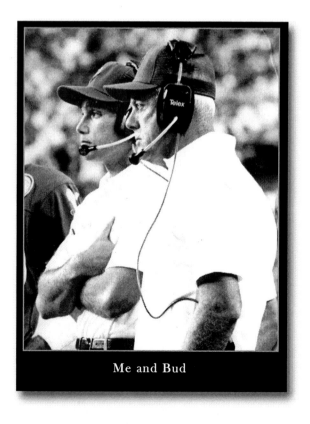

Me and Bud

orities of coaching, taught us to have fun doing it, and helped us grow. He saw something in us and he wanted to help us grow and mature as young coaches.

Once I got settled in I immersed myself in learning the new offensive system. I was now part of the Viking history which I had become an expert in over the last 20 years or so. I was learning the same offense that Fran Tarkenton, Gary Cuozzo, and Joe Kapp had learned to take the Vikes to the Super Bowl four different times. Amazing. I was on hallowed grounds and I was loving every minute it. My office was even just a few short steps down the hall from Bud Grant. I was living my dream.

A few weeks into my new job, Bud walked into my office one day and asked me what I thought about Bernie Kosar. Of course, I carried on about his intelligence, leadership qualities, character, as well as the hope and "it factor" he brought to each and every play he was involved in on the field. I was so caught up and passionate to answer the question, Bud had to slow me down. He then proceeded to tell me that the Vikings were going to make him our first pick in the 1985 draft. He just wanted to get my opinion of him beforehand. I was floored. I was so excited and had to do everything I could to hold back the tears. I thought to myself, "How amazing is this? I am going to get to coach Bernie for the rest of my career and we are going to do nothing but win Super Bowls."

Look, I knew why I had made it to the NFL — it was because of the success Bernie had at Miami. He had been my ticket. That's how it is in this league. I mean there aren't too many Hall of Fame head coaches in the NFL who didn't have a great quarterback on their roster at one time or another. Shula had Griese and Marino, Landry had Staubach, Walsh had Montana, and on and on. These men were unquestionably great coaches, but they also knew that they couldn't win the big games without those outstanding quarterbacks leading the way.

Bud used to say all the time when asked what made a successful coach: "A patient wife, a loyal dog, and a great quarterback... and not necessarily in that order." The answer was clear and concise. That was Bud, but this truth speaks true to any coach. You just gotta have a great quarterback if you want to be successful at this level. I then asked Bud how we were going to pull this off, given the fact that we only had the No. 4 overall pick in the draft, and that Bernie was going to go either No. 1 or No. 2? He just said not to worry, the team was in the process of working out those details.

Okay, this is where it starts to get a little bit confusing. Bernie, who had decided to forgo his final two years of eligibility at Miami and declare for the draft, came out publicly and said that he wanted to play for his hometown Cleveland Browns. However, because he had not yet officially graduated, he was not technically eligible for the draft. Instead, he was eligible for what is known as the supplemental draft, which was a separate draft altogether for a handful of players that fit certain eligibility requirements.

Buffalo held the first overall pick and they went out and signed Virginia Tech defensive end Bruce Smith several weeks before the draft. Shortly thereafter, Vikings general manager Mike Lynn traded two picks to the Houston Oilers in order to move up to the second spot of the draft. Later on the same day, Cleveland traded a pair of first round picks to Buffalo in exchange for their first round pick the following year. As a result, since the Bills had the worst record in the 1984 season, they held the first pick in both the regular NFL draft as well as the supplemental draft in 1985.

When a selection was used in the supplemental draft, that team then forfeited their pick in the next regular draft. This meant the Browns could now use the Bills' 1986 regular draft first round pick as the first pick in the 1985 supplemental draft. Confusing? Hang with me. Because Bernie had foregone his eligibility in college, he was now eligible to be taken in the supplemental draft. It was a loophole the brilliant Browns General Manager Ernie Accorsi figured out and it was a bombshell. Nobody saw it coming, nobody.

This was extremely unnerving to all of us, including our GM, Mike Lynn. Mike immediately went on the offensive to try to protect the Viking's interest on the matter and began to make a plan to try to neutralize the Browns. I was torn, because on one hand I selfishly wanted Bernie to join me in Minnesota, yet on the other hand I wanted him to be able to play in front of his hometown fans. I more than anyone understood the dream of playing and now coaching with the team you grew up with and the emotional attachment that is involved.

A few days later, Commissioner Pete Rozelle announced the four teams involved in the two trades (Buffalo, Cleveland, Houston and Minnesota) would be able to present their cases at a hearing. What ultimately transpired from that was Rozelle announcing he would leave the decision up to Kosar as to where he wanted to go. But, and this is important, he permitted the Vikings to try to persuade him to enter the regular draft with the condition they could not negotiate a potential contract with him. Translation... we still had a shot.

With the green light to talk to Bernie, we immediately put our plan into place to go out and recruit him. In what seemed like just a few hours, Bud and I got onto a private jet along with Jerry Burns and Mike Lynn and flew to Akron, Ohio. Why? To pick up Bernie Kosar Sr. and Geri Kosar, Bernie's parents. We then took off immediately on the approximately two and a half hour flight to Miami. Once there, we checked into the Hyatt on the marina and met up with Bernie for dinner. We then proceeded to work him hard and let him know we really wanted him up in Minnesota.

When I got back to my room I received a call from Bernie's agent, John Galetka. I have known John for years and he is a stand-up guy. John's message was brief and succinct. "Marc, as much as Bernie wants you to coach him, he wants to play in Cleveland. There is nothing left for you to do."

John simply reinforced what I already knew. Bernie Kosar was going home to play for the Browns. If the roles were reversed, I would have done exactly the same thing. Bernie grew up dreaming of playing for the Browns, and it was finally about to happen. Soon after, he informed the league of his decision and signed with Cleveland. I wished him well. I knew it wasn't personal, it was just business.

We talked later, and he told me he figured it would be easier for me to go to Cleveland than it would be for him to go to Minnesota. I never really believed him now that I was home in Minnesota, but later, to my astonishment, that is exactly what happened. As for the Vikings, we drafted University of Pittsburgh defensive end Chris Doleman, who went on to become an eight-time Pro Bowler. So, it turned out all right because both teams got great players in the end.

As for my job, learning our new offensive system proved to be incredibly complicated. It had been ingeniously piecemealed together over the past quarter century by the longtime members of the coaching staff and was very difficult to learn for someone new to the system. It was great for the players and coaches who had been with the team for years, but extremely difficult for those of us working at it for the first time. I remember calling my parents and telling them I had made the worst decision of my life. I was so discouraged. I remember at one point being just totally lost and didn't think there was any way I was ever going to figure it out.

While it was incredibly difficult to learn and memorize, the schematics of it were ingenious. In fact, 49ers Hall of Fame Coach Bill Walsh would later tell me that the basis of his legendary West Coast Offense came from Jerry Burns, our long time offensive coordinator. Yes, the prolific Viking offenses of the late 60's and 70's were the precursor to Bill Walsh's incredible Super Bowl offenses starring Joe Montana, Jerry Rice, and company.

Jerry pioneered the concept of the quick throwing game. A major part of the offense was the quarterback not holding the ball for long and throwing off to the running backs. Jerry's offense, which was inspired by legendary coaches Sid Gillman and Paul Brown, truly revolutionized the game. Bill said he studied it, and studied it, and eventually put his own spin on it. His Fran Tarkenton became Joe Montana and the rest is history.

Finally, after countless hours of studying, it began to all come together for me. Throughout the entire ordeal I stayed true to myself, which I was proud of. When I didn't know something, I asked my players or a coaching staff member. I was always straightforward with my running backs with the fact I had never played the position, but that I was going to do my best to prepare them to the best of my ability and to the highest professional standard. I am no different today. If I don't know, then I ask a coach, player, or even pick up the phone to ask coaching friends around the country. I am always going to be in an R&D (research and development) mode when it comes to football. When you have 11 on 11 (or in the CFL, 12 on 12), the variables and possibilities are infinite. The game continues to evolve on so many levels, and you have to stay ahead of the curve.

The other thing I learned early in coaching is you can't fake it. If you try to get by a situation with a player or fellow coach, you will lose their confidence and credibility immediately. As a leader of a football team today and as confident as I am with the years of experience I have, I can truly say I am still learning, asking questions, and telling those around me that I don't always have the information to give them the best answer.

It was baptism by fire as far as my learning curve. Jerry didn't have time to hold my hand and he expected me to not only understand the system, but to be able to teach it to the players. My first year in the NFL was much different than most rookie coaches. Most are trained in quality control. This means they don't do any coaching but are tied to the computer and need technology skills to even get in the door. In 1985 there was very little technology, but most first year coaches had more entry level job descriptions like drawing plays for the game plan, collecting statistics and opponent tendencies, and helping with scout teams. That was not the case for me.

I was thrown right in head first without any of that type of training. In many but not all instances, Jerry would simply tell me to gather the quarterbacks, running backs and receivers for meetings. Our young receiver coach, Dick Rehbein, and I would run the projector and just coach — calmly making corrections and complementing players as was appropriate. Here I was 28 years old, with a year and a half of experience, coaching veteran players — many of whom were older than me. Stuff like this never happens in professional football. Well, at least not nowadays. No way. It was crazy, but that was my indoctrination into the NFL coaching fraternity.

Before long I started working more closely with the quarterbacks, which accelerated my learning and confidence. This necessitated my initiation to weekly quarterback meetings. I was excited about working with Wade Wilson and Tommy Kramer, as well as Steve Bono (the former UCLA quarterback), our third stringer who later had a few good years with the 49ers. I even got to signal plays in from the sideline to our quarterbacks as Jerry called the plays from the press box.

I also had Bud listening on the headset during games as well. What an incredible learning experience. I realized quickly over the years that because Bud had so little turnover in coaches, I was one of the select few who would ever hear him coach on game day. What an honor. When people saw Bud Grant on the sideline for all those years they referred to him as "stoic." He may have appeared quiet, expressionless and indifferent, but I can tell you he was working his tail off managing the game. Bud was not a micromanager though, he delegated and let his coaches do their jobs. On Sundays, however, he was the leader and it was his job to manage the game. He got after officials and players, managed the clock, made critical decisions, and even found the time to calm down a very hyper and emotional Jerry Burns from time to time.

One thing Bud taught me early on was how to coach without drawing attention. This applies at practice or on game day. You have seen this with the likes of Tony Dungy, Bill Belichick, and other great coaches during the course of games over the years. You can get a lot of things done over the headsets on game day, and Bud found a way to get it done without drawing attention. He had a great feel for situational football, would reprimand a player for an undisciplined play, and would keep Jerry Burns (the funniest coach ever, a true football genius, and at times an emotional basket case) calm enough during the course of the game to make the next call. Bud saw things out there that 99.99% of normal humans would never see. He, of all the coaches I have worked for, was a master of observation. He could judge people quickly, see the game development, and then make the right decision at the proper time.

Our first game of the 1985 season was at home against Bill Walsh, Joe Montana and the World Champion San Francisco 49ers. Bud knew that they were obviously a great team, but he also reminded us that they weren't used to playing in close games. He told us that if we could keep it close into the fourth quarter and win the turnover battle, then we would win the game. Incredibly, that is exactly what happened. Not only that, but late in the game Bud predicted through keen observation that one of the 49er players (who I can't remember) would fumble the ball soon because of the way he was carrying it. Sure enough, the next series that same running back was stripped of the ball and the Vikings recovered. Welcome back, Bud!

It was a real lesson for me as a coach too. Whenever you are playing a team better than yours, even if it is only on paper, if you can keep it close and can be competitive until the end, then you've got a shot to win. Teams that are used to being way up at the end of games are forced to change their game plans in those situations, and that can be very disruptive.

I was getting an unprecedented education, a PhD of sorts in football, in what was and is my lifelong passion. All the while, I was getting the opportunity to coach alongside my childhood hero. He gave me clarity and perspective early on in my coaching career that has still never changed. He hired good people who he could trust and then let them do their jobs. I just learned so much from Bud, it was such an amazing experience for me.

I will never forget going to my first practice on the opening day of training camp. Now, in football, professional or otherwise, practice usually begins with stretching. Not with Bud. Instead, he had the players do 10 quick up-downs (hitting the ground on all fours and then quickly hopping back up) to break a sweat and that was it. Bud used to say: "What the heck do we need stretching for? That is for track runners, we are football players."

In football programs everywhere, sections of practices are organized with scripts that inform players and coaches what plays will be called. This script is a pre-set plan with every play to be run written down so it can be followed by the coaches and players. Bud, meanwhile, had his own unique

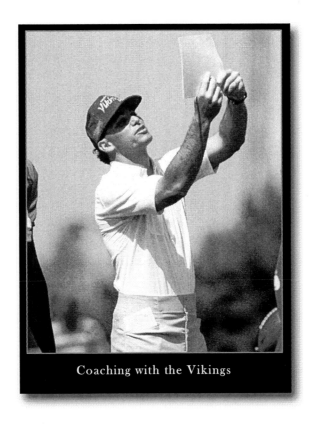

Coaching with the Vikings

way of doing things. He would blow his whistle and everyone would run over to him. He would then put the ball down on the ground and Jerry would begin to call the plays. That was it. It was chaos from a coaching perspective, but what I learned was that there are different ways to accomplish the same task. Most importantly, and I still do it every practice, was to make it so hard and so chaotic in practice that the games became easy. Without scripts, communication had to be better, players (and coaches) had to be focused. We had to think quickly on our feet, that was for sure. Beyond that, Bud could let us run plays until we got it right, without the worry of getting behind some pre-set schedule. There was a method to Bud's madness, and I was living it. What a lesson. This was priceless preparation for what the future would bring.

In those days there wasn't all the free agency that there is today, so there was a lot of continuity amongst the players from season to season. When we had our first practice we didn't even have a meeting before we hit the field. Guys would line up and start running plays, no walk-thru or anything. They all knew them for the most part. The few new guys who were there would just fall in and figure it out as we went along. This was unprecedented at the time and certainly would be so today as well. It was incredible. There were no mini-camps back then either. Nowadays, you have to reinvent the wheel every training camp. You may have a 50% turnover in players and need to start at square one. Back then though it was totally different.

Unquestionably, Bud's strengths were in managing and observing people and in identifying issues that could be problematic. He had been a very good college and professional player and his experience as a Grey Cup winning head coach in the CFL set the stage for his success with the Vikings. He didn't want to waste time doing things he felt were not relevant. He wanted to coach his team, spend time with the family, and most importantly — save time to hunt and fish. All of the other stuff, the intangibles, were for his assistants and support staff. Bud definitely kept it simple.

When we were on the field it was all about football. But quite frankly, Bud's genius as a leader and manager extended far beyond the football field. There were life lessons driven home, especially to Pete and I, on almost a daily basis. While eating meals at training camp, the cafeteria at Mankato State was set up so the coaches had a raised table overlooking the player's tables. Bud would oftentimes come sit next to Pete or myself, which made us both feel pretty special. This one particular evening I was doing my usual routine, which consisted of basically choking my food down as quickly as I could so I could get back to my room to review practice and prepare for the evening installation. Bud came over and asked: "Why are you eating so fast? Slow down, enjoy your meal. Try to take the time to taste your food. Your work will still be there, just a few minutes later. All you care about is getting back to your office to try to figure out how you are going to find the next first down." What Bud was telling me was to take some time to relax and recharge after what already was already a long day. We all know how unhealthy it is to eat fast, but also and maybe more importantly, it was at time to observe and gather information about the team. Simple, yet profound.

Since that time almost 25 years ago, I have used team meals to slow down and become aware of my surroundings, including which players eat together all the time and which make a point of eating and visiting with different guys each night. I have been able to discover so much by just watching and observing the demeanor and actions of my players. I therefore get so much more value out of them on the field. As a head coach I have been able to sit back and see things I never saw as an assistant. When it is your team you are so much more aware. Bud was so insightful, he really was. The man didn't say much, but when he did, it was like scripture. I could always tell he was interested in helping me get better.

Bud's family was certainly a prime focus in his life. He made it clear his wife, five kids, and tons of grandchildren took precedence. As important as it was for him to be the best head coach he could be, it was way more important for him to be a great husband and father. Sadly, Bud lost his wife Pat in 2009, she was an amazing lady. She, like so many coaches wives, was selfless, supportive and patient.

Bud went home every single night to have dinner with his family because it was just that important to him. He would leave around 5:30 almost religiously and then return to the office around 7:00 to get his head coaching duties done. Often, he would stop in my office on his way back in and spend a few minutes with me. He never seemed concerned with the football stuff either. Without inhibiting my drive to do great work, he mostly spent time slowing me down and making me more aware and appreciative of what I had. Bud still lives in the same house today he lived in back then. Nothing flamboyant or extravagant, just down to earth and modest — the same way he is. The guy just really had his priorities straight. During our training camp staff meetings, Bud would create dialogue at times that had nothing to do with football. It was his way of getting our minds off of football and allowing us to relax and decompress before the next practice. For example, one day we all sat down for our daily afternoon meeting and Bud said, "Hey Marc, do you know where the Khyber Pass is?" I was like, "Ah, no, not really." "Why don't you find out and then tell us tomorrow what you learned." So, I went out and looked it up and then the next day I told everyone it was this obscure mountain pass that links Pakistan and Afghanistan. He was simply trying to distract me away from my obsession with football.

Bud knew I wasn't used to a six month football season filled with so many games. He always reminded the young coaches that when we got done with Game 11 (which included four pre-season and seven regular season games), that we weren't even halfway through our season. He wanted us to remember that it was a marathon, not a sprint. Bud was aware that some of his young coaches like myself were coming out of the gates too fast and he wanted us to pace ourselves for the long haul. To this day I am constantly passing that very important message to young coaches joining our staff.

Another time I was at practice working a drill and Bud came over and stopped right next to me. I said, "What's up coach?" He looked at me, fixed my collar, and then said, "Did you see that?" "See what?" I asked. "Did you see that monarch butterfly?" "No, I must have missed it," I said. "Well, you should have. It just flew right past you, it was beautiful." Then he said, "Do you know where it was going?" I said "Ah... not really." "Why don't you find out, and then get back to me tomorrow." Then he just walked away.

I ran out to the library that night and looked it up. The next day I told the staff all about how the monarchs all fly down to Mexico every winter. What did that have to do with football? Absolutely nothing. That was the point. Understanding there are more important things than football and being aware in the moment are important life skills. Last year I had our players focus on effort awareness. In doing so, it made them actually pay attention to how hard they were working during certain parts of practice. I am confident in knowing that it made us better.

106

I will never forget the time Bud stopped practice when a red fox came out of the trees and lied down right on the field. We all just stood there and watched it. He wanted us to focus on it and think of nothing else. He would do the same thing in his office when deer came by. He would grab me and pull me in to watch the deer as they came over to eat hay out of the trough that he had placed adjacent to the practice field. He loved that stuff. It was these moments that defined a lot about who he was and what he was all about in my eyes.

Another time as the staff was leaving an afternoon meeting before a training practice, Bud told me to wait up. I walked out the side door of our dormitory where we were staying at the time and saw a horseshoe pit he had set up along the side of the building. He wanted to get in a quick game and I was going to be his pigeon. We played for five minutes and then he said to me: "You look like you're in a hurry. Don't worry, I have the whistle and nobody is going anywhere until I say so." At Vikings training camp, nobody left the locker room for the practice field until Bud blew the whistle. Period. And on this day, Bud was kicking my butt in horseshoes... so nobody was going anywhere!

That was Bud. He wanted me to stop and smell the roses for a minute. He wanted me to relax and clear my head. We would do this more than once, and he would always try to teach me a life lesson of some sort while we were there. I never forgot that and I have always tried to do the same with my young assistants, to pay it forward and share some of the wisdom that was handed down to me over the years. These were legendary moments in the making in my eyes.

Knowing what I know about Bud now, it is obvious why he loves hunting and fishing so much. He loved to get away and to enjoy the moment. He is a Zen guy. He had the ability to be "present" and he never seemed distracted. Even though he was a fierce competitor, when the game was over, it was over. This philosophy I am sure helped him overcome four bitter Super Bowl losses. He recognized that three hours on a Sunday, whatever the hype may be, was not going to take away from the six month journey the team had been on, not the mention the adversity and success they had all experienced.

This is exactly what I said to our football team after losing the Grey Cup in 2008. It was a bitter defeat, and with all due respect to John Hufnagel and the great game Calgary played, I believe we could have won. I really do. We all took the defeat hard, no doubt about it. But why after so much dedicated work, growth in relationships and culture between players and coaches, and spectacular play, would we let three hours on one day in that year diminish what we accomplished? No way. That was Bud, and I learned it first from him. That is still what I carry with me and who I am today. This allowed us to enjoy what we had accomplished in 2008 and build the "edge" and confidence in each other that we needed to return to the Grey Cup in 2009 and win it.

Nowadays, whenever I get rushed or panicked, I just slow down. I even eat slower, but I still have to work at it. I spend a lot more time in meaningful conversations and I ask more questions to coaches on how they and their families are doing. And most importantly, I mean it! I also really listen to their answers. Believe it or not, that kind of stuff might be just as important to winning as finding one more perfect play. These are times when the barrier of roles is eliminated and authentic relationships are formed that create a bond between members of an organization working in highly competitive environments. That guy will trust you and he will work hard for you when he knows you care. People enjoy being around other people who are good listeners. I have had to work hard at that because my mind just goes too fast at times. I am getting better though, because I am truly interested in what people have to say. It brings quality and value to an existing relationship and it often can be a true difference maker.

As previously mentioned, Bud didn't say a whole lot. However, he had this unique ability to communicate in sound bites. He could get his point across by saying very little, which was a real gift in my opinion. He would listen and observe before commenting and was very disciplined in that regard. He knew how to read his players and could find out the things that made them tick. He wanted smart players with strong character who wouldn't make mistakes. Those were the leaders on his teams and the guys who he wanted to lean on. He connected with them and treated them like men.

Bud also had a unique ability to get on players without embarrassing them in front of their peers or in front of the fans. The players respected that big time, this was a huge thing. As a result, those players took ownership of the team. They, in turn, would handle the disciplinary problems that would arise in the locker room and essentially lead the team both on and off the field. Bud didn't feel like he had to connect with everybody on the team, just the leaders. He would tell me about Jim Marshall, a defensive end who played for the Vikes in the late 60's and into the 70's. Jim was a warrior and one of the Vikings true leaders. He set the NFL record for consecutive games started (it was recently broken by Brett Favre in 2009) and his durability and dependability were unmatched. Bud would say to me, "All I had to do was get Marshall to buy in and the rest of the team would follow." Bud worked hard to connect to his team leaders. It was masterful and the team would essentially take ownership and responsibility of itself. The leaders had the credibility and the leverage with the other players to get things done.

It was a brilliant strategy, and one I worked hard to duplicate in my first year with the Alouettes in Montreal. I worked hard to really get to know the veterans first. I tried to find the strength of our leadership, that was key. I would then pound on the priorities of respect, trust, accountability, and a humble hard working approach — from there I hoped that they would buy in. The fact I was blessed with a brilliant quarterback in Anthony Calvillo and a core of vets who had championship experience only helped to expedite the process.

Bud was really principled too. For instance, he refused to talk to the officials. He wanted nothing to do with them... nothing. It was his way of protesting to the NFL that officials were too important to the integrity of the game and the coaches' livelihoods not to be full time. He really believed it, and although it hasn't been done to date, the demands and requirements of professional football's officials is much higher today. He felt strongly the officials wielded too much power and could dictate people's lives by their actions. So, that was sort of his form of protest, the fact he would not acknowledge the refs before or during the games.

It was actually pretty funny. Before games, when officials would come to the locker room for pre-game meetings, he would not allow them to enter. Bud would send one of his assistants to meet with them outside in the hall. He often had me do it and he would always tell me in a serious tone, "If you shake their hand, you're fired! Keep your hands in your pockets." It was believable, although I do think he was kidding.

Lastly, Bud was not a yeller. When he infrequently raised his voice it got everybody's attention, including mine. His quiet demeanor had a sort of soothing, calming effect on everybody. I remember one time in practice he asked me to get the video crane moved. This was a big platform on wheels that rose way up into the air so we could videotape practices from an aerial perspective. Well, occasionally we needed to move it from Point A to Point B around the field. I went over and yelled up to our video director on top of the platform and tried to get his attention. He didn't hear me, so I yelled his name even louder.

I then felt a hand on my shoulder. It was Bud and he said: "Marc, you don't have to yell at him. Just step back a few feet and get his attention, he will see you. You can just use your hands to gesture to him where you want him to go." Then he walked away, like it was nothing. Sure enough, I backed up and gestured to him, and he moved the crane. Now, I didn't think much of it at the time, but later I realized not yelling and screaming was part of Bud's philosophy of not drawing attention to oneself. He didn't feel it was necessary to draw attention to situations by yelling. It was so interesting to me that he would take the time to reach out and give me new perspective. What a gift.

I learned and have applied so many of Bud's life lessons to my own coaching style. He invested in me and now I do the same for my assistants. The infinite number of situations and possibilities that come up in the preparation, practice, and game of football leave an open door each day to learn something new. That is what this game is all about... learning something new, teaching it to others in time, and getting better at football while at the same time getting better in life.

We ended up with a 7-9 record that season, good for just third in the NFC Central Division. We were inconsistent and lost our last two games of the year to Atlanta and Philly. It was interesting speaking to Bud about the season though. Even with the team ending up at 7-9, it was one of his most enjoyable seasons as a head coach. I think being retired and then coming back to coach the team again gave him perspective on his own love for the game. He also enjoyed coaching his new young coaches, and of course his team which was full of high character players.

That off-season Bud decided to re-retire, this time for good. He simply had enough of the grind and was anxious to get back to his real passion — hunting and fishing. Bud always told me he believed he coached in the

NFL at the right time and he got out at the right time. In the years he coached, the off-season was a time for coaches to relax, decompress, and get refreshed after a six month and seven day a week grind. But the game changed and so did the role of a head coach. There were now more free agency issues, shorter off-seasons, and higher salaries, not to mention the greater demands and pressures on head coaches due to all the increased media such as ESPN, as well as all the talk radio. Bud was old school and that was not what he was about.

The game had changed and Bud could see his days in that new world would be numbered. So, he got out on top, leaving on his own terms. I totally respected his decision, but I was really sad to see him go. His life lessons for me were simply invaluable. I stay in contact with him nowadays and recently had lunch with him up in Minneapolis. His mind was as sharp as ever and his insights still profound. Thanks again, Bud.

With Bud stepping down, there were all sorts of rumors as to who was going to take over as the team's new head coach. Once again to my amazement, I was on a staff where the head coach voluntarily elected to leave, and I was standing there with no idea whether I would even have a job. Luckily, Jerry Burns was promoted to head coach and all of the assistants were kept in place. It was a huge sigh of relief for all of us.

In his place, Jerry then hired his good friend, Bob Schnelker, who had been the offensive coordinator of the Green Bay Packers. My role stayed the same as running backs coach, so not much really changed for me. In fact, in some regards, my duties decreased, because Bob served as the quarterbacks coach as well, which was something I had gotten more steadily involved with over the course of the previous season.

Originally, I thought everything was going to be the same, as far as our systems and coaching philosophies. A few days into training camp that next season though, everything got turned upside down. Bob was a black and white kind of a guy, with very little room for gray areas in how he saw the game. He was a very regimented thinker, very analytical and disciplined in his approach to the game, and had been very successful. He came in to our meeting one morning and said, "Guys, I can't do this. I can't learn this offense, it doesn't work for me and for the way I coach." I certainly knew where he was coming from because I was in his shoes a year earlier. Well, Bob decided with Bud gone it was time to re-tool the entire offense.

He asked me how I felt about it and I told him that I thought it was a logical time to make the change and that I was behind him 100%. I even encouraged him to convince Jerry to take this big leap of faith. As a result, we restructured the terminology with regards to the naming of plays and routes and coverages. Everything changed. We now had a symmetrical system where everything was interrelated, could be easily taught to new players, and was more functional throughout. It was essentially the same offense with different terminology. We had what I would call trickle down learning issues, in that if you learned something in one area of the offense, it would trickle down into another, and so on. The new system made a lot more sense to the players too, so it all worked out in the end.

For me, I went from memorizing an archaic, hodge-podge offense that made no sense, to learning a new one that was extremely sensible to everyone. It was still Jerry's offense, but it was redesigned so Bob could function in it, and players could easily learn it. As a result, our offense that 1986 season was very productive. Our record improved to 9-7 and we finished second in the division behind the Chicago Bears. We missed the playoffs, but I think we got better as a team. "Burnsey," as we affectionately called Jerry, handled the transition to head coach beautifully.

Bob Schnelker was an exceptional coordinator and a great play caller. One of the best the game has ever seen I would say. I learned a lot from him. All in all, things were going well for me. I felt like I had sort of settled into the lifestyle of being an NFL coach and I was happy. As for being back working and living in Minnesota, it was great. I could see my friends and family, and get away from the business of football much more than when I was in Miami. Yes, life was good both on and off the field.

That off-season I got a call from Ray Perkins, who had just taken over as the head coach of the Tampa Bay Buccaneers. Ray had been at the University of Alabama, and had also been the head coach of the New York Giants prior to that as well. I didn't know him at all, but he had heard about me and was familiar with my work. We started talking and he then told me that despite the fact that they had Steve Young as their quarterback, they were going to select Vinny Testaverde with the first overall pick of the upcoming draft. He then asked me if I was interested in becoming his quarterback coach.

The job was appealing to me not only because it would be a chance to reunite with Vinny, but also give me the immediate opportunity to coach the quarterbacks. With Bob as the quarterbacks coach and coordinator in Minnesota, I didn't know how long I would have to wait to coach the position again. Coach Perkins wasn't going to hire an offensive coordinator. He was going to serve as the head coach as well as the offensive coordinator, which meant I would essentially be his right hand guy. Plus, I was still single, so I figured moving at that point would be no big deal — especially back to sunny Florida. I also didn't want to miss out on another opportunity.

A year earlier, back in early March of 1985, John McVay, the vice president of football operations of the 49ers, called Vikings GM Mike Lynn and asked him for permission to talk to me about becoming their new quarterback coach. Mike turned him down, not wanting to lose me, and instead the Niners hired a young coach by the name of Mike Holmgren. That job, of course, eventually catapulted Mike into a high profile coordinator position with the 49ers. He coached Montana and Young and then moved on as a Super Bowl-winning head coach with the Packers. Those were the days when the Niners were a dynasty under Bill Walsh and he was a "king-maker" with all of his assistant coaches going on to become head coaches around the league — guys like Holmgren, Denny Green, and others. You know, Mike Lynn told me about it and then gave me some good advice. He said, "Marc, you can never look back in this business." I agree, but in retrospect, that is one job that could have been a big game-changer in my life.

I wanted to be mentored by coaches like Bill Walsh and was hungry for opportunities to advance my career. I wanted to be a quarterback coach, but with Bob Schnelker firing on all cylinders as the Viking's offensive coordinator and quarterback coach, my patience was being tested. My exuberance and drive to be a great coach told me to take this new position with Ray, and I had nothing holding me back. It was a completely new system and I was getting in on the ground floor. I told Jerry I did not want to pass this one up. He thanked me and wished me well. Little did I know at the time, but I had just made a huge mistake. Huge. To this day I look back and wonder why in the world I would leave my team in my hometown with Bud Grant still in an office just a few feet away (continuing to work with the team as a consultant). What was I thinking? Was I crazy? To this day I am still not sure.

I owe Jerry a lot and feel very indebted to him. He threw me into the fire as a young coach with no experience and I learned a great deal from him. He was an older coach and he looked just like Burgess Meredith. He would always say to me, "Hey boy, get down there and coach those guys up!" I really enjoyed coaching with him. He was fun, extremely bright, and just a really good guy. The F-bombs flew like crazy with him and there was never a dull moment when he was around. He was truly a "player's coach." The guys loved his personality and respected his foot-

"Marc came into the Vikings organization as almost a gopher, at the bottom of the assistant coaching ladder. He just dove in and did whatever we asked him to do though. I could see early on that he had all the mental capacities to be a good coach. He is a really bright guy. Had he remained as a lawyer, as he originally went to school for, he would most certainly be a very wealthy man today. He has a passion for the game though and that has kept him in it for all these years."

"As a coach he absorbs things very quickly and is able to put it into a proper perspective. He knows how to manage people and he really understands the game of football. He has brought it down to a simple denominator. He realized that football is not as complicated as people like to think it is. He has worked under a lot of systems and has worked with a lot of outstanding coaches over the years too. He has been to two Grey Cups in his first two years in the CFL and has been named Coach of the Year. In my opinion, he is more than ready and prepared to take on an NFL head coaching position. He has done a great job and his opportunity will come."

"The world is full of wannabe coaches and Marc has shown what it takes to actually make it. It takes a pretty resilient person to stay in the business as long as he has, so I give him a lot of credit. He has moved around a great deal and that vagabond lifestyle has had to have taken a toll over the years. It is hard to raise a family in that environment. To his credit, he has been able to survive all of that and still come out on top. That is what it takes to succeed in this business, determination and hard work. He has hung in there for a long time and I am really rooting for him." — *Bud Grant, Hall of Fame Coach, Minnesota Vikings*

ball expertise. He was a one of a kind. We had a very solid, positive relationship together and as you will find out later on, our paths would cross yet again down the road.

As for my parents, they understood my decision to leave. Sure, like any parents, they would have loved for me to stay, but they wanted me to be happy and to advance my career. These were very selfish times in my life. I was married to my job at that point and didn't give of myself in those days like I should have. It took for me to have children years later to realize the importance of family. I was so focused on climbing the ladder, I couldn't see anything else.

Not fighting for an opportunity of a lifetime in San Francisco, the league's premiere franchise, haunted me and I felt somehow cheated. I didn't want that to happen again, so I abruptly left a good situation to join a franchise that had struggled mightily over the years. At the time they were the league's least respected team. Why I left still doesn't make any sense to me, even today. I was drifting in the wind and letting fate, not brains show me the way. But at the time, I just knew I needed to keep having more responsibility and I needed new challenges which would eventually lead to me being promoted to a coordinator and eventually a head coach. With my abundance of life lessons learned from Bud and the others in Minnesota, I was off to Tampa for the next chapter in my life.

CH. 6) A "STRIKING" REUNION WITH VINNY IN TAMPA BAY

Successful leadership starts at the top and there must be organizational buy-in for success to be achieved. Lifelong relationships really matter and the quality of those relationships matter even more, because friends help friends out when they need it the most (i.e. when it is time for a leader to head in a different direction from the current organization because of lack of buy-in). Leaders build relationships through trust and respect. Often these relationships propel leaders in their careers and through adversity. Many aspects of adversity are out of a leader's control. To make it through, leaders must be adaptable, prepared and ready to bounce back when given the opportunity.

Going to Tampa was an exciting time for me. I was certainly apprehensive because the team had finished in last place the year before, but I was anxious to meet up with Vinny again and to be back coaching quarterbacks. When I first arrived there, Steve Young was the guy, but I wasn't sure if he was going to be there to mentor Vinny or not. We crossed paths only briefly in Tampa before he was traded to San Francisco prior to the April draft. Steve, of course, moved on to back up Joe Montana and eventually led the Niners to a victory in the 1995 Super Bowl. He would go on to be inducted into the Hall of Fame and is now doing a magnificent job as an analyst with ESPN. Fortunately, our paths would cross again down the road.

I hit the ground running as soon as I got to Tampa and was immediately working ungodly hours trying to learn Ray's new system. I found out quickly my experience as a running backs coach in Minnesota had made me a more well-rounded teacher of the quarterback position. I had gained a much better understanding of line blocking schemes, running lanes, and about how the running backs fit into the overall offensive system. I was looking forward to taking that knowledge I had gained over those two seasons with the Vikings and applying it to my new team as it pertained to the quarterback. Also, Ray was aware I had come out of two great offensive systems in Miami and Minnesota and embraced the opportunity to pick my brain to complete our offensive package. That boost of confidence meant a great deal to me.

In many regards going to Tampa was like starting over because we were going to be developing a new offensive system from the ground up. We had some great coaches on our staff though to take on the task, including: Sylvester Croom, who would go on to become the head coach at Mississippi State, and Richard Williamson, the longtime receivers coach for the Carolina Panthers. We all had come together to create this new, exciting playbook and really looked forward to seeing it come to fruition down in training camp.

Vinny Testaverde

In late July we began training camp at the University of Tampa. We worked really hard, and despite the fact that there was high humidity and several life threatening lightning strikes throughout our afternoon practices, things went well. Working alongside Ray was a unique experience to say the least. He was tireless and extremely self-confident. He was also a micro-manager and as such wanted to do everything himself. He was the head coach, offensive coordinator, chief scout, general manager, and team president. It was amazing how one guy could possibly think he could wear so many hats and be effective at all of them. Despite all of that, I really enjoyed working for him because I respected his passion for the game. He was a former player so the players respected him too. His biggest asset was his sincere love for football and his ability to pass that on to the players and coaches.

Late in camp that year we heard that the NFL players were going to walk-out and go on strike because of differences over their collective bargaining agreement with the owners. We never thought it would happen, but it did. You see, the union had been battling with the owners over free agency and monetary issues, and everything came to a head in the summer

Coaching the Bucs

of 1987. So the owners, not wanting to lose any money from their television commitments, had us use replacement players, or scabs as they were known. It was awful. The games actually counted in the record books too. We had to prepare entirely new simplified game plans for these guys, knowing full well none of them were going to be around when the strike ended. We also had to prepare game plans for the real players in case the strike ended in the middle of the week. It was messy and utterly exhausting for the staff.

Eventually, after a handful of games, the players resolved their issues with the owners and returned to the field. It was a very difficult time and the only thing going for us was every other team was in the same boat. Incidentally, there was a movie that came out a few years back that highlighted the whole incident called "The Replacements." I was actually hired to train actor Keanu Reeves and teach him how to play quarterback. I had a conflict come up though at the last minute and had to pass. My big Hollywood moment... and I blew it.

Eventually we got things figured out on the field and started to come together as a team. With Vinny being a rookie, Ray was reluctant to throw him to the wolves early in the season. So, we wound up going with veteran Steve DeBerg at quarterback. With this plan, Vinny could learn the system under him and then slowly gain some confidence before taking over. Steve had an incredible personality and was a stickler for preparation. I learned a great deal from him. He was several years older than I was and he helped train me as a young quarterback coach. He affirmed to me how demanding a quarterback coach had to be by clearly explaining what he expected from me. He was tireless and relentless in his preparation and knew what was necessary to achieve success in the NFL. He made me realize that a quarterback coach's work is never done. On Fridays and Saturdays after practice, when most players and coaches left the facilities, he and I would review film, study pass reads and audibles, and work on the game plan for the upcoming game. He used to grab me after a Saturday walk thru and say, "Marc, let's go!" The guy just loved to be pushed. He was very funny too, a real practical joker. He could be goofing off one minute and then dead serious a minute later. The players loved him and he was a huge asset in the locker room. He respected the game and I respected him. Working with him was like hitting the jackpot, it really was. He just taught me so much about what it took to be a professional in this league.

As for how our season went, it was pretty much a disaster. We lost our final eight games to finish with a pathetic 4-14 overall record. It was a big disappointment. We struggled in every facet of the game, and never really recovered from the time we lost during the strike. Steve played for the first half of the season and then we transitioned to Vinny for the second half to get him the experience necessary to take over in year two of the Perkins era. Tampa Bay had a history of futility and as I learned, it is always difficult to change a losing culture that runs throughout an entire organization. Ray and the staff had a lot of work to do and it wasn't going to happen overnight. I certainly wanted to do my part and as the team's quarterback coach I felt a strong responsibility to do work with Vinny as much as possible during the off-season so he could get up to speed that next year. Ray was mentally tough and assured us that we could turn things around. We all bought into it and were confident we could get over the hump.

Then, in early January of 1988, I got a call out of the blue from Bernie. Yes, that Bernie, as in Kosar... the soon-to-be Pro Bowl quarterback of the Cleveland Browns. Bernie had spent the last three years taking the Browns to three straight playoff appearances and two AFC Championship games. He had already (and not surprisingly) become an iconic figure in Ohio. Bernie asked me if I could get out of my contract because Lindy Infante, the Browns Offensive Coordinator, had become the new head coach for the Packers. Marty Schottenheimer, then head coach of the Browns, was interested in hiring me as the quarterback coach. Wow, this was big. I really wasn't quite sure what to do.

To say this was a dilemma would be an understatement. Stay and be a part of Vinny's development on a team that was no where near making the playoffs; or go and work with Bernie as a member of a franchise that was poised to win a Super Bowl. I was torn between my two guys and it was a tough decision. I knew that I was going to be letting one of them down and that was difficult for me. When it was all said and done though, I came to the conclusion that I was just not comfortable with the situation in Tampa. I enjoyed the guys on the staff, but at the end of the day I knew I needed to move on. I was respectful of Ray's passion for the game, but it was a losing environment in Tampa in those days — nothing like it is now. Although I was determined to help the program, I didn't think it was going to change any time soon.

With that, I had Marty contact Ray directly and ask for his permission to release me from my contract. Ray was quick to allow me to interview with them, which was interesting because ultimately I think he wanted a bigger hand in Vinny's development. You see, Ray's legacy was going to be tied to whether or not he could get Vinny to succeed in the NFL and he wanted to do it by himself. I understood completely. It turned out to be a win-win and luckily for me, Marty had come to the rescue. Bernie was right when he said I would have to go to Cleveland to coach him, and I was now on my way!

CH. 7) NEXT STOP: BERNIE AND THE BROWNS

Leadership requires accountability and for every decision to be made in the best interest of the organization. Leaders must also demand accountability upon those they lead in order to create an environment of responsibility and burden sharing. Leaders that are accountable for their actions build loyalty with their subordinates, and encourage continued hard work and respect. When demanding others to be accountable, leaders must be sure to not humiliate or retaliate because it's not personal, it's just business, and there are specific standards that must be met by everybody within the organization.

Upon moving to Cleveland I took a little time to reflect. I had been coaching for four and a half years and had already worked for six head coaches in four cities. It was surreal. But being relatively young, in good physical condition, and unmarried with no girlfriend, I was free to continue this unique adventure. I was now working for a great organization, with a winning tradition, and that had an unbelievable fan base. The Cleveland Browns had made three playoff appearances in Bernie's first three years in the league. Bernie had started every game and already led the team to the AFC Championship Game on two occasions. The Browns were the kings in Cleveland and at the time Bernie was "the man." The fans love him and he just owned that town. The team was on the verge of getting to the Super Bowl and I couldn't have been more excited about joining such a quality organization. I was working for a very sharp head coach in Marty Schottenheimer and I was anxious to dive in head first. Everything on paper looked good for me but in reality, my transition onto the Brown's coaching staff was much more difficult than I ever could have imagined.

Coming in as a new coach can be an extremely difficult transition, especially if you are not wanted — and that is where I suddenly found myself. Over my coaching career, I have put myself in some very tough positions. One of those tough positions comes from accepting jobs where I am what I would call a "mercenary coach." This occurs when an outside coach is hired onto an existing staff, of which members of that staff hoped and expected to get your job. Such was the case for me in this instance. Almost unilaterally, all of the other coaches on the staff made it pretty clear I was not welcome. I know these are words that sound of paranoia, but they are absolutely true. Looking back, had I had known it was going to be like that, I would have never taken the job. Ever. These guys did not want me around at all and it was really tough to take. After Lindy Infante had left, other assistants felt like they should have been promoted to be the offensive coordinator and quarterback coach. All these guys figured that Bernie made Marty bring me in and that didn't sit well with them. Marty, meanwhile, had appointed himself as the offensive coordinator, which also didn't sit well with a lot of the guys. I was happy to have Marty's support, but I was uncomfortable with what was about to become a very hostile environment for me.

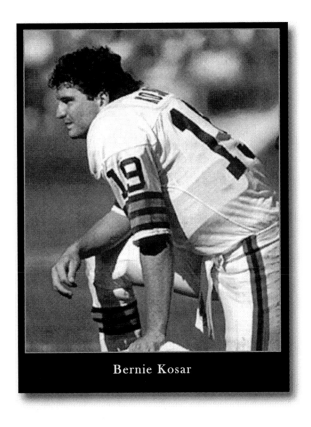

Bernie Kosar

Marty, also a micro-manager, was extremely thorough and detailed, and worked the team hard. He was also a great listener, communicator, information gatherer, and a quick study when it came to calling plays. He was tough, but fair, and a real task-master. I didn't ever really sense the feelings Marty had for me. We weren't close, but we got along and respected one another. I knew I was going to have my work cut out for me from the get-go, and he challenged me with his high intellect and confident demeanor.

I dove in and worked my butt off. My job would entail working with Bernie as well as our backups, Gary Danielson and Mike Pagel. They were a great group of guys and I was looking forward to working with them. I was also determined to earn the respect of the other coaches. I even lived in a hotel next to the team's training facilities for the entire season, just so I could put in the hours necessary to be successful. Every waking moment of my life was spent in my office or on the field. I was doing a lot of 18 hour days, it was pretty intense. Most of us on the offense were morning guys. By that I mean we got in early because it was when we got our best work done. One would think the earlier you arrive the earlier you could leave. Not in this business.

I learned quickly during training camp that it was not going to be easy. After evening meetings, we had a staff meeting which started a little after 10 p.m. and would usually go for more than an hour. After that, Marty would lead an offensive staff meeting that lasted well into the night. I mean late, like two or three o'clock in the morning. The staff then had to be up early to script and prepare for practices. This made for some of the most physically exhausting times in my coaching career, and it carried on throughout the entire season. But, I wasn't going to let them get me. After all, the first year of law school had prepared me well for times like this. I had survived that and I would survive this, regardless of the circumstances. I loved my job as an assistant coach and I was determined to succeed. It's like I always tell my girls: the Trestman's never give up!

The 1988 season started out with so much promise, but went south in a hurry when Bernie got injured. His backup, Gary Danielson, a smart veteran who had been with Detroit for most of his career, soon got hurt as well. We then had to go to our No. 3 quarterback, Mike Pagel, who incredibly also went down. It was unbelievable. From there we had to go with Don Strock, a 15 year veteran who had played behind Dan Marino in Miami, that our GM Ernie Accorsi had brought in midway through the season. Don was a good guy, I really liked him. He showed the kind of champion he was too when he arrived in Cleveland after being in Marino's shadow down in Miami. I was happy for him to finally get his chance to showcase his talents.

Don came in and had to learn an offense that was like learning a foreign language late in life. He couldn't make sense of it early, but he worked at it. I remember calling him on the Tuesday night of the week he was scheduled to start against the Eagles. The staff was game planning and I wanted to ask him if the pass list I had just sent him was acceptable. He said he was having a glass of wine with his wife, was excited about the opportunity, and really only needed three of the passes to get his job done on Sunday. That was Don, he just liked to keep things simple. He played really well for us in that game as well as in some other difficult, cold weather games against some really good teams. In fact, we just rode "Stroke" all the way to the playoffs. It was an amazing run, it truly was. Nobody thought we could do it, but we did. As the quarterback coach, I was especially proud of what we had accomplished considering all of the hardship we had endured that season.

I remember the last week of the season Don led us to an amazing comeback victory at Cleveland Stadium over the Houston Oilers to clinch a wild-card spot. Don had thrown some early interceptions during the first half, yet he overcame the initial adversity to beat the Oilers in a snowstorm. It always makes me laugh to think about seeing him out there in that blizzard, looking calm, cool and yes, tan— he just loved to hit the tanning salon. What a character. I never can laugh at the guy's guts though, he was as tough as they come.

From there we went on to play the Oilers yet again the very next week at home in the first round of the playoffs. Don got hurt in that game, but Pagel came in and wound up throwing a touchdown pass to Webster Slaughter late in the fourth quarter to pull us to within a point at 24–23. We then had three chances to recover an on-side kick, because of some opposition penalties. The Oilers recovered the ball, however, and ended our comeback bid. It was a tough loss and we were all just emotionally spent afterward. We finished the season with a very respectable 10–6 record and I was very proud of the way our guys responded to all the adversity. Believe it or not, as I look back I would have to say it was one of my most satisfying years in coaching. It was almost an impossible situation too, between the dysfunctional offensive staff, the injuries to our quarterbacks, and the horrendous hours. Personal differences aside, the guys on that staff were terrific coaches and we all overcame a very messy situation.

Much credit has to go to Marty for an amazing coaching job. With all the adversity on and off the field, he was somehow able to hold it all together. Marty never got the credit he deserved for that year's success though. He certainly didn't get it from our owner, Art Modell, who fired him a week after the season. For whatever the reason, those two just didn't see eye to eye. It was my understanding, although I don't know for sure, that Mr. Modell wanted Marty to promote me to be the offensive coordinator so he could focus solely on being the head coach. Marty apparently didn't agree with that though, so they parted ways.

Marty was quickly hired as the new head coach of the Kansas City Chiefs and he wound up taking about half of the staff with him. One of whom was our secondary coach, Bill Cowher. Bill was as fine a young coach as I had been around. He was everything you want in a coach: passionate, knowledgeable, and extremely bright. He related very well with his players as well. It was obvious early on to me that he had great leadership skills and potential. I saw this on the field, but in the year we were together, we had little or no time to get to know each other. If we weren't practicing, then we were meeting as an offense. There was no time. He would, of course, go on to win a Super Bowl in 2006 as the head coach of the Pittsburgh Steelers. Fortunately, Bill and I have recently reconnected and gotten to know each other as friends. He is a great person and I think the world of him.

As for Marty, I had a lot of respect for him. He was a great leader and very loyal to his staff. I will never forget one time during a game early on in the season where our relationship got tested. It was just seconds before the end of the first half in Houston and we had one timeout left. We had just run a play and the clock was running down, and I saw Marty trying to signal to Bernie to call a timeout. I yelled over to him: "Marty, don't worry, Bernie will handle this. Don't worry about it, he will take care of the clock." Bernie was a human computer with clock management, just amazing. He knew what to do. As such, Marty stopped trying to signal for a timeout and let Bernie handle the situation as per my request. Well, sure enough, the clock ran out before we could run a play. Had we called a timeout, we would have at least been able to kick a field goal. But now we got nothing. It was the worst case scenario.

As we were running off the field for halftime, I ran over to Marty to tell him I was sorry and that I really screwed up. He didn't say a word and he just kept running. I felt awful. We wound up losing the game too, by just a couple of points. I couldn't sleep that night. I was beside myself. The next morning I went into his office and apologized again. I told him I had no reason to believe Bernie wouldn't do his job and never could have foreseen the outcome that transpired. The reality was that we put Bernie in a situation that could have been avoided. I made a crucial mistake that was huge to the outcome.

So, I told Marty that I felt like he had every reason to fire me over what happened. I told him it was my fault and it was my mistake. I owned it. The responsibility fell on me, not him. He just looked up at me and said, "Marc, you work for me. You gave me information and I made the final decision not to call the time-out. Period. Now go back to work." That was it. He shouldered the responsibility for it and I respected that. Marty was that kind of leader. By shouldering the ultimate responsibility for mistakes made during the course of a game, Marty proved his loyalty to me. In turn, my loyalty to him went deep.

That off-season the Browns went out and hired New York Jets' Defensive Coordinator Bud Carson to serve as the team's new head coach. Bud was the architect of the famed Pittsburgh Steelers "Steel Curtain" defense back in the '70s which had won a bunch of Super Bowls. I was excited to work with him. I was even more excited when I found find that the Browns had hired Bud under the condition that I was to be the new offensive coordinator. Here I was, just 33 years old, and I was now the youngest offensive coordinator in the NFL. I had to pinch myself.

Even with all the loyalty I had for Marty, I was really relieved for this change. At the end of the day I was extremely uncomfortable with some of the confrontational styles within the coaching staff. I did my best to stay focused on Bernie and the other quarterbacks, and on doing my job, but it was an extremely dysfunctional work environment. At times I wondered if I would be better off just quitting. I never would, but it certainly crossed my mind.

Football aside for a moment, I was so blessed during the '88 season, because I met and fell in love with a beautiful young woman named Cindy Degennaro. I was shopping with my dad one day at the Beachwood Mall, on the east side of Cleveland. We were walking through this clothing store called Hemisphere and I saw this woman helping out a customer. She was beautiful. In fact, I didn't notice her first, my dad did. Dad shot an elbow in my ribs and said, "Look at the girl over there!" Good taste dad! But, that was it, and we left.

Then, about a month later, I met a friend of my uncle's daughter, who also lived in Cleveland. I coincidentally ran into her in the mall a month later and found out she worked at Hemisphere as well. I walked her back to the store and she introduced me to Cindy. I then asked Cindy for her phone number and the next day I called and asked her out. I had a couple of free tickets to the Cavaliers vs. Bulls basketball game, which turned out to be our first "official" date. One thing led to another and we started spending time together. We found that we were very different, but shared football as a common passion. It was great because Cindy loved football and was a huge Browns fan. She knew everything about the team and loved to talk football. I had never really made time for a serious girlfriend prior to that, so this was a big change for me.

Cindy is the most important person I have ever met in my life. Not because she has become my best friend and the mother of our children, but because she so clearly saw my many flaws. She changed my life because it wasn't just about me anymore. It wasn't about this relentless drive to achieve and it wasn't just about football. Cindy got me focused on the importance of balance, family, and to sometimes just take time to smell the roses. She had a great family that knew how to laugh and have fun. These were principles Bud Grant had taught me but that I had quickly forgotten as I drifted from Tampa Bay to Cleveland. She has made me a much more complete and well-rounded individual. She not only helped me recognize my flaws, she forced me to change — even when I resisted. She also brought out of me many good qualities that I never knew were there. I love her, she's the best thing that has ever happened to me.

Meanwhile, Coach Carson hired almost a completely new staff of coaches, including four new coaches on offense. They were all friends of his and as a result, this again unfortunately made for an extremely difficult working environment. There was politics and agendas, which was not fun to deal with. I am sure he was not thrilled to find out that Mr. Modell wanted me to be the offensive coordinator either, but that was a non-negotiable part of the deal as I would later learn. I quickly realized that working with Bud was going to be a challenge. Bud was 65 years old and very set in his ways. He was demanding and at times completely unreasonable, which made it very tough to coach under him. I worked hard for him though and was committed to being a positive resource for him on a daily basis.

As for my on-field duties, I was excited about having more responsibility and more credibility. In addition to serving as the team's offensive coordinator, I also kept my job as the quarterback's coach as well. I was going to be busy, but I was up for the challenge. Working directly with Bernie and the offense was a tremendous experience and we wound up having a great season. In fact, in my first year as an offensive coordinator we made it all the way to the AFC Championship Game. The season wasn't without its share of drama though. As time went on, I was told that Bud was very paranoid of me being 33 years old and hand-picked by the owner for the job.

Cindy and I

Early in the spring one day I overheard a conversation he had on the phone while I was waiting in his secretary's office. In it he told someone on the other end of the line that if we had a good season that year, then he was going to fire me. I couldn't believe what I just heard; in fact I refused to believe it. I was in total denial. This really happened, but at the time I just calmly let it slide because I was just determined to make the best of the situation and work hard. It got more and more difficult as the season went on though because as time went by and we kept playing well, all I could think about was getting fired. I coached the entire season that way and it felt awful. Halfway during the pre-season our general manager Ernie Accorsi called me to specifically ask me if I thought Bud was trying to undermine my ability to succeed. I lied and said no. I just simply could not be insubordinate to my head coach. I made a mistake that day. When your boss asks you a question, tell them the truth.

Anyway, the '89 season turned out to be a pretty wild ride. Taking over as the team's offensive coordinator was a big deal because in my mind, I wanted the job and the imminent challenge, but still was unsure whether I could handle it. The only way I was going to find out was to do it. Again, I go back to my own insecurities about never having a mentor and about never being formally trained as a coach. Being totally self-taught, I sort of unconsciously put myself on that island, for better or for worse. Regardless of the situation I was in, however, I just dug in and prepared to do whatever it was going to take to help the team win. I felt very strongly early

Patrolling the sidelines with Bud Carson

on that if Bernie could stay healthy, then we had a legitimate chance of making it deep into the playoffs. We had a very good team on both sides of the ball.

The season started out great. We beat the Jets and Steelers in our first two games and then, after losing some close games to Cincinnati, Miami and Pittsburgh, we got on a roll and won four straight games. We then lost four in a row in November before winning our last four games prior to heading into a bye and the playoffs. Bernie was playing well until late in the season when he suffered a pretty serious ligament tear on the index finger of his throwing hand. I was worried everything was going to fall apart at that point, but Bernie was mentally and physically tough enough to play through it — even with a make-shift sling on his finger.

As I have said, Bernie was extremely tough, both physically and mentally. He was also very articulate and had the ability to get his team to respond with his words. I remember one time while listening to him speak to the team, I literally had to turn away because I had started to cry. I was just so proud of him. Bernie was a true field general in its purist form. Even though I wasn't much older than him, it was like we had fostered this big brother type relationship. To watch his development since our time in Miami and now to see him having this kind of success, it was just amazing. I felt so blessed to be able to work with him on a daily basis. He made everyone around him better, especially me.

Bernie was a great leader and as such he was very demanding of everyone around him. His high standards applied to me as well. The evening before games I always went over the plays with the offense, including the initial third down situational calls. Bernie put a premium on these meetings as all quarterbacks do. I remember one game in particular where we got to our first third down call and I sent in a play that Bernie wasn't prepared for. We failed to convert and he came to the sideline pretty upset. I mean there was practically smoke coming out of his ears. Then he got in my ear and says: "Hey bro, what the hell are you doing? That wasn't the call we discussed!" What a moment. Bernie could not have cared if I was his mother at that moment. He was angry, and rightly so. This was business and he was holding me accountable. This was big and goes to the dynamic of trust that is so important between a quarterback and his coach. I had let him down and I wasn't going to ever let it happen again.

Looking back, that was a moment in my career that has helped me dramatically. Every football decision I have made since then is always measured by what is best for the team. If I have a player or coach who is not doing what they say they are going to do, or is not meeting the standard which has been set forth in the job description, I let them know. If I am not living up to my own standards then I am hopeful someone will say something to me as well. I believe I am way more demanding on myself than of others. The bottom line is that when you are in the people business, you have to build levels of trust and respect in the work environment. That's so important. It can be done without threats of retaliation or humiliation too. I would never say something to embarrass anyone or draw attention to myself. I have always worked very hard at that, and over the years I have gotten better, at least I think so. But, Bernie really pointed it out to me on this Sunday afternoon. The team really does come first, and when you are not doing your job properly, then you need to know.

We went on to beat Minnesota and Houston in our final two games of the year to clinch the AFC Central Division title. From there we edged Buffalo at home in a tight one, 34-30, behind Bernie's three touchdown passes to advance to the AFC Championship Game. It was incredibly exciting as we flew to Denver for the big game. As I was sitting on the plane, going over my game plans, I took some time to reflect. It was now five years since I had left Miami and almost seven years since I graduated from law school. It was hard to believe, but here I was just one win away from coaching in the Super Bowl. It was the opportunity of a lifetime.

Facing the Broncos on their home field in Denver was going to be no easy task. This would be the third time in four years that the Browns had faced the Broncos in the conference finals. These two teams had established THE rivalry of that era and we knew it was going to be a tough battle on both sides of the ball. Bernie and Denver quarterback John Elway already had two storied battles in 1996 and 1997, with John and his Broncos winning both of them. Denver jumped out to a 10-0 lead, but Bernie got us back in it after connecting with Brian Brennan on a 27-yard touchdown pass. Elway took over from there though and we could just never get back into it. Bernie threw three interceptions down the stretch and we lost the game, 37-21. It was a very difficult loss for me, the Browns, and all of northeast Ohio. It was a long flight home.

Two weeks later, Cindy and I were off to Hawaii. It is a tradition in the league that the losing coaching staffs of the conference championship games are rewarded by getting to coach their respective teams in the Pro Bowl. While in Hawaii, I was hearing rumors I was going to be fired from my job. Feeling uneasy, I went in to talk to Bud in his hotel room and he said it was absolutely not true. He completely denied it and said not to worry. He told me I had a great year, that we had done well offensively, and I had a bright future ahead of me with the Cleveland Browns. I was extremely relieved to say the least.

With that, we played the game and even had a little bit of fun on the sideline. It was nice to be coaching in a game that had no meaning in the standings for once. And, it was a thrill to be coaching so many outstanding players in that "all-star" environment. Anyway, after the game I asked Bud if it would be all right if I took a week off to spend some time touring Hawaii with Cindy. He said of course, as the entire staff would be off as well. He told me to have fun, and that we would catch up back in Cleveland.

Feeling relieved, Cindy and I took off to go tour the islands. It was great to be with her and to not have to worry about football. In fact, while on the island of Kauai, the tropical air took effect and I proposed. Luckily she said yes, and from there we said, "Why wait?" It was a spur of the moment decision, but it just felt right. So we exchanged our vows on the 16th hole of the Westin Kauai Lagoon golf course. As parents today we are disappointed that we made this decision, but we made amends by later having wedding parties in both Cleveland and Minneapolis.

Early on the morning of our wedding day, Cindy and I ran into 49er Offensive Coordinator Mike Holmgren in the hotel. Mike and I knew each other from his visit to Miami when I was the quarterback coach there. We had just won the National Championship and he came by to talk football. He was in Hawaii celebrating his 49ers Super Bowl win over the Broncos with his wife Kathy. We started talking and I invited them to join Cindy and I at our wedding ceremony. He agreed, and the two of them joined us as our only guests, believe it or not. How ironic, four years earlier, Mike was the quarterbacks coach at Brigham Young at the same time I was the backfield coach of the Vikings. As discussed earlier, the Vikings refused to allow me to speak with Bill Walsh about an available quarterback coaching position, so the 49ers went to BYU and hired Mike instead. Now we play the "what if" game. If I went to San Francisco, I cer-

133

tainly don't meet Cindy, and it is very possible Mike Holmgren does not have one of the best tenures of head coaches in league history. A twist of fate, and now he was going to be the only guest at my wedding. This was absurd and surreal.

As for the ceremony, it was perfect. It was a beautiful afternoon and I couldn't have been happier. We were on top of the world and nothing could have been better. We then walked back to our hotel room as husband and wife, I will never forget it. When I got into the room and sat down I saw the message light flashing on our phone. So, I picked it up and listened to the message. It was from Bud Carson, and he wanted me to call him right away. Not wanting to ruin the moment, I asked Cindy if I could please just call him quick to see what was up. She reluctantly agreed and I called him. Boy, what a mistake that was. Sure enough, the first words out of his mouth were that he "wanted to go in another direction" and I was being let go. All I could do was just stand there, speechless. I was stunned, I really was. No more than 15 minutes after I marry the girl of my dreams, my world comes crashing down on top of me. Needless to say, we had yet to actually consummate our marriage, and I had gotten

Our Wedding Night in Hawaii

fired. Talk about going from ecstasy to agony!

Cindy and I were absolutely devastated, both personally and professionally. I mean Cindy was a die-hard Browns fan, she grew up in Cleveland and loved Browns, and we loved being close to her family. I was enjoying the Browns as well. It was brutal. I had always figured I would be the heir apparent to Bud, and eventually be moved into the head coaching position. Mr. Modell had even talked to me about how Bud was 65 years old and about how I could learn the game from him for a few years before taking over. In the end though, Bud had gotten his wish — to get rid of me. Bud felt threatened by me and wanted me out of the picture. I was the youngest offensive coordinator in the league at the time and had just coached the offense to the AFC Championship Game. What was my reward? My "Thank you for all of my hard work?" A pink slip. Amazing.

The politics had finally gotten to me. The only vindication I got out of it was the fact that Bud's Browns went 1-15 the following season and he was ultimately fired. He let his ego get in the way and it got the best of him. I was there to help him reach his goal as a head coach, but Bud didn't get it. It cost him and I both. It ultimately cost the Browns as well. Believe it or not, that was the last time the Browns have been to the playoffs. The person I felt most badly for was Bernie. He did not deserve what happened, neither did his teammates, or his hometown. He would ultimately play nine seasons with the Browns before eventually finishing his career with the Dolphins in 1996. To this day I believe Bernie should be in the NFL Hall of Fame. He was an iceman who was able to play under tremendous pressure as a hometown hero. He was a winner on a team that went to the playoffs in his first five years in the league. He turned the Browns into something special and ultimately played in three AFC Championship Games in those five years. If it had not been for the brilliance of John Elway, in my opinion Bernie would be in Canton today, just a few miles from his hometown of Boardman.

Looking back, the whole experience in Cleveland was pretty unbelievable. But isn't that football and isn't that life? Nothing is perfect. There will always be internal and external obstacles getting in the way of achieving our objectives. But we can't give up or lose focus when so many others are depending on us. The great thing about my Cleveland experience was that I learned so much about how not to do things. When my time came, I decided I would create an environment built around trust and respect, not

"I first got to know Marc when I was the general manager in Cleveland and we brought him in to be our quarterback coach and later as our offensive coordinator. I am very proud to call him my friend. As a person, there is such a genuine nature to Marc, he is really an authentic human being. He is so unique in this industry, given his educational and legal background. He is very direct and sincere, and there is a real sensitivity to him that you just don't find in our business."

"As a coach, Marc is incredibly smart. I mean he has an amazing intellect. He sees the game, from an offensive standpoint, unlike anybody I have ever known. He is so innovative. Marc has a real passion for the game too, and that passion has carried him through some tough times and bad breaks over the years. He is very resilient and determined. I really admire that about him. He is not a politician. He doesn't try to manipulate people or maneuver for jobs either. He is very humble and has a lot of humility, almost to a fault."

"The one thing I learned about athletes a long time ago is that your control and influence over them is based on your ability to help them succeed. Period. That is what they care about. I mean they can like you or dislike you, but at the end of the day they are there to succeed both individually and for their team. They have to be convinced in their mind that their coach can help them get better and win. Having said that, in my opinion, the quarterback is the most critical and important position in all of sports. As such, the quarterback coach is also one of the most important positions. That relationship is key to the overall success of the team. Players have to respect your knowledge of the game first and foremost. Beyond that, they have to trust you. Marc had both. Not only do his quarterbacks trust him, they know that he is a brilliant tactician and extremely knowledgeable of the game."

"Everywhere he goes, the offense succeeds. He has a proven track record. As such, I think Marc going to Montreal was a really good move for him. He has all the experience in the world, but now he will get to prove that he is great leader. Marc has finally gotten his opportunity to be a head coach in the CFL and he has already impacted the Canadian game. Make no mistake, Marc is a great leader." — *Ernie Accorsi, Longtime NFL General Manager*

fear and paranoia. I was going to be a facilitator and mentor to those who worked for me and do everything I could to promote their good work in order to achieve their professional goals. As a head coach today, I do the staff hirings. When an assistant coach leaves our staff, all potential replacements are interviewed by the coordinator, who must "sign off" on the new hire. This way the new hire knows he answers not only to me, but to the coordinator, and is accountable to him for his work product.

We had success in Cleveland because many of us put the team ahead of ourselves and overall it was a tremendous learning experience because of what we had to overcome in order to succeed. No regrets, just memories and new life experiences that I was now going to be able to apply to the next stop in my coaching journey.

CH. 8) HEADING BACK TO THE LAND OF 10,000 LAKES

Preparation and a forward looking mindset is key to good leadership. Good leaders act with a plan and a purpose. Often that plan goes astray and in those circumstances survival is determined by adaptability and the ability to stay calm and make determinations that are best for all parties involved.

When we got home from Hawaii I immediately started calling around to find out what coaching jobs were going to be available for the upcoming season. I figured there would be a number of good opportunities waiting for me considering the fact that I was the offensive coordinator on a team that made it all the way to the conference championship game, but sadly that was not the case. The media back then is nothing like it is today, and it wasn't like I was a hugely known commodity either. In many cases today, the job I did very well may have catapulted me into a head coaching position. But things were different in those days. I had not been in the league long enough to have developed a lot of strong relationships, and I'm sure this hurt me. Either way, I was extremely concerned about starting my married life unemployed. Fortunately I had a year left on my contract, so I wasn't worried about finances, but I was concerned about having to potentially sit out the season without a job.

One of the first people I called was Mike Lynn, the GM of the Vikings. We always had a good relationship and he told me that he would speak with Jerry Burns to see if there was an opportunity on the staff. A few weeks later Jerry called me to offer me the job of "administrative assistant to the head coach," a nebulous title that would get me back to Minnesota. I have never been more grateful. I would be working for a great organization with a staff of good guys who I already knew, and even better — I was going to be able to move back home.

It also gave me some personal relief because Cindy could have some family support after moving away from her home town. I was happy to be going home to Minnesota, but it was certainly bittersweet for Cindy. Before being let go in Cleveland, we had moved into her apartment and were hoping to buy a house near her folks. That, of course, was not going to happen now. Instead, we bought a house near Cedar Lake in Minneapolis, literally three blocks from where I grew up. We were both avid runners and roller-bladers, so it was great to be able to walk out my front door to go blading or jogging around the lake. Overall, life was good.

One of the guys who I was excited about working with this time in Minnesota was my old coach when I was with the Gophers, Tom Moore. He was the Viking's offensive coordinator and quarterbacks coach. I had a lot of respect for Tom and was very self conscious to not get in the way. He had recently left the Pittsburgh Steelers to come to Minnesota, assuming he would take over as the team's head coach when Jerry retired. I figured

Jerry Burns

that scenario was great for me too, because when Tom took over for Jerry, then I would probably be promoted to his position as the offensive coordinator. I now had a plan and purpose and things were starting to look up. I was also learning the administrative issues a head coach goes through while assisting Jerry, which certainly has helped me in my job today.

Tom was brilliant and was totally prepared to be a head coach from his work on the Steelers Super Bowl teams of the 70's under Chuck Noll. He knew how to reach players, get under their skin, and get them to play at a high level. Unfortunately for Tom, however, the opportunity for him to become a head coach in this league would ultimately never present itself. He would go on to do a tremendous job during his years with the Indianapolis Colts, which included winning the Super Bowl in 2006 working alongside his former protégé, Tony Dungy, but in my opinion circumstances just didn't go his way.

Wade Wilson was our quarterback in Minnesota and he was an older veteran at this point in his career. He played well, but eventually the job went to Rich Gannon, who had the arm strength, athleticism and potential to be a very good quarterback. The season was a rollercoaster. We lost five of our first six games, then rattled off five straight wins, only to finish the season with four straight losses. We ended up with a pretty disappointing 6-10 record.

The next year I became the team's quarterbacks coach. I was really excited to be able to work closely with Rich and the other quarterbacks. We had a very good offense that year but struggled defensively. It was another rollercoaster and we ended up with a slightly better 8-8 record. As a result, Jerry got fired after the season. The ownership group decided to bring in Stanford Head Coach Denny Green and he obviously wanted to put together his own staff. I understood, but it didn't make it any easier. I just couldn't believe it. I had gone from being the offensive coordinator on a championship team and getting fired, to being the quarterback coach on the No. 4 rated offense in the league and was about to get fired for the second time in as many years. What had I done to deserve this?

I was genuinely concerned as to how this was not only going to effect my professional life, but also my personal life as well. I was desperate, disturbed, and frankly discouraged. To make matters worse, Cindy had also gone through three failed and very difficult pregnancies over the past two years, but miraculously became pregnant again towards the end of that '91 season.   As such, I was determined to stay in Minnesota for the remainder of her pregnancy so not to disrupt her in any way or cause any stress to her. I made up my mind, were not leaving Minnesota for any reason. None.

So, I went and met with the team's new head coach, Denny Green. I asked him to please consider keeping me on in any position he felt would help the team, even offering to take a demotion. I did everything I could to try to get a job on his staff and he ultimately agreed to keep me on for about a month, but in the end he wanted to go with his own guys. Denny was a good coach and had great success with the team for the next several years. He clearly had a plan and knew what he was doing. I understood, but it put me in a really tough spot.

Wanting to make sure nothing complicated Cindy's pregnancy, I decided to take a leap of faith and just take the year off. I had time left on my contract, but this would be the first time in almost 25 years I had entered the Fall not playing or coaching the game I loved. I figured I would just relax for a few months, take birthing classes with Cindy, and enjoy some free time — something I hadn't really ever experienced in my adult life. I was going to just sit back and watch the NFL season unfold in order to determine where the coaching vacancies would be in the next upcoming season.

CH. 9) TAKING TIME OFF TO PUT MY FAMILY FIRST

The ability to reinvent is a trademark of a great leader in times of adversity and unknowing. Leaders recognize that there is more to life than just the current job for both themselves and for those who work for them. Taking time for family is healthy because behind every good leader is a great support system.

We were blessed with the birth of our first daughter, Sarahanne, in the summer of '92. It was one of the greatest moments of my life. The time I was able to spend with her and Cindy was amazing. My folks were elated too, getting to spend all of that quality time with their first granddaughter. I spent that summer relaxing, changing diapers, and reflecting on life. Family-first is the life-lesson I took from this experience. I have no regrets about it either, none. It was a blast and although it is never fun and always stressful to be jobless, it couldn't have come at a better time as Cindy and I began our family. Taking a step back sometimes, to reflect and to do the right thing for your family, is so important. Being a coach is a selfish job. You are gone a lot, you move around a lot, and you work ungodly hours. It is imperative to marry a person who not only understands this, but embraces it. Thank God Cindy was on board with me, or I don't know where I would be right now. So for me to take this time with her and our newborn was simply incredible.

That Fall I got a call from my old work-out buddy in Miami, Sean Clancy. He had become a partner in a financial firm that managed municipal bonds for private investors in Coral Springs, just a few miles north of Fort Lauderdale. He was calling to say hello and catch up. We started talking and he told me the firm was doing well and that they were looking to expand and bring in some new blood. One thing led to another and eventually he asked if maybe I would be interested in talking about it. I was inquisitive enough to say yes, so Cindy and I flew down there to meet with he and his partners. It is always a compliment when someone is interested in speaking to you about a job opportunity. I have always listened because you really don't know where it will lead.

Cindy and I were impressed with what they were doing at the firm and we talked for a long time about whether we were ready to make a change our lives. After much consideration, we decided to take a leap of faith and move to Florida. Having taken the time off to be with my daughter made me realize that there were other things in life besides football. I was ready to try something else and this just seemed right. It was only natural my parents were disappointed we were moving with their new granddaughter, but they knew I needed to get my new career going.

I wasn't sure if I was going to love it or not, but unlike coaching it would give me stability and feed my family. The way I approached it wasn't just to get my mind off of football for a while either. In my mind I was now done coaching and out of football for good. In fact, I had no desire to coach again, absolutely zero. I looked at this new job as an entirely new career path for me to start over with. My perspective had totally changed after Sarahanne came into the world and I did not want to be around football. I loved the game, but it had treated me so cruelly after I had sacrificed for it and given it the ultimate respect I believed it and the players deserved. Enough was enough. I was done, and I was focused and disciplined enough to put it behind me. I just wanted to raise my kids and be a good husband and dad.

The first thing I had to do was study for a board exam to become certified to sell municipal bonds. This was something I vowed never to have to do again after graduating from law school, but I sucked it up and did it anyway. It was a difficult test, but I studied hard and passed. With that, we packed up and headed south. Once there, we rented a modest townhouse in the city of Boca Raton, which was about two miles from the beach. I dove in and immersed myself into my new job and tried to learn as much as I possibly could about the investment business. I was happy to be doing something different and came to the conclusion that I either really didn't miss football or I was in a complete state of denial. Either way, I was moving forward with my new life.

A year later, during the summer of '94, we were blessed with our second child, Chloe. It was amazing to see how Sarahanne interacted with her new sister. We moved into a larger house and settled in. I wanted to reflect and learn some new things about my family and about life. Looking back, I had burned myself out at a young age and needed to recharge my batteries. I was put on salary my first year, but then after that it was 100% commission. This was pretty stressful, especially since I had a growing family to take care of. For the first time in my working life, my income was not guaranteed. The NFL sure was a good place to work in that regard because there are terrific perks that come with the job including great insurance, pensions, and of course the salary. This was totally different. Now that I was out of football, I realized for the first time how hard it was to make a living. Making $100,000 dollars a year selling bonds was a heck of a lot tougher than making $100,000 dollars a year coaching. My respect for those who have to work in the "real world" grew immensely, and my appreciation for the NFL and what it had provided me over the years was affirmed. I also realized that when I was coaching I was doing what I loved. As long as the hours were, I was never really "working." Well, I was now "working" for a living. Big difference.

Bonds were a safe and secure investment. It didn't take a financial genius to manage them and I had great mentors like Sean at the firm. I worked hard and used my football network to get to agents who were managing million dollar athletes, and then helped them set up portfolios. I had carved out a nice business. I found true satisfaction in helping others invest securely and protect their assets so they would have a quality retirement or smooth transition into "civilian" life. Eventually, however, after two years of selling bonds, the luster wore off and I started to get uncomfortable with the job. My desire to make more money began to force me to be away from my family more than I wished to be. To be really good at that job, I had to get up, put on a suit and tie, and go out and continuously network to find new clients. Over time I simply became uncomfortable with this lifestyle. I had enjoyed being able to come home for dinner every night, which was something that had been totally foreign to me in my previous life as a coach. I began to realize if I was going to make a larger income, then I would have to put in more hours and make more sacrifices.

As I began my third year away from the game, I started doing a football radio show with Hank Goldberg. Hank was the former voice of the Miami

Dolphins, an ESPN correspondent, and a local talk radio guru in south Florida. I had the itch to get back into football and this proved to be a great way for me to scratch it. I could still be "around" the game, but I didn't have to deal with the business or politics that came along with being "in" the game. Then, as luck would have it, Bernie Kosar came back to Miami to back-up Dolphins' quarterback Dan Marino. Several of my old coaching colleagues joined the Dolphins' coaching staff as well and just like that, it was like old home week for me over there. In addition, I had gotten to know the team's legendary head coach, Don Shula, who had been buying bonds from me. He used to let me go over to the Dolphins' practice facility on Saturdays before games to check out the action. I would oftentimes even bring Sarahanne with me, who was just beginning to walk. Coach Shula was always hospitable, and it was fun to go by the locker room afterwards to see Bernie and some of my old friends.

Later that fall, one of my friends on the Dolphins coaching staff, Gary Stevens, interviewed to become the head coach of the Philadelphia Eagles. One day out of the blue he called me to ask if I would be interested in joining his staff if he got the job. It totally caught me off guard, but after thinking about it for a few seconds I just blurted out "Yes!" Incredibly, a few days later I got a call from Don Shula, who told me if Gary got the job and left the Dolphins, that he wanted me to join his staff as well. Wow, I guess when it rains it pours. I couldn't believe what was happening. After three years of being out of the game, just like that I had two coaching offers! I wasn't even thinking about getting back into football, and I was now getting hit over the head with footballs.

Then, believe it or not, I got a call from a friend of mine at the University of Miami, who encouraged me to apply for the head coaching position that had recently become vacant after Dennis Erickson was let go. I talked to Cindy and she agreed that I should throw my name in the hat and apply for it. She could tell that I wasn't happy selling bonds and that it was time for me to get back into the game. Oddly enough, I then got a call from Butch Davis, the defensive coordinator for the Dallas Cowboys, who had just interviewed to be the Oakland Raiders head coach. Butch and I had crossed paths briefly at UM in 1984 when Jimmy Johnson brought him in to be the defensive line coach. Butch was an awesome guy and had great success as Jimmy's defensive coordinator in Dallas. Anyway, Butch had just spoken with the team's owner, Al Davis, and told me that if he got the job that he wanted me to be his offensive coordinator. He wanted to know if I was interested. Again, I said, "Yes!" He then proceeded to tell me he was also a candidate for the University of Miami head coaching job, and that if he got that one, he wanted to know if I would be interested in being his offensive coordinator there as well. I then told him I had just interviewed for the job too. We both just laughed. I was starting to get dizzy from everything that was happening.

In the end, Butch wound up getting the University of Miami job. Sure, I was disappointed that I didn't get it, but I was happy for him, I really was. So, he called me and invited me to come over to his office. While I was over there, I ran into Steve Young, who was in town to play in the Super Bowl. His 49ers were practicing at the University's training complex and he just happened to be leaving for the bus back to his hotel when we crossed paths. We stopped and visited for about 15 minutes and had a nice conversation. I was amazed at his patience, demeanor, and willingness to stop and talk to me. We had gotten acquainted in Tampa Bay only briefly before he was dealt to the Niners, but he was cordial and completely interested in what I was doing. I wished all him the best in the Super Bowl, told him how truly happy I was for his success and the ob-

Don Shula

stacles he had overcome, and we parted ways.

I didn't think anything of it at the time, and then proceeded to walk over to Butch's office to talk to him. When I got there he offered me the job as his offensive coordinator and assistant head coach. I was blown away. I asked him when he needed to have an answer, and he told me there was no rush and that I could take my time to think about it. I went home and told Cindy about everything that had happened. She was excited and so was I, but I wasn't sure if it was the best move for me to get back into college football. Regardless, none of the other NFL jobs had come to fruition for me at that point with Gary Stevens and Coach Shula, and this was the only offer on the table at the time. We finally decided to just sit on it for a few days and think about it.

Shortly thereafter I got a call from my old friend from the Vikings, Jeff Diamond, who said that he had couple of extra tickets for that Sunday's Super Bowl game between the Chargers and 49ers. This was terrific, the game was in Miami and Cindy and I could take in all the pre-game activities in and around the stadium. As for the game, it was incredible. The Niners crushed the Chargers, 49–26, and Steve Young threw a record six touchdown passes en route to earning Super Bowl MVP honors. I couldn't remember the last time I was at a game to just watch and have fun. It was really an odd experience and to be honest it even made me feel a little uncomfortable. Then, towards the end of the game, I remember sitting there in the end zone watching this amazing game when Cindy leaned over to me and said, "Marc, it's just too bad that you never got to coach on a team like this with players like Steve Young, Jerry Rice, Brent Jones and John Taylor." Little did I know at the time, but my wife was on to something.

Unbelievably, three days later, while sitting at my desk in my office, my assistant called to tell me George Seifert was on the phone. I thought, "Yeah right, the winning coach of the Super Bowl is on the phone wanting to talk to me?" Figuring it was a prank by one of my buddies, I answered the phone. "This is Marc," I said, sort of laughing. But as I was about to learn, this was no laughing matter. The voice on the other end of the line then says in a dead serious tone: "Marc, I know you don't know me, my name is George Seifert, and I would like to know if you are interested in coming to San Francisco to interview for the offensive coordinator position of the 49ers." I just sat there on the line, speechless. I couldn't believe it. I had been out of the NFL and out of coaching for three full years, and now I get a call like this. I just blurted out, "Absolutely, it would be an honor!"

I hung up and just sat there, sort of numb, and not knowing whether to laugh or cry. I mean I had just watched this guy's team win the Super Bowl a few days earlier. Now he wanted to know if I would be interested in running his offense. What the heck was going on here? This was THE most coveted coordinator job in football. Bar none. The previous coordinator, Mike Shanahan, was on his way to Denver to become the head coach after running one of the highest powered offenses in the history of the game. He had followed Mike Holmgren, who had followed Bill Walsh. How in the world could I be next? It was crazy.

All of these offers were coming to me and I didn't even solicit them. How can someone NOT trying for anything, get opportunities like this? All I was trying to do at the time was feed my family. So, I flew out there to meet with George and his staff. While I was sitting there on the plane, a sort of warm feeling came over me as I stared out the window. I knew I was going to get the job. I didn't know why or how, but I just knew it. This was my destiny. I know it sounds crazy even as I write this, but I knew it even before the wheels hit the ground at San Francisco International. I got there and George brought me into his office. He said, "Marc, can you forget everything you ever learned about football up until this point in your life and start over by learning the West Coast offense?" I looked him right in the eye and said, "Definitely, I have no doubt about it."

When it came to the success of the 49ers during their glory years over the 80's and early 90's, there were three men who went virtually unnoticed. Yet, these men had as much to do with the success as anyone. The first was John McVay, who was Bill Walsh's general manager. John was Bill's right hand man as it related to personnel and the draft, and worked very closely with George as well. His reputation inside the organization was impeccable. Next was Neal Dahlen, who was a kind and even tempered man with a very even keeled demeanor. When it came to detailing out administrative issues or dealing with agents and coaches, Neal was the best. Lastly, there was Bob McKittrick. Bob was not just the offensive line coach, he also constructed the protections the West Coast Offense was built on.

From there I was taken down to Bob McKittrick's office, where we had an informal conversation that involved looking at 49er game tape and discussing our personal lives. We talked for 15 minutes, and after about 20 minutes of watching video, Bob turned off the machine, looked me right in the eyes and asked, "Do you want this job?" I quickly answered without hesitation that I not only wanted the job, but I believed I was up to the challenge. He then told me he was going to recommend to George that I be the guy. I was so excited. The thought of coaching arguably the league's most storied franchise was mind boggling. And, to get to run the West Coast Offense, that was just icing on the cake. It's what I would call the most quarterback friendly offense in the history of the game, and one that would ultimately enable me to have more fun coaching than I ever thought possible.

The next day after I flew back to south Florida. Shortly after I arrived George called and offered me the job. Amazing. Just like that, I was back in the game. With that, I hopped right back on a plane to San Francisco to sign the deal and start my new career back in the NFL. Accepting the job was one of the most bizarre and simply unbelievable things that has ever happened to me in my life. To say I was excited was such an understatement. To this day I cannot even fathom the series of events and coincidences that had to happen for me to ascend to that position. A coach with only one year of experience as a coordinator just does not get handed the reins to the best offense in the world. No way. But somehow I did and I was grateful. The stars were aligned perfectly and I became their man. Truth is, I not only knew I would get the job on the flight to the interview, but I was absolutely positive I could do the job. I had spent a lifetime waiting for this moment and I felt like I had just won the lottery.

Incredibly, barely a week after Cindy's prophetic comments at the Super Bowl, I had become Jerry Rice and Steve Young's coach. Beyond that, I remember watching the Pro Bowl with Cindy on TV the week after the Super Bowl. Al Michaels, the iconic announcer, was interviewing Carmen Policy, the President of the 49ers. He said, "So, Carmen, I understand you are going to hire a stock broker to be your new offensive coordinator." It didn't even register at the time, but seconds later we both figured out he was talking about me. Al thought I was a stock broker rather than a bond broker... but close enough. I used to kid Al about it whenever I would see him for Monday Night Football games after that. I would ask him how his stock portfolio was doing and if he needed any advice. We would both just laugh.

Before packing up to move to the Bay Area (Cindy and the girls would stay and move out in a few months), there were a few people I wanted to thank. First was Sean and his partners for the tremendous opportunity they had given to Cindy and I in south Florida. This had been a time to be a dad and husband, as well as a time to gain a unique perspective on what the business world was all about. It gave me great perspective of life on the other side of football. It was demanding and rewarding in so many ways, but it didn't create the passion, nor challenge me intellectually or emotionally in the way football had for most of my life. I then thanked Butch for giving me time and for not pressuring me into taking the Miami job. To this day I have not forgotten how understanding he was. Gary Stevens was next, and I couldn't be more grateful to him for having the confidence in me at a time in my life when I really needed it. Thanks to the great Don Shula, who I was so close to working for. What a privilege and honor that would have been. For him to even make that call was amazing in itself. Lastly, before leaving I thanked each and every person who trusted me with their money. I mean, that isn't an easy thing for even friends to do. I know I did you guys right though, even if I had to twist your arms!

ON SUCCESS...

"Success is an attitude. Success is your journey executed with integrity. Success is being in a position to serve others while empowering them to reach their fullest potential, ultimately leaving them with a desire to unselfishly pay it forward and give to others in return. Success is being able to balance family with your professional passion."

CH. 10)   LANDING MY DREAM JOB IN SAN FRANCISCO

Leaders protect their assets, care for individuals and what is important to them, and structure an environment to maximize hard work, enthusiasm, and productivity. They recognize other leaders and work together with them to better themselves. When adversity strikes, leaders refocus on the task and put the organization first. Leaders never settle and are always striving for the best. They want to not only maximize the talents and skills of those they lead, but also themselves. Leaders don't look back except to learn from mistakes and they never compare, because they understand their position and circumstances are always different and that what is important is that the organization's interests are always put first.

Three weeks later at a press conference seen by most of the football world, I was introduced as the new offensive coordinator of the San Francisco 49ers. Expectations were high and opinions of the 49ers new hire were mixed. They ranged all across the board from brilliant and progressive, to absurd and ridiculous. I could take the negative stuff, I had already developed pretty thick skin. But the positive stuff? That was another story. It wasn't the first time in my life people had seen more in me than I had in myself, but now it was finally time for me to believe it. These were the Niners, they were the best of the best. They had set extremely high standards both on and off the field from the ownership down to the coaching staff and every other team in the NFL was looking to somehow duplicate their success.

The offensive staff remained essentially the same once I arrived, except for Mike Shanahan and Gary Kubiak (Gary was the team's quarterback coach and is currently the head coach of the Houston Texans), who were on their way to Denver. The defensive staff was also in place except for defensive coordinator, Ray Rhodes, who was on his way to Philadelphia to become their head coach. He would be replaced by none other than Pete Carroll, my former coaching buddy with the Vikes. So here we were, "Bud's boys," back together again — this time as coordinators of the most respected franchise in football. What a thrill! This was big for me to have Pete on the staff. He was brilliant and understood both sides of the ball as good as anybody I knew. Pete and I would be in the press box together on Sundays and he was a terrific sounding board for me during the course of games. He was also the guy I sat next to for two years on every flight from coast to coast. Pete is unique and worldly in ways that go beyond football. Our conversations would run the gamut from politics to the supernatural. These were very good times and our conversations never disappointed. After nine seasons and two National Championships at USC, in 2010 Pete took over as the head coach of the NFL's Seattle Seahawks, where I am sure he is destined for even more greatness.

When I got settled I just assumed that I would begin by spending time with the staff and getting their help in learning the offense. Nope. Instead, I spent the next two months sequestered in a hotel room doing nothing but watching video of Bill Walsh, Mike Holmgren, and Mike Shanahan install the West Coast Offense. Then, as minicamp approached, the team flew me to Denver for three days to meet with Shanahan and Kubiak in an attempt to allow me to gather even more information about the offense and the organization. It was enlightening to say the least.

While watching the installation tapes, I was able to see the presentation styles of all three brilliant coaches, and the way they worked to stimulate their audience of players. I also was able to learn the details of the system and its unique concepts and terminology. I also learned that the West Coast Offense was a lot more than the quick passes. It was about everything from how to effectively install game plans, to practice structure and development, to a code of ethics that accounted for player safety and more. This only scratched the surface of what I was about to learn, and I hadn't even started to get to know the character, intelligence, and passion of our great head coach, George Seifert.

I felt as though I was dreaming. I had entered into a world very few others had ever seen. I was now part of an historic family. I honestly thought I would never get an opportunity to be a part of the organization after Mike Lynn had denied me permission to interview for a job with them years ago when I was with the Vikings, a position that ultimately went to Mike Holmgren. Nobody ever gets a second chance in this business, yet here I was. The timing wasn't right then. I mean if I would have gotten the opportunity in 1985, I would have been all alone. Now I had the chance to continue this amazing journey with Cindy and the girls, which was a miracle in itself. And speaking of my family, after being away for nearly three months I was finally able to get back to south Florida to pack up for the big move. We wound up settling in Los Gatos, a suburb just outside of San Francisco, to begin what we felt was going to be the adventure of a lifetime.

Over the remainder of the spring I continued to work diligently and tried to get to know all the coaches and the players. In those days, players weren't around as much as they are now in the off-season, and especially in the Bay Area where the cost of living for many of the players was just too high to live year round. A week after the draft in late April the players all came together for our first mini-camp. It was there where I got my first opportunity to be introduced to the team and to address the offense. I was both nervous as well as excited.

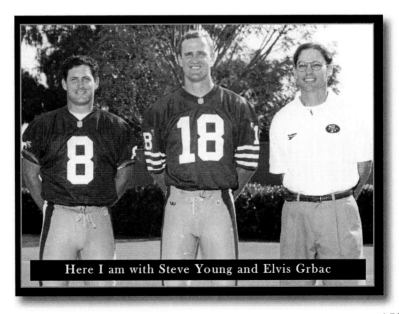
Here I am with Steve Young and Elvis Grbac

Three months prior, I was crunching numbers at a desk in south Florida, thinking about municipal bond rates. Now I was standing before the offense of the world champion 49ers with Steve Young, Jerry Rice, Brent Jones, and John Taylor, just like my wife had somehow foreshadowed several months earlier. Standing there was like an out of body experience for me, absolutely surreal. These guys were legends in my mind and now I was going to be coaching them. I addressed the offense briefly and began to install the passing game for the day's practice. Afterward, as I concluded and walked outside to practice, Steve Young walked by and said to me, "Great job with the meeting Marc, now relax, we will take care of things from here." I was like, "Wow, don't wake me from this incredible dream." What Steve was saying was, "Don't worry, we know this stuff... you just call it, we will execute it." And that is exactly what happened. I prepared the game plans and called the plays, like any coordinator does. But at the end of the day, Steve, Jerry, and the rest of the guys did the rest.

Besides being a man of the highest character, Steve Young is one of the most brilliant and courageous quarterbacks of our time. He had to follow one of the greatest quarterbacks of the era in Joe Montana, and the expectations placed on him were like no other. As such, he could genuinely empathize with my situation of having to follow Mike Shanahan. He had taken the monkey off his back by leading the 49ers to the world championship six months earlier, having an incredible season statistically, and a career game in the Super Bowl against the Chargers. Despite all the no-

George Seifert and I, talking shop...

toriety and adoration, however, Steve was as humble a man as I had ever been around. He didn't have an arrogant bone in his body. He was also extremely tough and courageous. It was such a privilege to be able to work with him. Over the years he has always been there if I have needed him, even as his own family continues to grow and he grows and prospers in business. I always tell him I wish he could see the coach I am now as opposed to the one I was after being out of football for three years. He always told me not to apologize because he knew how hard I had worked and he knew I did my best under what would prove to be some very challenging circumstances.

The 49ers had a really unique organization. It was so different from any I had ever been around before. Everything about it, from the players to the management, was just first class. They had an amazing reputation, yet they were also sort of an enigma. They didn't really let outsiders in that much and were sort of shrouded in mystery to some extent. Coming in as an outsider myself, it was very eye-opening. One of the most defining moments for me as a coach was when our team president, Carmen Policy, spoke with everyone in the organization at our Santa Clara offices prior to our Summer break. Carmen, a brilliant attorney in his own right and lifetime friend of our owner, Mr. DeBartolo, told everyone in the room other than the coaches that they all had one job to do. One. That job was to be the best resource they could be to help the coaches do their job. When a coach needed assistance, that task went to the top of the list.

He then made a second point which hit me even harder, when he said, "The most important people in the organization are not only the coaches, but their wives!" Are you kidding me? Did these people get it or what? You were so right, Carmen. Without the support of his wife, there is no way a coach could in good conscious do his job because there are too many hours, tremendous pressures, and times away from family. If the wives weren't happy, the coaches were distracted and couldn't get the most out of their work. The 49er management would not allow that to happen. As such, flowers, phone calls, and occasional shopping trips were all a part of the cost of doing business to the organization. If it made the coach and his family happy and content, then in their eyes it was money well spent.

Pete Carroll and I actually started our tenure with the Niners by flying to Colorado with our wives to celebrate the world championship. I asked

George if I could stay back and work, as did Pete. We had no business being on that Boeing 747 that took off from San Francisco International that Spring with the players, coaches, wives, and everyone else in the organization, but they insisted. The 49ers wanted to show their appreciation for hard work, loyalty, and accountability and they wanted us to share in the perks of success too. Pete and I were floored. It was pretty much "carte blanche" too, at the exclusive Broadmoor Resort in Colorado Springs. There was golf, water sports, and spa treatments for everybody. On the final evening there was a magnificent party held for everyone, a performance by the group "Boyz to Men," and an appearance by World Heavyweight boxing champ Evander Holyfield. The night was capped by the presentation of the Super Bowl Rings to every employee of the organization, which even included my old roommate at Moorhead State, Pat Richie. It was impressive, I mean really impressive!

The Niner organization did everything in a big way, even the team's Christmas party. The support staff would personally shop for every member of the organization's children. Not just players' kids, not just coaches' kids, I mean everybody's kids. Then over the Holidays, working around that

Just soaking it all in with Steve Young

156

week's games, we would go over to a local hotel and a beautiful meal and party would await us. The first year they had live deer in the lobby for the kids and they always had Santa. And not just one Santa either, they had a white Santa and a black Santa. This was a team that treated its people right, and that all started at the top with the owner, Mr. DeBartolo.

Mr. DeBartolo was a very generous man as well as a very appreciative and supportive owner. He was truly unique. I will never forget when our small dog was hit by a truck on our street during my first season with the team. Mr. DeBartolo called Cindy to the office about a month later and presented her with a new dog. We were blown away. To thank him, we appropriately named the dog after him — "Eddie," as in Edward DeBartolo. He was genuinely upset for our loss, because he knew our dog had been such a big part our family. You could just see why the guy was so successful in business and in life, he just "got it."

Meanwhile, I did exactly what George Seifert had asked me to do: to forget everything I had learned about the game and start new. I used my training from Cleveland and Minnesota as a foundation to learn the offense, and my mental discipline to do the rest. There was so much structure in every aspect of the game within the organization and they even had a term which symbolized their own unique standard of performance. It was called the "49er way" and it started with extremely hard work. The focus was on the details and on the mindset of each and every player. Each player had to have a common respect for his teammates throughout the course of practice every day. The organization did not want any players to get hurt and made player safety a priority. Because of league salary cap limitations, with regards to being able to replace a quality player, we all focused on it. George Seifert always made it very clear to his team that a safe practice environment was his most important job as the head coach. In fact, nobody was ever allowed to inhibit the running routes of Jerry Rice or the throws of Steve Young. They took it that seriously.

This place was special. From meetings, to walk-thrus, to practices, there was a unique and very business-like mentality to everything we did. There was a level of accountability that quietly and humbly showed we were exceptional, and that nobody did it better. Everybody bought in and as a result, nobody wanted to let anyone down. I have termed this with my current players in Montreal as understanding that we are all truly interconnected and that what I do and you do will affect our team. This was a big part of the "Niner swagger," or confidence. This special culture had snowballed due to the leadership of Bill Walsh and George Seifert, and the quarterbacking of Joe Montana and now Steve Young.

As businesslike as things were, however, there was also a time for a sense of humor. This was stressed by George and was a big part of the philosophy of the organization, because a sense of humor helps teams through adversities and successes alike by keeping the team loose. Bill Walsh illustrated this in an early Super Bowl in Detroit. When the team arrived at their hotel early in the week, Bill was there to meet the team in a doorman's uniform and hat. This was classic. I have always stressed to my teams that there is a big difference between having a sense of humor and silliness. Mature football teams always know the difference. At the time we had guys like Harris Barton, Ken Norton Jr., and Gary Plummer, who all kept everybody loose. These guys were the real deal; they knew when it was time to be serious, and when to laugh. This is often a fine line in an environment where there was only one goal every year, to WIN THE SUPER BOWL.

As much fun as it was to be part of it, there were many players who lived in a constant underlying fear of being released. Many of these players were very good and there was no way they would be going anywhere. That was kind of the 49er way. It was clear that while some coaches in the league would stick with a player while his skills would begin to diminish, Bill felt it was better to release these players early. It happened to Montana and Rice, so players felt it could happen to anyone. As often as I talked to Bill, I learned this was not done with malicious intentions. It was believed to be good business and in the team's best interest. Releases aren't ever easy for either the player or the organization, but they are just a reality of life in the NFL. Believe it not, we had a number of players who were in constant fear of being released. I just wanted them to enjoy their journey, work hard, and play fearlessly. Whether player or coach, we were living our dream by working in the NFL. This was amazing to me

"One of the most attractive qualities of Marc is that he possesses an in-depth overall knowledge of the offensive game. He is one of the brightest coaches I have worked with." — *George Seifert, Head Coach, San Francisco 49ers*

and I have done everything over the years to help my teams look at the game in this manner.

The 49er practices were fast and furious. At times we would go two or three practices without a ball even touching the ground. No kidding. There was a frenetic pace and chaos that was like nothing I had ever seen, but it all made sense to me. The team even had a "Practice Code of Ethics" which was followed each session meticulously. They figured the more chaos and speed in practice, the more the games became easy. In addition, the players were expected to run to each drill. They wanted practices to be short with consistent energy throughout. Whenever there was a change in drills, they wanted guys hustling on to the next work station. They didn't want that time to be diluted by players slowly moving from different areas of the practice field. Coaches did their coaching on the run. Otherwise corrections would be made later by reviewing videotape. They took it very seriously but still were able to make it fun. In fact, sometimes I would literally race Steve from drill to drill. Over the years I have since made it a point to pick different players from practice to run with from drill to drill. The guys love it!

George's "work fast—practice fast—play fast" philosophy was a big part of the "49er Way" and it was brilliant. He had learned it from his mentor, the great Bill Walsh, and made it one of the cornerstones of his system. The structure of practice, speed of practice, and the ability of players to co-operate in a way that would protect them from injury was a high priority in San Francisco. Every bullet point on the list was a way to maximize each minute of practice as well as protect every player, but most importantly the quarterback. Injuries in practice which were the result of somebody not following the practice code were simply not tolerated. Period.

Expectations were obviously through the roof going into my first season, given the fact that anything short of repeating as world champions would be considered a failure by the 49er organization as well as the fans. We played solid football and had a good season, going 11-5 and securing the NFC West Division title. It wasn't easy either when Steve went down with an injury midway through the season. At that point we had to go with a young quarterback named Elvis Grbac. He was very tall at six-foot-six, extremely bright, and very competitive. Elvis came in and played well for us. In fact, he even had three, 300-yard passing games, which would later earn him a $20 million contract with the Kansas City Chiefs. He made a name for himself beating the Cowboys in Dallas midway through the season. We were 5-4 at the time, and not really playing our top end football. We went into their house and Elvis cut-up a very good Cowboy defense. This ultimately started us on a five game winning streak which culminated with us winning the Division.

Between the Steve and Elvis, we led the league in passing and finished No. 2 in total offense. Jerry Rice, meanwhile, was amazing. He had 122 catches for a record 1,848 yards, plus 15 touchdowns — an NFL receiving record that still stands today. We were poised to make a big run in the playoffs but unfortunately got upset in the first round at home to Mike Holmgren, Brett Favre, and Green Bay, 27-17. It was heartbreaking.

As I look back, my first year in San Francisco was a blur. To think I called every play during that 1995 season and to have the results we had after being away from the game for three years is so amazing to me. It was an adjustment in nearly every aspect of my coaching style. I really coached under the radar that entire year in what I felt was a quiet and professional manner. I coached with a completely different demeanor from the passionate, outgoing coach I was in the classroom and on the field. Steve and Brent Jones, our great pass receiving tight end, tried hard to bring it out of me early in the year. I regrettably never just let myself go. To this day when speaking to Steve and Brent, who I have stayed close to, I apologize to them, because they never got my best. In 1995, we were very productive and the chemistry was good amongst the players and coaches. We worked hard and prepared well, but in the end we just came up short.

About a week after the season ended, George came by my office and said, "Marc, you came into a situation after being out of the game for three years and learned an entirely new offense. You are as far along as the two Mike's (Holmgren and Shanahan) were at this time, and I am expecting even bigger and better things from you next season." I needed that from George, because as productive as we were even without Steve for the entire 16 games, there were some in the media who felt the 49ers were not the team they were the year before. George told me he was really excited about our prospects going into the '96 season though. I was really excited about getting a vote of confidence like that, it meant a lot to me. He had been with Holmgren and Shanahan, he watched their growth as coaches, and I knew him well enough to know he meant what he said.

Then, a few days later, George called me into his office and told me that Mr. DeBartolo had decided to bring back former Head Coach Bill Walsh as a consultant. Bill had just gone through a personal tragedy and I think for the most part Mr. DeBartolo wanted to bring him back in order to give him something to do on a daily basis. Bill was still as cerebral as ever, and had never lost his passion for the game. He still had value in many ways and Mr. DeBartolo thought the time was right to bring him back. Plus, from a public relations standpoint, Bill was an incredibly popular and beloved figure throughout the Bay Area. As for me, I wasn't quite

THE 49ER'S PRACTICE CODE OF ETHICS

What Will We Look for on the Practice Field?

• Common Respect for Each Other and Player Safety

• Everybody Knows to Stay Away from the Quarterback

• No Bull Rushes

• Stay off the Ground

• Keep Your Feet Moving

• Run from Drill to Drill

• Everybody Finishes

• No Grabbing or Pulling Jerseys

• No Batted Balls

• Explosive Movement

• Players Carrying the Ball Have it Properly Secured

• No Collisions

• The Ball Stays off the Ground

• Fighting Wastes Time

sure what to make of it at the time.

Shortly thereafter, when the news of his return was announced, a media frenzy ensued. A lot of so-called experts assumed he was coming back to help me with the offense, but in reality he was going to be helping the entire organization, in a very limited role. The media was really rough on me that off-season and it was tough. They made it sound like I was incompetent and that Bill was going to straighten it all out. They wanted to make it about me, which wasn't right. It also cast a shadow on my perception from some of the players as to my competence as their coach. It was bad and it got worse as the media ran with the story.

In fact, I was advised by several people close to the situation to just quit. There were a number of people who had worked with Bill previously who told me having him around, perceptively looking over my shoulder, was going to be a nightmare for me. So, I considered my options at that point. I figured I would be marketable because of my work product and association with the team. I knew George would help, as would guys like Steve and Brent, and Jerry's remarkable year was irrefutable. I started to won-

Talking shop with Bill Walsh

der if maybe I should see what other opportunities were out there. Maybe I could resurface in a better place where my work would be appreciated?

Finally, I just decided to make the best of it. I believed I could handle it. I didn't want to turn the situation into a negative. It was only about positives for me at that point. Bill was an invaluable resource and I was excited to be able to learn whatever I could from him. In fact, our relationship would evolve and we got close. I utilized him as a sounding board and he became a mentor to me. I would ride the bus to games with him, have lunch with him, and I was like a sponge whenever I was around him — soaking up all of his wisdom. He was just very supportive of me and I really appreciated it.

Early in the '96 season, I asked Bill to speak with the offense early in the season just to give them his perspective on the state of things at the time. He did a great job, but the episode was leaked to the press and they spun it as if he was taking over. It was ridiculous; I mean the fact of the matter was that Bill wasn't around all the time. He would come in late morning, go to lunch at times with friends, and then leave early. He would always put his thoughts to paper or stop by to give me his thoughts though, and that meant a great deal to me. The guy was brilliant. You know, they use the term genius loosely in sports these days, but in my experience with Bill Walsh, it was absolutely correct to refer to him as such.

I was able to weather this early storm by just focusing on football and coaching this tremendously talented group of players. Things eventually calmed down and we went back to business as usual. We started out strong that next season, winning seven of our first nine games, and I felt very confident in leading the offense. Later in the year, however, I had an interesting dilemma come up when I was interviewed for the head coaching position at my alma mater, the University of Minnesota. It was something that really caught me off guard. I was intrigued, so I met with the Gophers Athletics Director, Mark Dienhart, on the tarmac of the San Jose airport. It was late at night, during the middle of the week, and completely under the radar. I was not well prepared and was dealing with the exhaustion of the season. Also, in the back of my mind was the fact I never really saw myself in the position of a college head coach. I was the offensive coordinator of the 49ers and my next job would be NFL head coach. I didn't disrespect this opportunity, but we were on a run to the Super Bowl that year, and I felt this would be somewhat of a selfish distraction.

I confided in Bill. Surprisingly, and without hesitation he told me if offered the job I should take it. He told me when you have an opportunity to become a head coach, do it, and don't look back. He went on to tell me it was a rare chance to be a head coach and that I would probably regret passing it up. Bill believed once you were a head coach, you were never perceived any other way and more doors would open for you. In retrospect, Bill was exactly right. But at the time, I thought I was in the right place to achieve my ultimate goal of being an NFL head coach, and removed my name from consideration. At the time, I was also blind to the fact that change was around the corner for the 49ers. In retrospect, I think Bill knew that George was going to be fired at the end of the season, and Minnesota would have been a great exit strategy for me.

Regardless, I stayed loyal to George and stuck with the team. My focus was on doing everything possible to win the Super Bowl. That was my only concern. Plus, I knew if history was any indicator, I would be rewarded if we had a successful season. If that were to happen, then I too would be in line to follow in the paths of Mike Shanahan and Mike Holmgren, who got head coaching jobs in the NFL after their third seasons as 49er coordinators.

We finished up the season by posting a solid 12-4 record. We headed into the playoffs full of confidence and blanked the Eagles in the opening round, 14-0, in a driving northern California rainstorm. It was a huge win, but it proved to be costly too, because Steve wound up breaking some ribs on a quarterback draw play that I will never forget. You see, I used to sit up in the coaches' box and call plays down to the field. Bill would sit in an adjacent press box with team executives, who at times wore head sets to hear play selection. This led some in the media to speculate and even insinuate that Bill was in fact the one who was actually calling the plays during games and not me. This was ridiculous; in fact, Bill went out of his way to keep his distance from me during games and never wanted to get in my way. He knew his presence was a distraction and he genuinely wanted to help me.

It happened once though, on that specific play against Philly. Bill came over and put a note on my desk during halftime, telling me to run a quarterback draw. So, during a critical red zone situation early in the third quarter, I called for Steve to run a "quarterback draw" play — which would have him fake the pass and run the ball himself. Steve ran it flawlessly

"Marc and I became great friends when wound up as roommates together up at Moorhead State University. It was quite a mix, a Jewish kid and a future minister. We hit it off right away though. I remember a lot of late night conversations while we were lying in our beds, talking about the meaning of life. I could tell early on that he had a plan. I didn't know what it was at the time, but he was such a smart guy — you could just tell that he was destined for greatness."

"Marc and I share many of the same values and I think the world of the guy. He is a very thoughtful, very kind person. He is a person with a lot of depth and character. He is always concerned about others too, which is a great quality. He was such a smart guy, yet so humble. I remember when he was in college, he was a finalist for a prestigious Rhodes Scholarship. He didn't get it, but just the fact that he was even in the running for it was a really big deal. He didn't even tell anybody about it though, that was just not his style."

"We would remain friends for years and then got to reconnect when he wound up coming to San Francisco to be the offensive coordinator for the 49ers. I was serving as the team chaplain at the time and it was great to rekindle our friendship. I will never forget how I found out. I got a phone call one night out of the blue from Brent Jones, our tight end, who was in Hawaii playing in the Pro Bowl. He called to congratulate me on the fact that my old roommate had just been hired as the team's new coordinator. I was shocked. Sure enough, a few hours later I got a call from Peter King at Sports Illustrated, who wanted the inside scoop on this guy who had been out of the game for a few years and had now been given the best job in football. It was a pretty amazing story."

"I had worked with Bill Walsh and George Siefert for several years and I knew what Marc was getting into when he got there. I was so excited for him, to be coming into a situation like that at such a young age. He fit right into the culture that we had up there and thrived. I knew he would be able to handle the pressure, the guy is brilliant. He certainly doesn't carry himself like your average football coach though, that is for sure. He just never bought into all of the 'coaches-speak' and all of the other stuff. He did things his own way and never really cared about being in the limelight or anything else. For Marc it was all about helping people and all about helping the team win. That was it."

"He wound up putting up some huge numbers when he was with the Niners and it was unfortunate that it didn't work out for him in the long run. But hey, that is football. Had we had a few bounces here or there, who knows? Maybe Marc would have gotten his big break and would have gotten a head coaching position. He has persevered though, that is for sure. He has gone through so much over his career and he always seems to bounce back. I really admire that about him. He is a wonderful person." — *Pat Richie, Team Chaplain, San Francisco 49ers*

and wound up scoring a touchdown. The problem was that he took a big hit at the goal line and went down hard. As a result, the No. 1 quarterback in the NFL was lost for the remainder of the playoffs. I was sick. I really didn't want to call the play for just that reason, but my thick skin wasn't so thick at that moment. I had pacified Bill, but had possibly caused our team a run at the Super Bowl. It remains as one of most memorable calls

"I first met Marc when he came to San Francisco to coach with the 49ers. He and I hit it off right away. He came in with a lot of credibility and we were excited to get him. To be the offensive coordinator of that team in those days was quite a pedigree. There was a lot of pressure on him and he produced. I could tell right away that he was an incredibly bright guy, and so knowledgeable about the game of football. I watched him grow into his role with the team and gain his confidence, it was pretty special."

"As a coach, Marc was extremely analytical. He had a gift in terms of being able to convey those thoughts to his players too, which was unique. He could really relate to the guys and we respected him. He was the best I ever saw at preparation and he was a great communicator too. He also knew how to motivate people at their own unique levels. That was one of his greatest strengths, for sure."

"You know, I think sometimes the media expects coaches to be tough, like Bill Parcells or Bill Belichick, and that wasn't Marc. He was a humble guy and was more of a quiet leader. When he had something to say though, guys would listen. He was a great listener as well, absolutely. He had such a great understanding of how the game is played, especially on the offensive side of the ball. He was just an offensive genius and is really respected in the football community."

"Marc has such an amazing passion for the game. I mean the guy eats and sleeps football. I can't wait until he gets his shot as a head coach in the NFL, he is going to shine. He is such a great guy. I can't say enough nice things about him. He has a great perspective on life and it is a pleasure to be around him. He has a great family too, which says a lot about him. I am just really proud to be able to call him my friend." — *Brent Jones, Pro Bowl Tight End of the San Francisco 49ers*

in all my years of coaching, I will never forget it.

We flew to Phoenix the next day to get out of the Bay Area's wet weather in order to practice somewhere warm and dry. I remember meeting with our team doctors at the Arizona Cardinals practice facility and was so relieved to learn that they felt Steve would be ready to play that next Sunday in Green Bay. He would need some rest and a shot before the game, but he would be okay. Or so they thought. You see, Steve was actually not okay. While warming up before the game, it was evident that he was simply in too much pain to throw the ball. As a result, he had to sit out and the Packers won on that muddy and rainy evening in Green Bay, 35-14.

We had a Super Bowl team in 1996, I know we did. But the fact that we didn't make it was a very big disappointment to ownership. A week after the season Mr. DeBartolo asked George to step down as the head coach, and I was right behind him. He was replaced by Steve Mariucci, who had been Brett Favre's quarterback coach in Green Bay. It was the Super Bowl or bust for George, and he knew that. Those were the expectations in San Francisco at that time and when he went, we all went. It was tough. I mean how does somebody get fired after being a member of a staff that wins 24 games in two seasons; a coach of the top rated quarterback in the NFL; and the coordinator of a team that produced top-five ranked offenses in back-to-back seasons?

I will never forget the moment I found out my fate; it was January 15th, my 40th birthday, and I was down at the Senior Bowl in Mobile, Alabama. I remember watching George's exit press conference on TV in a hotel bar down there when Mr. DeBartolo came to the podium to take questions. When he was asked about my status, he quickly blurted out, "He's gone!" I was floored. How could this be that I was fired after having so much success? As surprised as I was to have gotten the job, I was shocked to have been let go. Then to have been disrespected like this publicly made no sense to me. Not long after, Mr. DeBartolo artfully apologized and we moved on, but my work had been thrown back at me, and my family life would again be dramatically turned upside down.

Being let go after two years with the team was very difficult. The media was tough on me after it was announced we were all being let go, and in some regards I was made out to be the scapegoat. That was hard to swallow. I learned so much during my time out there and from being around such a first class organization though. They set extremely high standards and expected to win because that was the essence of the "49er Way." I admired that a great deal. I also learned from the Walsh's, Holmgren's, and Shanahan's before me, and then tried to make it my own. I learned how to practice, how to set the tempo, how to process information, how to take notes, how to conduct walk-thrus, how to dissect video, and how to deal with players — it was amazing. I also learned to respect my opponent, but that the guys on the other side of the ball were nameless and faceless. I learned that it really didn't matter who was over there. It was all about us, about our preparation, our effort, and our performance. It was the most enlightening time in my coaching career and really where I started to become the coach I am today.

As for George, all I can say is thank you for the opportunity of a lifetime. George was a very intelligent coach and a good person. He was an in-

"Marc is a great football coach, he really is. Off the field, we have become friends over the years and I think very highly of him. On the field, he is a very cerebral and thoughtful tactician. He is very smart, very patient and very competitive. He is also very aggressive, yet he is never afraid to make tough calls. He loves to throw the ball too, which was great for me because I got to air it out a lot in his system."

"We connected right away because our styles were a perfect fit for each other. His style is one of accountability, so players who are self-accountable and mature really thrive in his system. He sets very high expectations for his players and he demands excellence. He treats people like professionals too, and I really admired and appreciated that about him."

"The football world is full of coaches who yell and scream and berate players, but Marc's approach was totally different. He is wired differently, his personality, and he was able to relate well to his players. It wasn't just about finding any means to an end with him either, he wanted to get there the right way. He was all about winning, but he wanted to do so with hard work and by respecting the game. We share a lot of the same values in that regard, and I respect that about him."
— *Steve Young, Hall of Fame Quarterback, San Francisco 49ers*

tense guy and could get very emotional at times, especially when he wanted to make a point to the players. He lived under a lot of pressure. There is a saying in this business, "You don't want to follow ghosts," which means don't take a job where you're replacing a legend — and that was exactly what he did when he took over for Bill Walsh. I had a lot of respect for him. He won over 100 games as the head coach of the Niners, including a pair of Super Bowls in 1989 and 1994. George was very business-like in his approach to coaching too. He delegated things very well and then he held those people to a very high standard. He didn't interfere with me doing my job and I appreciated that a great deal.

All in all, San Francisco was a great experience. Heck, we were 24-8 in two years. Sure, I wish we would won a Super Bowl and that things would have turned out differently, but what I took away from there in terms of knowledge and experience was priceless. It was the most enlightening time in my career and where my philosophy of coaching began to take root. I had no regrets about not pursuing the Minnesota job either, and for staying with the team to pursue my goal of being an NFL head coach, as the coordinators before me had done. For me, it was about moving forward at this point. I refused to look back except to learn, and I refused to compare my journey to those of others. I had been in this situation before and it wasn't easy, but I knew that I would bounce back. It's in my nature.

"Marc is one of the most capable and knowledgeable coaches in the game." — *Bill Walsh, Hall of Fame Coach, San Francisco 49ers*

CH. 11) STARTING OVER IN THE MOTOR CITY

Leaders face the possibility of failure and adversity square on by reassessing assets and talents, and by finding the problems and priorities to mend. They seek responsibility outside of their comfort zones when success is not guaranteed and they work hard to create an environment that enables others to be successful. Humbleness and respect are crucial. It is always important to think about where you came from, the adversity you overcame, and who helped you along the way to get to where you are today. Arrogance can create a downward spiraling effect, but teamwork and respect builds rapport and strengthens organizations because everybody feels that they are contributing to the team's success and working towards a common goal.

After being let go from the Niners, I had some serious soul searching to do. Usually you get fired when you lose, not when you win. Having been fired first in Cleveland and then in San Francisco, after coordinating both teams to the playoffs, I started to wonder if there was somebody out there with a voodoo doll or something. It was crazy. I regrouped though and started to call my network of friends and allies in the business. That is what all coaches do in these situations; we get on the phone and try to land on our feet. It's always a difficult time, but we all know the drill. Most everybody who coaches at this level has been fired many times over.

One of the first coaches I spoke with was Jerry Sullivan, a former LSU assistant, who I had crossed paths with when my friend Mike Archer had been the head coach down there. Jerry had recently been the wide receivers coach with Bobby Ross at San Diego. Bobby had recently been fired by the Chargers and was now the new head coach of the Detroit Lions. Naturally, Jerry was going with him. Jerry knew I had been fired and asked me if I would be interested in coaching in Detroit. He told me it wouldn't be as a coordinator, but as the quarterbacks coach. Sylvester Croom, a coaching friend from my year in Tampa, was to be the coordinator. I spoke with Sly and he was excited about the opportunity, so I told him that I would like to interview for the position. Bobby and I hit it off and he offered me the job as the team's new quarterbacks coach. I gladly accepted it. I had a lot of respect for Bobby and for what he had accomplished at Georgia Tech, where he won an improbable National Championship in '90, and then with the Chargers where he made a Super Bowl appearance in '95. I was looking forward to working for Bobby as well as with Sylvester and Jerry.

It wasn't ideal, given the fact it was a demotion of sorts, but it was a decent situation considering everything I had been through. I just figured I would have to take one step back in order to take two steps forward. This was an opportunity to professionally catch my breath. Cindy and I were devastated to be leaving the west coast. We loved it there. The only conso-

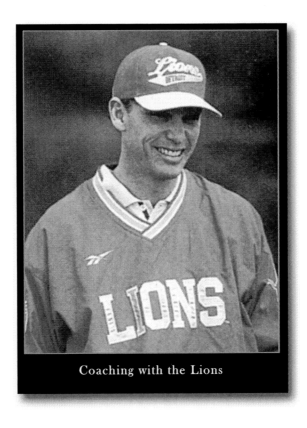

Coaching with the Lions

lation of being back in the Midwest, where we would be closer to our two families in Cleveland and Minneapolis. So we packed up and moved to the Motor City.

One of the biggest positives about my situation in Detroit was the fact the entire coaching staff was all coming in together. Whenever you join a staff that is already in place, you have to deal with a lot of distracting and uncomfortable situations early. The politics can kill you. A coach has left, after being either fired or promoted, and there are often remaining members who are uncomfortable because you are getting the job they thought they deserved. This was totally different and it was really a nice change of pace for me. We all hit it off right away too, which was pretty neat. We ate together, hung out together, and even lived in the same hotel together. We just bonded. We all learned about the city and the organization as a group, which built a lot of chemistry for us as a unit. I was able to start on the ground floor with the new staff and we installed the new offense together. This was big and I really enjoyed this very unique dynamic.

I knew going in that coaching in Detroit was going to be a challenge. The team had finished in last place the year before, but they had a core of very talented players on offense. They had two excellent wide receivers in Herman Moore and Johnny Morton. Their running back was the incomparable Barry Sanders, and they had a big strong lefty quarterback by the name of Scott Mitchell. In 1995 the offense performed remarkably well under the tutelage of none other than offensive coordinator Tom Moore. Things fell apart in 1996, but the talent base was there. We had a chance to be good, and to do it fast.

The Lions were one of the only teams in the league that had never been to a championship game in the modern era. But what I found out when I got there was that they were in fact one of the better managed teams in the league. The Ford family was a great ownership group and they treated their employees very, very well. Mr. Ford and his son, Bill Jr., were extremely generous in many ways. GM Chuck Schmitt did an awesome job of managing the day to day life of our organization as well. We also had a terrific group of scouts that included Tom Dimitroff, now the GM of the Atlanta Falcons, and Kevin Colbert, who is now the head of football operations with the Pittsburgh Steelers.

Bobby Ross fit right in. He was extremely well organized, a good communicator, very understanding of people, and a terrific X's and O's coach. He had hired an outstanding staff of coaches and we were all hopeful that we could turn the organization around in the right direction. His wife, Alice, was an astute woman who did a great job of bringing the wives together and making them feel important. The Lions leadership had holiday parties and did little things to make sure coaches and their families were paid well and treated with respect. Before I had taken the job, I spoke with a number of coaches who had worked over the years in the Lion organization. They all had the same thing to say, that Mr. Ford, his son Bill, and Chuck did things first class and treated the coaches well. As I would find out for myself, they were exactly right.

Our off-season meetings went very smoothly. Sly focused on the installation of the running game, and it was my job to format the passing game — which was basically the 49er passing attack plus some additional plays that Scott Mitchell felt comfortable with from his last few years in Detroit. The season started off slowly for us, but we then came on strong, winning five of our last six games down the stretch to finish at 9-7. We beat the Vikings and Jets in our last two games which even put us in the playoffs, which was huge. A first year program headed to the post-season, that was something we could all feel pretty good about. All of our hard work that season had been validated to a certain extent. We ended up losing to Tony Dungy and the Tampa Bay Bucs in the opening round, 20-10, but it was definitely a big turn-around for the franchise.

That season we had one of the top offenses in the league and much of that was due to the amazing play of Barry Sanders, who rushed for 2,053 yards, third most in NFL history. It was unbelievable to watch this man practice and play the game at a level most others playing in the league could only dream about. He had a sense of humor, was extremely bright, and it was really a privilege to watch him day in and day out. He was a quiet leader and a tremendously hard worker — a true professional. I remember watching him stay after practice sometimes to run 100 yard wind sprints at full speed. In 1996, a year earlier, he was chased from behind on a couple runs that prevented him from scoring. He was determined to not let that happen in 1997 and all of his hard work paid off for him because he had a bunch of 50+ yard touchdowns for us that next season. He was a quiet man with a champion's heart. I was in awe of him, I really was.

One of the things that I admired most about Barry was the fact that when he scored a touchdown, he would humbly hand the ball to the referee. He never spiked it or attempted to draw attention to himself, that was just not his style. This spoke volumes about his character and about his level of respect for the game. In Montreal we actually have our players practice what I call "touchdown demeanor." This is not a pre-designed choreographed celebration, but rather just a bunch of guys going to touch the ball while expressing honest emotion and a sense of equal participation in the play's success. The idea is that a player should not do anything that draws attention to himself by performing some overactive display of emotion or choreographed celebration. This is about respect — respect for the work each player has added towards the team's success, the game, and the opponent. Barry exemplified class and respect in every facet of the game, so his quiet celebrations were really no surprise when you think about it.

Our passing game also flourished under our quarterback Scott Mitchell, who threw for nearly 3,500 yards, second most in team history. He also threw 19 touchdowns that season, with most of them going to Herman Moore and Johnny Morton, who each had over 1,000 yards receiving as well. I really enjoyed working with Scott and related strongly to him. He was incredibly easy to work with and he picked up the offense easily. He signed with the Lions as a free agent from the Dolphins for more than $20 million a few years earlier. He came in with a lot of hype but remained quiet and unassuming on arrival. The media and city were very hard on him, but they didn't know him the way I did after spending time around him in the off-season. This guy gave the Lions everything he had. In the winter before the 1997 season, Scott worked extremely hard off the field getting physically ready to play. We spent a lot of time together in the classroom too. He was a very smart player who was passionate in his preparation and a quiet team leader.

Our backup quarterback, Frank Reich, was outstanding as well. Frank had previously been Jim Kelly's backup for several years up in Buffalo with the Bills. People might remember Frank's performance at the University of Maryland when he rallied the Terps back from a 30-0 deficit to beat the Miami Hurricanes in 1984. I was the quarterbacks coach at the time and I certainly never forgot it. He also led the Bills to an unbelievable comeback against the Oilers in the '92 playoffs, which is widely regarded as one of the greatest comebacks in NFL history.

174

These two quarterbacks were men of such high character. I really enjoyed coaching them. They gave me everything they had and more. In fact, I remember waking up Christmas morning in 1997 and there the two of them were, knocking at my door. They wanted to come over and personally deliver a present for me. As a coach, I can tell you stuff like that doesn't happen very often. I was really touched by that. That was an important moment to me. It told me I was valued and that I was making a difference in people's lives.

Helping the team to the playoffs and getting the team pointed in a new direction was very gratifying to all of us. In fact, it was probably one of the most enjoyable years I have ever had in the league. It was a very different situation in Detroit as opposed to San Francisco, where I did everything myself with regards to putting game plans together. In Detroit, we did this together collaboratively as a staff, which was very refreshing. It was difficult for me at first because I had to learn to let go and not fight my urge to jump in and take over. That ultimately helped me become a better coach though, which I have never forgotten.

Another positive about Detroit was the fact that I was able to stay out of the limelight and just focus on coaching. I enjoyed working for Bobby too. The players respected him. He was very human, very approachable, and just an extremely kind yet very competitive guy. Despite the fact that he was a micro-manager and was involved in every aspect of the game — from personnel, to scouting, to special teams — he had specific tasks and roles for all of us and just let us do our jobs. When you didn't do well as a coach or as a player for Bobby, you felt like you were letting him down. He had that kind of demeanor. He was a great people person and he knew how to motivate people extremely effectively.

After the season I went in and met with Bobby for what is basically an annual performance review. This is where you are evaluated and where contract issues are brought up. He told me he was going to give me an extension and a raise, but then told me something pretty interesting. He said "Marc, we are thrilled to have you here, but I personally think that you are on the wrong career track. You have got to get back on track to being a coordinator and eventually a head coach. That is where you belong."

He then basically told me he would help me find a job as a coordinator if that was what I wanted. That meant a lot to me. I enjoyed the staff and my day to day work with the quarterbacks, but I knew Sylvester had done a great job with the offense and that I wasn't going to be taking over for him any time soon. So, I told Bobby I would talk to Cindy and take a look at the NFL landscape, but that I certainly was more than comfortable coming back that next season. We had bought a house in suburban Detroit and were happy there. I thought I had gotten in on the ground floor of a young team with a new staff and figured I would just work my way up.

A few weeks later, while I was down at the Senior Bowl in Mobile, Alabama, I got a call from Wade Phillips, who had just gotten the head coaching job with Buffalo. He wanted to see if I was interested in becoming the new offensive coordinator on his staff. The very next day, Dave McGinnis, the defensive coordinator for the Arizona Cardinals, saw me at practice and introduced me to his head coach, Vince Tobin. The Cards had just fired their offensive coordinator and they wanted to know if I was interested in joining their staff. Again, sometimes when it rains, it pours. I interviewed with each coach and there were so many positives with both teams. It was a tough choice because both were really different jobs. Buffalo had an extremely rich tradition of winning, having gone to four Super Bowls in the early '90s. Arizona, meanwhile, had a perception of being a dysfunctional organization which had never won any big post-season games. Both were generous offers that represented unique challenges.

When I sat down with Cindy to talk about my two options, it became read-

The Trestman Family

ily apparent what her first choice was — someplace warm! With that, we took yet another leap of faith - this time to Arizona, where we would begin the next chapter of our lives on this crazy coaching carrousel. Cindy was thrilled to be headed back west and her support and excitement made me feel really good about the decision to move. Arizona had a talented young quarterback by the name of Jake Plummer and I was anxious to once again take on a new challenge. We hadn't lived in Detroit for even a year, and I already had to ask her to stay behind for a few months with two young children, in the middle of the winter in Detroit, while I picked up to go take on a new challenge. Such is life as an assistant coach in the National Football League.

CH. 12)   ECSTASY AND AGONY IN THE LAND OF THE RISING SUN

"Buy-in" is essential to being able to lead. Without buy-in, any and all efforts of a leader will go to waste because those they lead have to see, understand, and be on board with what is going on. Good leaders recognize when buy-in is not present and they do all they can to either obtain it or create a new vision. They also recognize when buy-in is impossible, often due to circumstances outside of their control, and are able to move on to make better uses of their talents when organizational stalemates occur.

Coming to Arizona was much like it was when I came to Detroit. The team had finished 4-12 the year before I got there, dead last in the NFC East. The expectations weren't as high coming in as they were with the 49ers, but I was anxious to help turn things around. The team had been through some really tough losing seasons, but I could see that they had some real talent on their roster — starting with Jake Plummer. My game plan coming in was simple, I was going to take everything I learned in San Francisco and teach it to the existing staff and players. I thought Jake would be great at running the West Coast Offense and I was anxious to quickly teach him as much as I could.

Not only did I want to bring in the new offense from the 49ers, I also wanted to bring in their practice culture. Bill Walsh's "work fast/practice fast/play fast" philosophy was a hallmark of the "49er Way" and I believed it would work here in the desert as well. Whenever you go in to a new team and try to install an entirely new system, it can be extremely difficult, especially with people who you have no prior relationship with. Such was the case for me with the Cardinals. They were not very open minded about buying in at first, but they eventually came around. Vince got on board early and that helped out a great deal. He had a very high character, a quiet yet highly competitive demeanor, and a common sense approach to his coaching style.

Things started out rough that season. I remember we were playing Dallas in the opener and they were up by more than 30 points late in the game. Their coach then kicked a field goal, which then really upset all of us. That was absolute disrespect for the game and for the people who play and coach it. In these situations, most coaches will not run up the score on the other team, and instead will simply have their quarterback take a knee to end the game — even if they are on the opposition's one yard line. In my opinion it is never appropriate to show-up the other team and kick them when they are down. Never. I always remind our players and coaches that everyone in this business works hard, and sometimes it just doesn't go well for the opposition. We've all been there. In those situations you just take a knee and get out of there. That stuff comes back to haunt you in this league. Why give a team a reason, or motivation, to

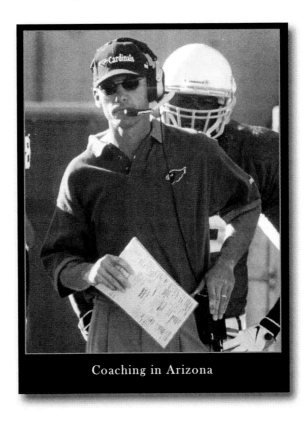

Coaching in Arizona

get up" to play you?

Anyway, that lesson aside, we were a very poor offense for the first eight weeks of the season. We had a very good defense, but in my opinion I wasn't doing a very good job with the offense. My new system was taking time to sink in and it was extremely frustrating for everybody. Our defense was so good that I found myself calling plays conservatively to protect Jake and the offense from being in a position to lose games. This just wasn't my style. I also talked myself into being inhibited by my staff. They were a group of very good coaches but just weren't familiar with the offense. The turning point came right at about the halfway point of the season when Vince came into my office one day and said, "Marc, I want you to open up the offense and start throwing the ball." It was like a weight had been lifted off of my shoulder. The next week we went to a no-huddle offense, which really neutralized our competition. We were able to set the tempo and that helped Jake's confidence to thrive. In fact, he threw for nearly 2,500 yards in the last eight games alone. It was incredible. Once we started winning, the fans started coming out too. Seeing 70,000 red jerseys in the stands every Sunday, for a change, was fantastic. Vince Tobin's

Watching Jake Plummer at practice

plan had worked and I was grateful to have gone along for the ride.

Jake was a pleasure to coach. He was very charismatic and he loved the game. His strength was his resiliency. He could throw an interception and it wouldn't matter because he would come right back, firing away. He was as mentally tough and resilient as anybody I had ever coached before. There are two kinds of toughness in football, physical toughness and mental toughness. Mental toughness is the toughest quality because it is very difficult to teach. Jake was mentally tough. In fact, I called him the "Ice-Man." We won six games in the last two minutes that year, which is an amazing stat, and was Jake the reason why. When you think of quarterbacks who are known for their abilities to rally their teams you think of guys like John Elway, Dan Marino and Brett Favre. Well, Jake Plummer was the best in the business at doing that in 1998. He just refused to give up and seemingly always found a way to make something happen out there.

We got hot at the end of the year and finished with a pretty good 9-7 record, good for second in NFC East. Most importantly, we made the playoffs for the first time since 1982. From there, we headed to Dallas to face the Cowboys in the opening round of the post-season. We were big underdogs heading into the game but came away with a huge upset victory, beating them, 20-7. It was sweet payback to the team which kicked an unnecessary field goal 17 weeks earlier. This was an amazing win for us; one of the greatest in the franchise's history, without question. We just played hard, stuck to our game plan, and we walked out of there with the organization's first playoff win in more than a half century. I will never forget landing at the airport in Phoenix after the game and seeing 20,000 fans out there to welcome us home on the tarmac. It was unbelievable.

The players prepared hard and were focused the entire week as we headed up to Minnesota for the divisional playoffs. Minnesota was amazing that season, with Randall Cunningham, Cris Carter and Randy Moss. They had the top rated offense in the league and were playing at home; we knew we were going to have our work cut out for us. They got up early and that Metrodome crowd really got behind them. It was a tough and hostile environment to play in. Needless to say, we played hard, but just got beat by a better team that day. We lost in a shoot-out, 41-21, to end an otherwise magical season.

I was excited about our prospects heading into the next year but everything started to fall apart that off-season when we lost two of our top players to free agency. Their departure would leave a gaping hole for us that we could just never dig out of it. We lost our chemistry and became a totally different team in the locker room after that. We fell apart. Everything changed and we became victims of our own success. I had never seen anything like it before.

Plus, we had a big case of the "the reason why we won was because of me" syndrome. And believe me, I was as guilty as everybody else too. I certainly believed I did a great job and had a big part to do in the team's success. At the end of the day, it was because of all of us doing our jobs collectively – not because of any one individual. In the game of football, you eventually learn that everybody must do their job at the highest standard to have team success. Nobody is more important than anybody else. When you start thinking you are the reason for your team's success, bad things will invariably start to happen. They sure did after the '98 season in Arizona.

Jake got hurt midway through that next season and Dave Brown came in as his back-up. We got hot and won four in a row late in the year, but then fell flat and lost our last four games to finish at 6-10, good for just fourth place in the division. I was very disappointed with myself and I felt that I had let Vince down. It got even worse the next year and we just couldn't seem to recover as everything spiraled out of control. Vince got fired during the middle of the year and our defensive coordinator, Dave McGinnis, took over. We were playing poorly and had a ton of injuries. Frank Sanders and Herman Moore, our top receivers were hurt, as was our starting center. Everybody was on the shelf for whatever the reason and it was really tough on all of us. Jake threw 21 interceptions that year and we struggled in every aspect of the game. We ended the season losing our last seven games to finish with a dismal 3-13 record, dead last in the division. It was awful.

Dave was forced by ownership to fire me after two unproductive offensive seasons. The media was all over me and in the end I had to take the fall. I had magically gone from a genius in 1998, to an idiot in just two years in the eyes of the media. That was painful. It wasn't personal that Dave had to fire me, just business. I totally understood. You know, I was the highest paid coordinator in the league during my years in Arizona, and the offensive stats weren't showing why. Mr. Bidwell was very generous to me during my time in Arizona and I sincerely appreciated that.

What I learned was that as a coach you can make a lot of money, but if you are uncomfortable in your work environment on a daily basis, and you are constantly fighting uphill battles, then it's just not worth it. The life-lesson learned here was that sometimes it's just best to move on, especially when there are issues beyond your control. We loved Arizona and were sad to leave. Our kids were getting settled and our folks loved to come visit too, but it just didn't work out. Career-wise, however, I was definitely ready for a change of scenery.

ON GETTING FIRED

"I have always been pretty resilient when it comes to getting fired. I am grateful for that and in most cases have looked at it as an opportunity in the making. In professional football, getting fired is just a natural progression. It has happened not only to me but most every other coach at this level as well. The important thing to realize is that, for the most part, it is not a result of your work ethic or ability. In football as with all business, everyone is interconnected and timing can enter into a coach's ability to have a long tenure in one place. The next thing to do is to 'hire yourself' with the job of finding a new job. When it would happen to me I would get up every day, get a workout in to relieve the anxiety and stress, and then begin to execute my plan for landing on my feet. Sometimes you get the job because of your efforts, other times random fate allows you to cross paths with the right people. At the end of the day, I believe there is no such thing as a coincidence."

CH. 13) A COMMITMENT TO EXCELLENCE IN OAKLAND

Game plans are important in any business. Leaders plan their work and work their plan. They must regularly analyze every aspect of their work environment, tendencies, and analytics in order to create a plan going forward for success. Often this assessment needs to go outside of the organization as leaders look at competitor's tendencies in order to stay prepared and ahead of the curve.

A couple of weeks after I was let go from the Cardinals I got a call from George Seifert, who had taken over as the head coach of the Carolina Panthers. He offered me an assistant position with his staff, so I flew to Charlotte to meet with him. It was a good opportunity in a beautiful city and one which I was grateful for, but Cindy and I wanted to stay out west, so I passed. I had a year left on my contract and didn't need to do anything right away. Soon after, I got a call out of the blue from an old friend of mine by the name of Jon Gruden. It was a call that was going to change my life.

I first met Jon back in '94 at the Senior Bowl. I was there trying to interest agents into considering municipal bonds for their millionaire clients. I was at a coaches social one night when a young, blonde-haired guy walked right up to me. He was much shorter than I but carried himself with an air of confidence and charisma that I had not seen before. He looked up at me, all five-foot-eight of him, and said, "Hi, I'm Jon Gruden; I'm the wide receivers coach with Green Bay. You don't know me but I've watched all your tapes from when you were with Cleveland. You put some great football out there with Bernie. Why the heck aren't you coaching in this league right now?" I was blown away. Somebody actually knew of me and had watched my tapes?

We talked and really hit it off. We stayed in touch and saw each other every year down at the Senior Bowl. We would go out for beers and sit for hours, diagramming plays together on napkins like a couple of real football nerds. He later went on to accept the offensive coordinator position with Philadelphia and we even coached against each other one time back in '96 when his Eagles faced my 49ers. I will never forget walking down the steps together after that game and somebody yelled, "Hey ass hole!" We both turned to look. We then looked at each other and just laughed. It was funny because we both felt like he was talking to us, individually. We still laugh about that to this day and say, "Hey ass hole!" whenever we see each other.

Anyway, somewhere along the line we made a pact that if either of us was ever coaching and the other was out a job and needed work, the coach would hire the other. Well, sure enough, a few weeks after I got fired in Arizona, guess who called? Jon Gruden, the fourth year head coach of the Oakland Raiders. Jon had already made a big name for himself by turn-

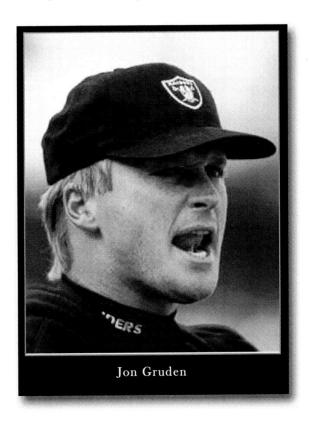

Jon Gruden

ing around the Raiders. He offered me a position on his staff with the nebulous title of "senior assistant." He told me that I could help out with quarterbacks and with game-planning, and that we would see where things would go from there. There were no guarantees, but I appreciated the offer and took it. Cindy and I were thrilled to be headed back up to the Bay Area.

From a career perspective, I was especially excited to be back in the game with a team moving in the right direction. Oakland had a lot of talent and fortunately I was able to assist the team even more by helping with the acquisition of Jerry Rice, who moved across the Bay from San Francisco to join the Raiders that season. They also had a great quarterback in Rich Gannon, who I was really excited about getting an opportunity to work with again. Rich and I had originally spent time together when we were both in Minnesota and I thought the world of him. Rich had been on an amazing journey himself over the past decade and was flourishing in Oakland. Jon had been trained by Mike Holmgren in San Francisco and Green Bay, and had his own version of the West Coast Offense which was extremely effective.

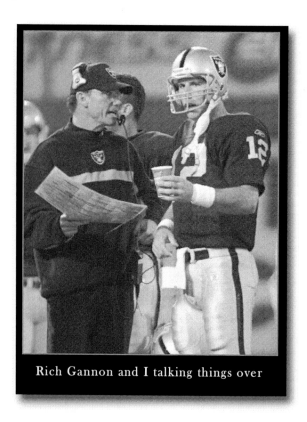

Rich Gannon and I talking things over

In Oakland I wasn't hired as a mercenary coordinator with the responsibility of coming in to turn things around. Rather, I was coming in to compliment a system that was already up and running smoothly. Big difference. I just was looking forward to working with Jon and his staff and doing whatever I could to help out in any way he saw fit. There were some aspects about coming to Oakland that were a bit nerve wracking for me though. I was somewhat familiar with the organization, from having spent a few years in nearby San Francisco, but they were a real enigma in my eyes. The team had a great tradition and truly a unique mystique about it and that all started with their owner, Al Davis, who was and is a legendary figure in the NFL. His notorious mantras of "Just win baby!" and "Commitment to Excellence" were the philosophy of the entire organization from the top, down.

I wasn't sure what to expect, but when I got there everything fell into place. I was excited about football again and had renewed my passion for the game. Working with Jon was invigorating, especially after two disastrous years in Arizona. I am not sure if I have ever known a harder worker in all my life. Jon was a morning guy like me. During my time in Oakland, Cindy used to have to kick me out of bed at a quarter to three in the morning to get up for work. This enabled me to beat the rush hour traffic and get a lot of things done. By getting to work early, there was generally a back end of the day that I could save for Cindy and the girls. As exhausted as I was, especially after driving the 34 miles of Bay Area traffic from our offices in Alameda to my house in Danville (an Oakland suburb) each day, I was able to read to the girls before bed and then talk to Cindy about her day. This was big to me and always has been. It has kept us connected during some very turbulent times and grounded in what is most important.

The more I got to know Jon the more I would say to myself, "Wow that was me, when I was 30," only I didn't have the confidence and swagger he had. I definitely saw myself in him though. He was really passionate about his work and was so focused. He didn't spend much time with our defense or special teams, but he micro-managed the offense. That was his area of expertise. He was very bright and articulate, with the ability to keep things simple for our players. He was also a tremendous salesman. When he stood before the team to install a game plan, his passion forced you to believe that it was special and that you as a player were individually a very big part of that plan. He was also a student of the game who researched and studied other teams. He would do anything he could to find plays that would help his Raiders move the ball. The guy was relentless.

Jon re-enforced in me the importance and power of great presentation skills, which I had always struggled with. In Oakland I began to really perfect my ability to excite our team and capture their attention during my game plan presentations. In many ways I learned that it was much more important than the actual plays themselves. The guys were going to buy in based on my demeanor and passion, so I knew that I had to connect with them. I finally came out of my shell in Oakland and as a result, football became fun again. To this day, I always prepare for a meeting by reminding myself that players (and coaches) will follow that which they see and feel. The demeanor and confidence with which you carry yourself is huge, and the more prepared you are the more this sets the tone.

The first few weeks of the season were extremely difficult. On the morning of September 11, 2001, word passed through our complex that the U.S. had been attacked by terrorists who flew planes into the Twin Towers in New York City and the Pentagon in Washington D.C. This was incomprehensible as we watched in utter disbelief on our televisions in Alameda. When disaster hit, it was a time for reflection on the things that were most important, like the health and safety of family and friends. At that moment seemingly every American as well as every citizen in the civilized world stopped to say thank you for what they had. This was certainly a message we not only had to cherish on that day, but one that should also stay attentive on each and every moment of every day. All we are really guaranteed is the now. This is certainly not easy to do, but it remains big for me today in how I approach the daily work with my team.

We had a good season in 2001, finishing with a solid 10-6 record and the team's second straight AFC West title. Rich threw for over 3,800 yards and 27 touchdowns. It was amazing. Jon and offensive coordinator Bill Callahan had the offense running beautifully. We beat the Jets at home in the Wild Card game, 38-24, and then headed to New England to play the Patriots in the next round of the playoffs. This one was memorable for all the wrong reasons and would go down in infamy as the "Tuck Rule Game."

The game was played in a heavy snowstorm, and late in the fourth quarter it appeared that Patriots quarterback Tom Brady fumbled when Charles Woodson hit him just as he was releasing the ball. The ball was then recovered by our linebacker, Greg Biekert. We were up 13-10 at that point and figured we had iced the game. The play was reviewed, however, and determined to be an incomplete pass by the officials. They said that Brady had pump-faked and had not yet tucked the ball into his body, which, by rule, could not result in a fumble. It was an extremely controversial call. As a result, New England retained possession and then drove for a game-tying field goal. From there, the game went into overtime, where Patriots Kicker Adam Vinatieri ultimately nailed the game-winning field goal to win it, 16-13. It was an absolutely devastating loss. The Patriots would go on to win the Super Bowl that season, which made it sting even more.

I was looking forward to sitting down with Jon after the season to go over his expectations of my job description for the upcoming 2002 campaign. Just days after the devastating loss to the Pats, however, the staff was called into the office by our general manager, Bruce Allen, who wanted to meet with us as quickly as possible. We soon found out that Jon was leaving and was going to be taking over as the head coach of the Tampa Bay Bucs. It was a huge story and his face was plastered all over the news. As for me,

Coaching Jerry Rice was a real thrill

the whole thing made my head spin. I had started my coaching career in Miami and in two years I worked for two coaches, then went to Minnesota where I worked for two head coaches, then to Cleveland where I worked for two head coaches, same in Arizona, and now it was happening again in Oakland. This just doesn't happen, but it happened to me. What was even more amazing was that many of these changes had occurred on winning teams, such as in Oakland. How do you explain that on your resumé?

When situations like this arise it is about remembering what is important and enjoying the journey along the way. Football is a game which has so many variables both on and off the field that are out of a coach's control. When you truly understand this and maintain an even keeled approach and appreciation for health and family, it makes the hardships that go with the job come easier. Nevertheless, the trade of Jon to the Bucs was unbelievable and unprecedented. It turned out that he really wanted a change of scenery and needed to get out of Oakland. His extended family was in the Tampa area and that was where he wanted to be. Ironically, he was going to replace my old college roommate, Tony Dungy, as the

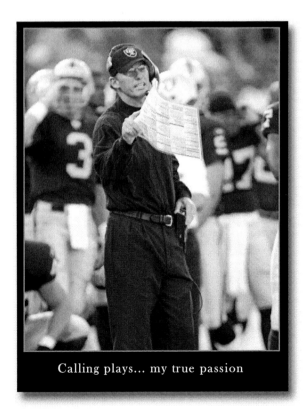

Calling plays... my true passion

190

new head coach of the Bucs.

The way it all went down was pretty extraordinary. Apparently Jon had gone into the office, taken his computer, cleaned out his desk, and left in the middle of the night. He was under specific instructions not to talk to anybody and that was exactly what he did. He was under contract with Mr. Davis at the time, so he was traded, as opposed to just leaving as a free agent. To my understanding, the Raiders received 2002 and 2003 first-round draft picks, 2002 and 2004 second-round draft picks, and $8 million in cash. This was a king's ransom. As for Jon, he signed a five-year contract and under the terms of the deal he couldn't take any assistants with him. I called him a few days later to thank him and wished him well. I was happy for him, he worked ungodly hours and he wanted to be near his family. More power to him.

Shortly after, it was announced that the team's offensive coordinator, Bill Callahan, would be taking over as the new head coach. Bill then immediately offered me the position of offensive coordinator and quarterback coach. What an amazing twist of fate. Wow. Hey, I was excited to have the opportunity and gladly accepted it. Bill was one of the most brilliant coaches I had ever been around. In fact, I would say that his understanding of the game was higher than any coach I had ever worked with. His passion, like Gruden's, was contagious. He was a master of the science and detail of the game, and like me, he was constantly in search of learning more football each and every day he came to the office. Bill and I had a great connection from the beginning and I enjoyed his cutting edge approach to the game. I worked hard to stay right there with him. I grew as much as a coach with Bill than I did in my other 15 years in the league.

Mr. Davis gave us a very long leash to try new things and that was very refreshing too. He provided an environment for us to be whoever we wanted to be. People today refuse to believe that Mr. Davis never got involved with the offensive side of the ball, but he really didn't. Oftentimes his interest was more on the defensive side of the ball and with preparing the organization for the draft.

A lot of owners like to be hands-on, but Mr. Davis let us go about our business. His focus was on assessing and acquiring talent and at the time he did a tremendous job with our draft boards. I used to call our draft meetings "The Draft by Socratic Method." It was amazing; the staff and scouts would settle in and get ready as Mr. Davis entered the room. He said, "Good morning" and would then ask us questions. He could start anywhere, and who was questioned was arbitrary with no apparent method to his madness. But Mr. Davis came to each meeting prepared with questions, of which he mostly already had the answers. This was the Socratic Method I had learned in law school, and that helped relieve my nervousness especially in the first year with the team. My ability to be prepared, combined with knowing the personnel in the league and AFC West, along with my historical perspective of the quarterback position all really helped my confidence. For whatever the reason, I was actually much more confident handling football questions than I was at handling questions about Contracts and Constitutional Law.

Bill and I made an important decision early in the winter of 2002. We were going to change our offensive philosophy from that of a conservative "run first — play action," to more of a spread out, drop back passing attack. Bill and I were from the same school of not putting square pegs into round holes, and we wanted our offense to best take advantage of our player's strengths. Going into the 2002 season we had three very good receivers who we wanted on the field most of the time in Jerry Rice, the great Tim Brown, and an up and coming young player with phenomenal athleticism in Jerry Porter. We had also acquired the fiery and dynamic all purpose running back Charlie Garner. The year before fullback Jon Ritchie had played a majority of the time in place of three wide receivers. We loved Jon, he was an outstanding player, but spreading the field with Porter and utilizing Garner's run and pass catching ability allowed us to put more explosive personnel on the field. We had no boundaries to the type of football that we were going to put out on the field. All Mr. Davis asked was to do was "Just Win Baby!", and that was our plan from the opening day of training camp.

I remember speaking to the players at the very first meeting in camp. I told them that if they were willing to put a the team first, then this was going to be one of the greatest journeys of their lives. That became our motto the entire season too. Whenever we came upon any adversity, I went right back to it and worked hard to get the players to re-purchase this philosophy. We had some great veteran players on our roster who had accomplished some great things up to that point in their careers, and thankfully they were willing to make the individual sacrifices that champions do. When they bought in, the rest followed and great things began to happen. This was Bud Grant's "Jim Marshall" philosophy to a tee.

With Bill constantly pushing for us to think out of the box, we became one of the most dynamic, aggressive, and outrageous offenses that had ever been seen in the NFL. It was the West Coast Offense in principle, but we took it to the next level. The man behind it all was Bill, who, in addition to being a line coach was also a former quarterback coach. Bill formatted the running game for each game plan and you would think, like most line coaches, he would want it to be "run first, throw second." But this was not the case as he believed wholeheartedly that we should throw the ball. We had a huge offensive line full of great pass protectors, a running back who was an explosive pass receiver, a pair of future Hall of Fame wide receivers, as well as an up and coming superstar receiver. During the season, I called the plays with Bill giving me the runs he wanted. But when he said, "Throw it Marc," I called the best pass available. This was unprecedented, and it worked magnificently. Bill and I were tied at the hip. We believed in each other and along with our staff of Aaron Kromer, John Morton, Skip Peete, Fred Biletnikoff, Chris Turner, and Jim Harbaugh, we put some amazing stuff out there that teams throughout the

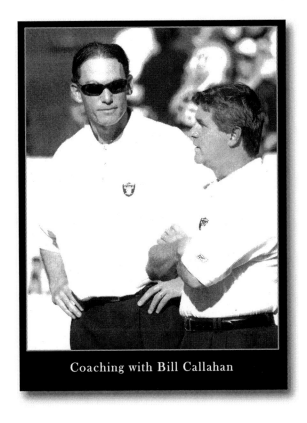

Coaching with Bill Callahan

NFL as well as the collegiate ranks still use today.

The season began with four dynamic wins, followed by four straight losses. We turned it around after that though and won seven of our next eight games. Our only loss in the second half of the season was to a pretty good Miami team. When it was all said and done, we finished with an 11-5 record and won the AFC West. We earned a bye week after the regular season finale and even clinched home field advantage throughout the playoffs. We led the NFL in total offense with 390 yards per game and in total passing yards with 280 yards per game. As a result, we had the top rated offense for 16 straight weeks during the regular season, which had never been done before. Rich played marvelously and was even named as the MVP of the league. I was extremely proud of what our players and coaches accomplished, but the journey was not over.

During the season, Bill did a great job of keeping us on a steady course. He and I had put together what we called our "First-15," which was a script of the first 15 plays that we ran each game. Week in and week out we mixed it up, but we would always follow that road map that we had laid out for ourselves. I remember in Week Two we beat the Pittsburgh Steelers in a nationally televised Sunday night game. They had an outstanding team that year and I knew that if we were going to have a chance to beat them, we were going to have to do some really radical things. The Steelers ran a slanting and blitzing run defense that was not a good matchup for our running game. So, we installed a really intriguing First-15 that set the tempo for one of best games I have ever coached. It started the night before in a Pittsburgh hotel ballroom where I stood before our offense and told them to get a good night's sleep and to be sure to drink plenty of fluids. I told them they were going to need it because that next night we were going to throw the ball more than any team had ever attempted in NFL history, and that we were going to do it from a no-huddle offense.

We had meetings that day with the ESPN production team which included my close friend Joe Theismann. Bill made me promise not to tell Joe our plan. I remained true to Bill, and Joe has to this day never stopped bugging me about not telling him. Bill and I, along with the entire staff, really believed that balance (our team's run/pass ratio) was not as important as doing whatever it took to best utilize the personnel we had to move the ball. This was a cutting edge philosophy at the time. Now, the week before we had a 40-rush, 200-plus yard rushing attack against the Seahawks.

This gave us the perfect element of surprise going into Heinz Field in Pittsburgh. We fully expected the Steelers to believe we would try to pound their vaunted 3-4 defense with our huge line and big running back, Ty Wheatley, like we did against Seattle. As such, there was simply no way they ever could have prepared for what we gave them that night.

From the moment he set foot on Heinz Field, Rich took control of the offense and played a masterful game. We threw on our first 15 plays and just kept on throwing from there. In fact, Rich broke nearly every major single-game Raiders passing record that night by throwing the ball an unheard of 64 times. By the time it was all said and done, he had 43 completions in 64 attempts for over 400 yards. Our receivers, Jerry Rice, Tim Brown, Jerry Porter and tight end Roland Williams had great nights. Pro Bowl Center Barrett Robbins and our offensive line protected beautifully and we dominated. We changed up our personnel, our formations, our tempo, and our protections. We ran the ball just one time in the entire first half, a surprise draw play that went the distance for a touchdown. We won the game, 30-17, and that really set the tone for us that season — we were going to change and adapt week in and week out.

Each week we changed things up based on our opponent's strengths and weaknesses. Thirteen weeks later in a torrential downpour in Oakland, we ran the ball 60-plus times to defeat the Chiefs en route to clinching the home-field advantage for the playoffs. Once again, against the Chiefs, it all started with the First-15. The night before the game, Bill and I, at Bill's suggestion, sat down and prepared an unprecedented two separate First-15's. One for good weather and one for rain. Sure enough, it poured relentlessly throughout the game and we were prepared. Was it worth the effort at a time when we were totally exhausted at week's end and would both rather have just gone to bed? Absolutely.

I have always enjoyed putting the First-15 together. It is during this quiet time that you are forced to review your entire scouting report and game

"I think Marc is like Bill Walsh, because he's one of those guys who you want to go out and lay it on the line for. He is totally committed, and players want to play for a guy like that." — *Jerry Rice, Hall of Fame Receiver, San Francisco 49ers & Oakland Raiders*

plan, as well as put the final touches on your call sheet. Late in the week changes due to injury, weather, crowd noise, final quarterback meetings, and tape study can also be very important to the process. We also focused on how we were going to neutralize key players and set the tempo that was the most conducive to our style of play. The First-15 takes time and tremendous concentration to do it right. But when you do, it can be a real difference maker.

Putting together a game plan in football is the same as in business. Plan your work and work your plan — that is a cliché I wholeheartedly believe in. When you sit down and analyze every aspect of the game and go over all of the tendencies and analytics, the picture begins to crystallize. You anticipate the opposition's moves and can attack and counter-attack on your own terms. Everything slows down. You want to make something that is very simple offensively look very complex from a defensive standpoint. It's the "game within the game." For a coach, when you draw up a perfectly executed game plan and it works, that is the equivalent of any athlete "being in the zone."

Over the years I formulated countless First-15's, usually alone in the confines of my hotel room, office, or team plane. It can be extremely challenging, frustrating, and exhausting. I found that I was always fighting with myself over every decision and the lack of feedback from another coach. It mentally and emotionally taxed me. And for me, the fight for perfection with every call only exacerbates the issue. That all changed when I got to Oakland and was able to collaborate with Bill though. He was more into planning and preparation than any coach I had never known.

He and I would spend literally the entire Saturday before a game together laying out the First-15. What was once an exhausting process became a completely exhilarating coaching experience for two guys who simply loved the game of football. The manufacturing of the First-15 became one of my favorite segments of the week because Bill and I worked without distraction, sitting around the office or in a hotel suite. We would

"Marc is a very intelligent coach and he really understands the game. I can't even begin to describe how far his depth goes in terms of knowledge of the game. He's a brilliant coach." — *Bill Callahan, Head Coach, Oakland Raiders*

order in some food and then breakdown the three hours of football that we were going to play the next day. Our time preparing was spent reviewing tape, discussing personnel, creating dialogue of game day scenarios, as well as formulating final thoughts on the best way to attack our opposition. It was a process that would take us in so many directions, but in the end we solidified our thoughts and had already played the game in our own heads. It was like chess.

To give you an example of how we proceeded, the first hour might be a general discussion over lunch, reviewing the week's practice. From there we talked about our player's energy levels and our injury situation, followed by reviewing the next day's matchups. We would then transition to putting our priority plays up on the grease boards. Then we spent time just talking about them, and articulating why we liked or disliked them. This was not always an easy exercise since we would go in with 125 to 150 passing plays and 25 to 30 running plays. In Oakland the process became even more exhaustive because of the quality of our receiving corps, as well as our other skilled players. I had to be sure to spread the ball early in order to capture their attention and involvement early in the game plan. That was key.

The season began with four wins in a row which were followed by four losses. As a result, the media was all over Bill and the team. Many believed the league had caught up with the offense, and many media people believed we wouldn't win another game. But Bill, myself, and the rest of the coaches and players did exactly what we should have done. We stayed close and didn't climb into a collective or individual shell. We continued to work hard. And maybe most importantly, we kept our collective sense of humor. Our guys knew this was a long season, a marathon not a sprint, and we kept on a steady course.

When I got together to create the First-15 with Bill the day before we played the Broncos, we knew it needed to be good. Really good. We were playing Mike Shanahan's Denver Broncos, who were well rested coming off a bye week, and on the 500th Monday Night Football game in history. Mike and Mr. Davis had a longstanding public feud dating back to when Mike was a coach with the Raiders and the media was using it to build the hype for the game. The atmosphere that night was electric. Putting the Denver First 15 together with Bill was one of the most memorable times in all my years of coaching. Bill and I filled up not one, but two huge grease boards with all the reasons why the Raiders should have "no chance," that's right, NO CHANCE to beat the Broncos that Monday night.

What I later came to realize was that by articulating the reasons why we had no chance to win, we clearly defined what we had to do to in order to be successful against one of the league's best defenses. My goal as a quarterback coach has always been to prepare the quarterback to play at an unreachable standard, and do the impossible — to play a "perfect game." That night Rich completed an NFL record 21 passes in a row, while Jerry Rice caught his 200th and 201st career touchdowns as we defeated the Broncos, 34-10, before a record Monday Night Football audience. Our players showed that they had a lot of backbone and I was really proud of them. That night Rich Gannon came closer than any quarterback in NFL history to playing a perfect game.

We eventually went on to beat the New York Jets in our opening game of the playoffs, 30-10. From there, we beat the Tennessee Titans in a vicious battle to win the AFC Championship, 41-24. Once again balance

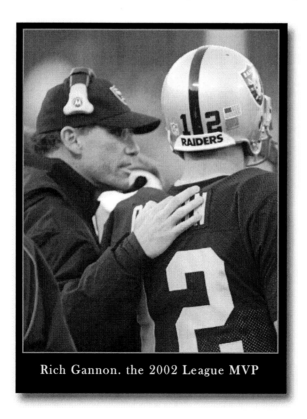

Rich Gannon. the 2002 League MVP

was not the issue as we threw the ball 29 times in the first half. It was a very physical game for our older football team, but we battled. Rich threw for nearly 300 yards and three touchdowns and our defense played extremely well. In an unprecedented moment in my life, I sat there just before the clock ran out, hugging every player and coach I could get to and then looked up to the stands to find Cindy and the girls. There was Cindy, crying and looking at me with such pride in her eyes as she blew me a kiss. She had been through so much over the prior 12 years. Sarahanne and Chloe were so excited too. In the next few days there would be paybacks. They were about to do what very few kids there age get to do — sit in a first class seat on a 747 headed to the Super Bowl. This was a part of our adventure I hoped they would really enjoy and certainly never forget.

When I arrived back in the locker room after the on-field celebration, one of the first people to greet me was my good friend Jeff Diamond. Remember Jeff, the brother of my best friend, Buddy; the son of my childhood dentist; and the Viking employee who in 1979 helped me get a tryout with the Vikes? Jeff was on a journey of his own after being named Executive of the Year with the Vikings. He was now the President of the Tennessee Titans, the team we had just defeated. Jeff is one of my closest friends and mentors. He had been on five losing Super Bowl teams and now his old neighbor was about to get his shot at it. That night he looked at me with such brotherly pride. Two guys from the old neighborhood had fought it out in front of the nation and only one could go. This was a very humbling moment as I thought about both Jeff and his wife Diane, and how surely disappointed they must have been to have lost that game. Jeff's reaction to my success spoke volumes to the person he was though, and it meant a lot to me that he came over to wish me well in the locker room that night.

The AFC Championship Game against the Titans in Oakland didn't get over until the early evening. That night we all went across the street to the Hilton Hotel where we had a celebration dinner. There, our GM Bruce Allen went over the ticket situation and Super Bowl itinerary. As a result, we didn't get home until late Sunday night. We were totally under the gun because the Super Bowl was to be played in San Diego the very next week, and not two weeks later as was typical in years past. They changed it up that year for whatever reason, and this inhibited not only our preparation, but also our physical recovery. Our team was relatively old and these guys needed to rest; I could tell right away that this was going to be an issue.

For me, I never had the opportunity to enjoy winning the AFC Championship. It was quickly back to business from the moment we boarded the flight and it didn't stop until the opening kickoff a week later. Looking back, I regret never getting to savor that moment. I really do. I mean winning the conference championship in some ways is bigger than actually getting to the Super Bowl. It is a huge mountain to climb and it should be enjoyed. Not in 2002, however, we had a game to play and the clock was ticking.

As fate would have it, we would be facing the Tampa Bay Buccaneers in the Super Bowl, who just happened to be coached by none other than Jon Gruden. As you could imagine, the hype surrounding the game was insane. The media jumped all over the "Mr. Davis vs. Jon Gruden" angle and just ran with it. It was a zoo. Normally, during game weeks our time is structured. Not Super Bowl week, no way. We had mandatory press conferences every day which took away from the normal flow of preparation and practice. As a result, we all worked our tails off. When it comes to work, I can go hard, but this week I was totally exhausted. The hours were ridiculous and I was completely sleep deprived. The only consolation was Cindy and the girls were having the time of their lives.

To make matters worse, the night before the big game we lost our Pro Bowl Center Barret Robbins, who went AWOL and apparently wound up down in nearby Tijuana, Mexico. He ended up in the hospital before the game due to an apparent bipolar condition. He was our best offensive lineman. It not only took us totally by surprise but it completely distracted everyone in the organization. Bill worked hard to get the team refocused but it was tough. There are certainly no excuses when you are playing in the biggest game of your life, but on that January night in San Diego, the real Oakland Raiders did not show up. And I was as much at fault as any other. I did not have be best game plan in place for my guys and I regret

"I think Marc is one of the most creative minds in football, and he probably isn't getting enough credit for what he has done as an offensive strategist in the NFL." — *Jon Gruden, Head Coach, Oakland Raiders & Tampa Bay Buccaneers*

it. My priority should have been to get more rest so that I was fresh. I remember lying in front of my locker before the game, normally a time for true meditation, but instead I was trying to get 30 minutes of sleep. I should have suggested less field time during the week and more rest for everyone. I could have done a much better job. The lessons learned that night were not forgotten and were a big part of our Grey Cup success in 2009 up in Montreal.

It had crossed my mind over the last couple of weeks that if we won this game, I would likely have an opportunity to be a head coach in the NFL. I knew as the coordinator of the No. 1 rated offense in the league, teams would come calling. We were perfect on the Friday before the game in our last dress rehearsal. The ball never touched the ground in a well orchestrated practice by Rich and the offense and I started to feel better about our situation. On that late Sunday afternoon, we ran onto the field. We prepared for an almost 25 minute wait on the field for pre-game festivities, but were not prepared for the 80 degree heat and the sun that had not set on our side of the field. Our guys burned up. We were already tired going in and that just made it worse.

We jumped out to an early lead on a Sebastian Janikowski 40 yard field goal, only to watch Tampa unload as they proceeded to score an unconscionable 34 unanswered points. It was a demoralizing evening. As we continued, it was as if we had forgotten everything we had prepared. We eventually put together a small rally behind a pair of Gannon touchdowns to Rice and Porter, but it was too little too late. The Bucs took it to us that night. When the dust finally settled, we lost the game in a blow-out, 48-21. It was a nightmare. Jon put together a masterful game plan and I had to tip my hat to him.

Rich didn't play the way he had all year, and I felt completely accountable. No player I had ever coached gave any more of himself to the game than he did. He of all players deserved to stand there that night embracing the Lombardi Trophy. He had so much love and respect for the game and had been on an unprecedented journey over the years. A week earlier he was named the NFL's Most Valuable Player. He threw for 4,689 yards and 26 touchdowns and his 418 completions and 10 games with over 300 passing yards were both NFL records. I was so proud and happy for him and his wife Shelly, who had stood behind him all those years. This unbelievable six month journey finished on such a sour note. I had experienced my fair share of losses on the gridiron over the years, but this one truly hurt.

Despite the loss, I was proud of what we accomplished that season. That one week was in no way a reflection of what we had achieved as a team. We led the league by scoring 450 points that year, while outscoring our opponents by 144 points. I remember getting a letter in the mail shortly after the Super Bowl from Bill Walsh that read: "Marc, you are the best in the NFL." I have that note framed in my office and it means a great deal to me. Bill and I used to get together for lunches together and talk about everything from politics to football while we were both in the Bay Area. Those were very memorable occasions for me. He tragically passed in the summer of 2007 after losing his battle with cancer. He was a legend and one of the greatest football coaches in the history of the game. The man was truly genius.

Historically, coordinators of Super Bowl teams get opportunities to interview for head coaching vacancies. Despite being named as the NFL Offensive Coordinator of the Year by American Football Monthly, however, this was not the case for me in 2002. I didn't even get an interview. So, I decided to just ride out the remainder of my contract. I put the disappointment of the Super Bowl behind me, reminded myself that I was not the exclusive reason for the teams overall success nor its Super Bowl failure, and went to work for the 2003 season. I worked hard to internally appreciate the incredible season that we had and was grateful to Bill for giving me the opportunity to be his offensive coordinator. I assumed there was no reason we couldn't get back to the Super Bowl and figured if that scenario indeed came to fruition, then I would be set either way — my contract issues would either be resolved or I would be a head coach somewhere else. What would transpire, however, was nothing short of a total disaster.

Little did I know that we would have 13 starters wind up on injured reserve and our top two quarterbacks would be injured for the entire year. It was terrible. As a result of all of that, and maybe because of the hangover of losing the Super Bowl the way we did, everything fell apart for us in 2003. We ended up going 4-12 and the walls collapsed in around us. At the end of the year we all got fired. I thought we would get a mulligan, a second chance, because of all of the injuries and because we had led the team to the Super Bowl, but Mr. Davis had other ideas and decided to clean house. There was no formal meeting with him either, it was just inferred through the media that we should all start looking for jobs. With that, we all went and cleaned out our offices.

In retrospect, maybe I should have signed the extension. Who knows? I remember calling Tony Dungy when I was deciding what to do and asking him for advice. He said I would have no trouble getting a job and I should wait it out. Everybody else I spoke with felt the same way. That is the nature of this business, you just never know. It is the ultimate high risk/high reward career. The problem for me at the end of the day was the fact that I really enjoyed living and working in the Bay Area and did not want to leave. I didn't want to pack up my family yet again and move off to another far away city to start all over again. The girls were getting older and that was tougher to do now.

With no contract in place and with just a few paychecks remaining on my contract, I eventually started to get nervous. In years past something always came up right away, but not this time. So I started making calls. A short while later I flew to Chicago to interview for the Bears' offensive coordi-

Bill and I looking things over

nator position under new Head Coach Lovie Smith. I thought the interview went well, but Lovie went another direction and hired somebody else. From there, I got offered the head coaching position at Cornell University. It was an interesting opportunity. Their Athletics Director, Andy Noel, did his homework and researched every aspect of my life. He wanted Cindy and I to fly up to Ithaca, NY, to see the school and meet the academic people and players. It was a beautiful campus, but we both felt that it would be a tough place to live at that particular stage of our lives. It was exactly the right place at the wrong time. I had always been told that Ivy League coaching jobs were some of the best around. Now I had one in hand and I turned it down. Andy Noel was a special guy who has become a close friend. Cindy and I actually cried over the decision, it was that tough. We did not want to turn it down. That stability of an Ivy League position was very appealing to me, but living in a small town was not the right fit for my family at this stage of our lives. I knew that the opportunity to coach kids of this caliber might never come around again, but that was a risk I was willing to take.

Then, on the day my contract expired I got a call from Norv Turner, the

A very proud papa

offensive coordinator with the Miami Dolphins. I did not know Norv very well, but I really respected him as one of the premiere play callers in the game. Norv told me that he and Head Coach Dave Wannstedt were interested in hiring me to be their quarterback coach. This was a unique opportunity, similar to my transition to Detroit, to regroup professionally and stay in the game. The prospects of staying in a warm climate just a few miles from my parents' place in West Palm Beach seemed like a pretty good option at that point too, so I took the job. Norv had come from a completely different offensive system and I was anxious to learn from him. With that, I flew to Miami to get settled while Cindy, for the fifth time in nine years, stayed behind until we could sell the house and get ready for the next move. The journey continued.

ON THE MEDIA...

"I recognize the media is an essential element to the success of our game. Those in the media have a job to do and we must peacefully co-exist for our game to continue to thrive. With that in mind I have three basic rules that I live by and give our team at training camp to help them understand this dynamic. First, the media (in most cases) are not your friend. They have a job to do, and when we interact with them we must remember that. Second, there is no such thing as speaking to the media off the record. You may say to them it's off the record and your comment may not be used in the next day or week, but there is likelihood that the information or quote will be used in some context or another in the future. Third, when the media wants to direct their questions at 'how great YOU are,' you need to turn it around and think about the TEAM first. Answering a question that relates to your personal success with an answer that credits the team is humble and respectful. You simply cannot be 'too humble' in this business. Humility is a byproduct of your acceptance that personal success is a result of the endeavors of so many others doing their job at a high level. It doesn't happen any other way."

CH. 14) A NIGHTMARE IN MIAMI

Leaders handle adversity and failure with resilience and per-severance. Beyond that, leaders must have a thick skin. Adversity is inevitable and leaders recognize this in order to mitigate the risk of failure. Successful leaders are selfless and recognize when their adversity is likely affecting others. As such, leaders will act in the best interests of the parties involved in order to meet the goals and needs of the organization.

A few days after I accepted the Miami position, I received a call from Norv. He said he was interviewing for the Raiders head coaching job and that he wanted me to stay in Oakland to remain on his staff if he got hired. I was floored. I thought about it and in the end figured it would be best for me to move on. To be honest, I am not even sure Mr. Davis would have let me stay in the first place. Who knows? Regardless, I consulted with Norv and did what I could to educate him on the ins and outs of the Raider's organization. He obviously made quite an impression because the day I arrived in Miami it was announced that Norv was taking over as the new head coach of the Raiders.

It was bittersweet to leave Oakland because we really enjoyed all that the Bay Area had to offer. There were no hard feelings about my time there and I had a lot of fun. The fans were fiercely loyal and so crazy, especially in the "Black Hole." At first I was really concerned for the safety of Cindy and the girls at games, but we came to understand that these were just loyal fans who loved Raider football. As for Mr. Davis, he was unique and eccentric in many ways, but a football purist at heart. I don't know if anybody has ever loved or respected the game more than has. He is a deserving member of the NFL Hall of Fame and a key figure in the growth and development of the league. We disagreed over some business issues, but he created an environment in Oakland that gave us a chance to win. We did everything in a first class manner and I am genuinely appreciative of my time there. I left Oakland an incredibly better coach and person and had no regrets.

I was excited about going to Miami because I always had an affinity with the Dolphins from my time with the Hurricanes. I had also gotten to a lot of the people in the organization when I was selling bonds in Coral Springs and hanging out in the locker room with Coach Shula. It's a storied franchise and I was anxious to be a part of it. I was looking forward to working with Dave Wannstedt, who had a solid reputation as a coach. He was the defensive coordinator with the Cowboys prior to coming to Miami and had already been with the team for a few years. I knew he was on thin ice with the organization, however, because the team didn't play that well down the stretch the year before. They finished with a very respectable 10-6 record that prior season and had a decent roster, but expectations were high. Once I arrived, I quickly realized that Dave wasn't getting the respect he deserved from media and fans, which made the 2004 season critical in terms of him keeping his job.

When Norv left I was hoping that Dave would promote me from quarterbacks coach to offensive coordinator, but he had already promised the

My Parents with their grandkids

position to one of his assistants — which I totally understood. Dave said he would make it up to me though by appointing me as his assistant head coach, which got me an increase in salary and visibility. I was especially appreciative to Dave for doing that and felt good about the way things started out. As I was about to learn, this was about the last time I would feel good about anything in Miami for a while.

I knew that joining a pre-existing offensive staff could be tough, but coming into this situation was unlike anything I had ever experienced before. I will never forget watching film the first day and then realizing that there was little or no interaction. I would ask questions about reads and quarterback progressions, and there were no answers. Norv left behind a very good staff, but nobody was really familiar with the details of the offense as it pertained to the quarterback because none of them were previously ever in Norv's quarterback meetings. This made it extremely tough on me. It was much different than the offense I had coordinated or trained previously, but fortunately I was able to use my training to try and piece it all together.

My time with the Dolphins was
an adventure to say the least...

The meetings did not improve and frustrations grew. When Cindy finally arrived with the girls in Miami I immediately began bringing my frustrations home, which is something I had never done before. This was different than anything I had ever experienced and felt just awful about it. For the first time in my career I felt completely out of sync with everyone else. In the first five weeks I was there, not one offensive coach stopped by my office to interact with me besides Dave and the team's running backs coach. It was insane.

Shortly after the draft in April, our offensive coordinator called me into his office and asked me to install the passing game for the team's upcoming minicamp. I told him that wasn't my job and that it wasn't appropriate, but he insisted. So I did it, reluctantly. I am serious; I did not want any part of this. I came to Miami to coach the quarterbacks, Jay Fiedler, A.J. Feeley and Sage Rosenfels, not to install the offense — that wasn't my role. But I eventually relinquished and installed the passing game as he instructed me to do. It was a very uncomfortable situation and one that to this day I regret getting myself into. I could tell early on that this was going to be a difficult situation for me to be in.

We lost our first six games and things went from bad to worse in a hurry. Our Pro Bowl running back unexpectedly retired in the face of drug abuse charges, another player was arrested for domestic abuse, and a newly-acquired star receiver got injured during training camp and was lost for the season. The offense under-produced and the defense couldn't stop anybody. We were falling apart at the seams. Dave quickly became the focus of intensified criticism and pressure from the fans and from the media. As a result, our owner, Wayne Huizenga, fired him just prior to Game Seven. We were spinning out of control. I felt badly for Dave, but he handled himself like a true professional. He is currently the head coach at the University of Pittsburgh, where he has enjoyed great success.

Our defensive coordinator Jim Bates was then named as the team's interim head coach. Jim was a good guy and in our short time together he taught me a great deal. This was his opportunity to show the organization that he could handle the job. Jim immersed himself in all areas of football, particularly the locker room. He was full of energy and worked tirelessly to get to know everybody on the team. He understood that he was in the people business and it showed. He did the job as if he had been a head coach for 20 years, but with the enthusiasm of a guy who knew he may only get one chance. He worked every day to get the most out of his team and I will always look up to him and respect him for the job he did that season. He was partially rewarded with a last minute win over the Super Bowl champion Patriots on Monday night later in the season, but it was too little too late. We limped through the rest of the season and finished with a 4-12 record.

I stayed focused on quarterback preparation and did everything I could not to feel sorry for myself by putting the team and the quarterbacks first. I really enjoyed getting to work with our three young quarterbacks: Jay, A.J., and Sage, and thank God for that, because they allowed me to keep my sanity that year. What a disaster. It was the sourest experience of any job I had ever had. Although I worked as hard as I could right up until the end, it was the first time in my career that I couldn't wait for the season to get over. After the season LSU coach Nick Saban was brought in to be the team's new head coach and I was fired along with everybody else. Nine months in Miami and I was already out of work. What had I done, and how much more could I do to once again disrupt the life of Cindy and the girls?

I can't speak about my time in Miami without mentioning Rick Spielman, our team's general manager. Rick was an awesome guy and very talented. After I was initially hired he arranged for the team to pay for my travel back and forth to Oakland each weekend to see my family. I would leave Thursday night after practice, get into Oakland later that evening, and return Sunday night on the red eye to start work early Monday morning. I will never forget Dave and Rick for allowing me to be with my family during this time. Rick is a stand up guy and a real family man. He understood and he made a difference. Rick was also great in the draft room because he was extremely organized, well prepared, and detailed. Most importantly he was a great listener. He gave every coach and scout a chance to be heard and to express their opinion. This was big when it came to putting a draft board together. Rick does as good a job as any in this profession and I have a lot of respect for him. He is currently with the Minnesota Vikings, where he serves as the team's vice president of player personnel.

Getting fired publicly is never easy. It goes right to your dignity and manhood. I have developed a thick skin over the years though, and this is the main reason why I knew when I finally became a head coach that I would have a chance to succeed. Believe it or not, it wasn't so much that I had prior success as an assistant coach and offensive coordinator, but rather it was because I had the resilience and perseverance necessary to handle the inevitable adversity that comes with this job. If you want to coach at the highest level, you have to be prepared for criticism even when things are beyond your control. How you respond to it and your ability to persevere are the keys to both survival as well as success.

I have somehow been able get through the tough times, but often I wonder how Cindy gets through it. She sees me getting fired on TV and knows she is going to have to pack up and do it all over again. She is the one who has to find the house, find the new doctor, the schools, and make new friends. It has been extremely tough for her and the girls, yet she has found a way to make it a positive adventure. She is an incredible woman. Rich Gannon may have said it best when he told me a few years ago, "Marc, the No. 1 reason you need to be a head coach is so that Cindy can be a head coach's wife. Nobody deserves it more!" Rich was right. Not only have I gathered a wealth of knowledge from adversity and success, but so has Cindy. She has seen it all from both a wife's as well as a coach's perspective. Although there are many perks to coaching in the NFL, it isn't an easy life. She has been around so many head coaches and their wives, and I knew that given the chance she would do great. This is more difficult in Montreal because the families are so far apart and visit infrequently, but Cindy knows how to give wives and families the respect they deserve. Her life experiences as a football coach's wife could be made into her own book. She's amazing.

We cried openly as a family after I got fired from the Dolphins because it was the toughest situation for us yet. The girls were in a school they loved and had made so many new friends in a very short period of time. How could I have done this again to my family? I even began to question myself and my ability to coach. My confidence was down and it was at this time I reminded myself that this is the NFL and that sometimes things can spiral out of control, leaving you as just a spectator. That was exactly what happened to me in Miami.

A few weeks after the season, I interviewed for the Detroit Lions' offensive coordinator position. Steve Mariucci was their head coach and although I didn't know him very well at the time, our paths had crossed in years prior and I felt a connection with him. I went up to Detroit and met with him, but after the interview, we both mutually decided that I would-n't be the best fit. Shortly thereafter that I got a call from Jim Haslett, the head coach in New Orleans, and we met down in Alabama at the Senior Bowl. He flew me in to meet with him and then offered me the offensive coordinator job with the Saints. Incredibly, I then got a call from Chuck Amato, the head coach at North Carolina State University, who I had met through a mutual friend. Chuck had heard that I was a free agent and offered me his coordinator position with the Wolfpack. Suddenly, I had options.

Ultimately, and after much deliberation with Cindy, I decided to turn down the Saints job. It was a tough call, because these jobs are not easy to get — there are only 32 of them and every assistant coach in the world wants one of them. I really respected Jim and was extremely grateful for the offer, but this time it was about more than just football. I decided that I had simply had enough. Cindy and the girls had done everything for me, now it was their turn. I had been a coordinator in the NFL on four different occasions, and all four times I had coached playoff teams. I had been blessed to have coached two No. 1 offensives, a league leading passer, a number of Pro Bowlers, the league MVP, and was still no closer to becoming a head coach. I started to wonder what the heck I was doing with my life. I mean if I had taken the New Orleans job, it would have been my fifth as an offensive coordinator, which to me suddenly looked like the definition of insanity. I kept doing the same thing over and over, and kept getting the same results. I had already proven myself four different times and felt like I was qualified for a head coaching job. So, I walked away on my own terms.

With that, I signed a four year contract to become the offensive coordinator at NC State University. We were moving to Raleigh, North Carolina, where we were going to put down some roots once and for all. At first I was reluctant to even consider coaching again in college, but soon I started to think that this might be exactly the type of change I needed in my life. I then made a promise to my girls that we would stay in Raleigh until they graduated high school, and I intended to keep it. Sarahanne was starting the eighth grade and Chloe the sixth. It was a big promise to make and it was going to be an even bigger one to keep.

CH. 15) GOING BACK TO SCHOOL

Leaders recognize important factors that go beyond the dollars and cents of an organization. Leaders are adaptable and recognize that success in the past does not make success guaranteed in the future. Circumstances change and different positions require attention to different aspects of the same industry. For example, in the NFL it's a coach's job to maximize talent in order to put a winning team on the field. In college football, meanwhile, it's still about winning, but there is a responsibility on the coach's part to develop the young men as well. Recognizing your role as a leader in any organization will maximize effectiveness and enable you to achieve goals and work toward your vision more efficiently.

I loved the NFL and really didn't want to leave it. It's the highest level, with the world's greatest players, in the greatest showcase. Professionally this was not a great move for me, but personally it was. That was the key for me in taking the job and Cindy felt the same way. She would much rather I had taken the Saints job, from a professional standpoint, but in the end our kids won out. We felt this would be the best fit for them and in the end it turned out to be a tremendous family experience for all of us. Raleigh is just a beautiful city and great place to raise a family. I know I was built for the job of being an NFL coach, but I had decided to put that goal on hold and worry about it down the road. For now I was going to give Cindy and the girls some stability in their lives.

I was going to be paid well by the University, but it was nowhere near what I would have made if I had taken the job in New Orleans. The value to Cindy and the girls, however, could not be measured in dollars and cents.

The girls went to school about two miles from my office and after class they would come and hang out with me. They would come to watch practices, they would attend athletic camps at the school, and they attended games with their friends. Chuck never micro-managed me and he let me spend time with my family on a regular basis. I was able to go see their sporting and school events and just be there for them, like so many other "normal" dads do. Chuck had two daughters himself and was fortunate to have raised them entirely in Tallahassee while he was coaching at Florida State, so he understood. He was giving me a tremendous opportunity and I worked hard for him to show my appreciation.

I had very high expectations put upon me on arrival. Chuck called me their "No. 1 Recruit of the 2005 Season," and I didn't want to disappoint him. As an assistant, I never really cared about any of that, but coming into a college town like Raleigh, I certainly felt there was more visibility than usual. As for my job, it started out eerily familiar. It was tough coming in as yet another mercenary coordinator, where the previous guy had been fired and none of the coaches on the staff really embraced you. Some of the guys were upset because they wanted my job, while others were just plain mad at me for having to learn my new offense. It was awkward to say the least. Often teams will clean house and bring in new staffs all at once in order to avoid these types of situations, but Chuck stood behind me and that made me feel really good. I made the best of it and eventually began to earn the respect of the other assistant coaches. They started to buy in and worked very hard to support my efforts. These were good men and with Chuck's help, we worked it out.

That August, Hurricane Katrina hit the Gulf Coast nearly wiped out New Orleans. So many people down there lost everything, it was so sad. I remember watching it on TV with Cindy and thinking about how lucky we were not to have been there. We hugged each other and chalked it up to some sort of divine intervention. In the aftermath countless families were displaced, including those of the Saints players and coaches. Jim Haslett ended up losing his job and the team was forced to play the season split between San Antonio, Texas, and Baton Rouge, Louisiana. I would have been divorced after that one, no doubt about it.

N.C. State was not an elite program at the time, but Chuck, an N.C. State grad, had developed a very good program with a solid foundation. Because he had been a long time assistant for Bobby Bowden down at

Florida State, they had a recruiting pipeline into Florida's top high schools, which was a big advantage over the competition. They had also recently built some great new football facilities, which was a big boost to the program as well. I felt like they were ready to be catapulted to the next level. They had a great quarterback just graduate in Philip Rivers, who would go on to stardom in the NFL with the San Diego Chargers, but the problem was they didn't have another star QB to take his place. I could tell early on that this was going to be a big issue.

We had a good first year and finished with a respectable 7-5 overall record. The highlight came against South Florida, whom we beat, 14-0, to win the Meineke Car Care Bowl. The game was played at Bank of America Stadium in Charlotte, which was great because so many of our fans could attend. We played in front of a packed house and our girls had a blast hanging out with the other coaches' kids. This was really a memorable moment for all of us, just a lot of fun. Overall, I was enjoying my job. It was different and in many ways very satisfying. You see, as a college coach I became a teacher, a father, a confidante, a mentor; not just a guy trying to make first downs. It was an entirely different mindset. I began to re-

Chuck Amato

alize that for some, I was the first male figure in their lives away from home. They became my children, in a sense, and I began to care deeply about each and every one of them in a way that went far beyond the game.

I knew that in order for our program to really get over the hump and be able to compete day in and day out with the Floridas, Ohio States, and Oklahomas of the world, that we needed to get a big-time quarterback. So, I went out and recruited a young man out of Lexington (Kentucky) Catholic High School. We red-shirted him and I was excited about watching him develop. Then, on the recommendation of our baseball coach, we worked out and signed a charismatic young man from a small private school in Virginia. Both were outstanding players with a lot of potential. I knew that it was going to take some time for them to develop, but I was very excited to work with them.

I was optimistic about our chances that next year, coming off of our bowl victory, but what ultimately transpired turned out to be a disaster. We lost a couple of big games early and our quarterback play was totally inefficient. We came back to beat Boston College and Florida State to get back to .500, but we collapsed down the stretch, losing our next seven games in a row. It was horrible. We were very unproductive offensively and that was especially difficult for me to deal with. I didn't feel like I was able to make a difference in what I was doing and that was especially frustrating. I was completely accountable and took full responsibility, however, because I was working for a good man who I felt deserved better.

I had a pretty good feeling that we were all going to be fired after the season and that is exactly what happened. Chuck had been to five bowl games in seven years and this was really his only bad season, so I thought he might be spared. But in the end there was a faction of prominent alumni who wanted him out, and that is just the nature of the beast in college football these days. It's all about winning. The boosters became the owners, and we were all out of work. I felt very bad for Chuck because it was unfair in my mind. He is a man of integrity, very enthusiastic, and a just an overall good coach. The guy was full of wisdom. He used to always tell our players, "I have been your age... but you haven't been mine." He had great experience teaching young men and building their character. He was an excellent and very honest recruiter too. He cared about the kids and knew when to give them a second chance with regards to disciplining them. He built up the program over the years and I thought he deserved better. At the end of the day I also felt partially responsible for him losing his job, and that was tough.

When it was all said and done, I took this firing harder than any job I had lost. I was bitter, angry, crushed, and just mad at the world. I know there are many who have far less than I have, and my family has been blessed with health and relative prosperity. But how could this be? Sarahanne was about to start high school and Chloe was finishing her second year of middle school. I was probably in the worst place personally and mentally I had ever been. I don't think I was depressed, but I was down, way down. The big silver lining for me though was the fact that I still had two years left on my contract, which meant I was still going to be paid my full salary. Because of that I was going to be able to keep my promise to my girls, which was so important to me. The Trestmans weren't going anywhere.

My Priority No. 1

CH. 16) REINVENTING MYSELF IN RALEIGH

Leaders know what they are working for and never give up prior to achieving their goals and their vision. They understand that there is no one way to achieving goals and that road blocks will come up along the way. When that happens they work hard to better themselves and to get back on the track to successfully completing what they originally set out to do. This is the same whether in an organization or working towards personal goals. Adversity is overcome by toughness, creativity, trust in oneself, keeping priorities in line (family first), and a passion to succeed.

Ironically, just a couple of weeks after getting fired, I got a call from a friend of mine who was an assistant coach with the Saints. He told me that they had a job opening come up and wondered if I'd be interested. Their head coach was Sean Payton, who had taken over for Jim Haslett two years prior. Sean and I had crossed paths over the years and had become friends. So, I called him up to inquire about the job and asked if there was anything I could do to help him out. I explained to him that I was out of work and that I might be able to help him with some game-planning or whatever else he may need. I figured if something worked out that I could travel back and forth as a consultant.

Sean was really appreciative and wound up inviting Cindy and I to fly down so we could meet. It was emotional to see New Orleans at that point, with all of the destruction still visible a couple of years after Katrina. I met with Sean and the staff and the interview went well. Then, as I was walking around their facilities, I had a "moment." What was I doing? What if they offered me a full-time position? I had made a promise to the girls, yet I found myself in survival mode. The normal thing for me to do whenever I had gotten fired in the past was to interview for a new job, to provide for my family. Cindy and I talked frankly on the flight home and came to the realization that we needed to stay focused on staying put for the sake of the girls. Sean reinforced our decision by telling me that he really didn't see me as a good fit with his staff at the time, which I took as a good omen.

With that, I immediately started networking locally in Raleigh. From there, I got connected with Gary Stevenson, who had been an executive with the Golf Channel and was involved in several sports-business start-ups. We connected and really hit it off. This man saw right through me in about 10 minutes. He looked at me and said, "Don't you realize how lucky you are? This is a dream come true, having two years of paid vacation to figure out what you want to do with the rest of your life. Nobody gets that chance, and you have it."

It was as if a light went off for me. He was right. I had sat in dark offices for the past 25 years, beating my head against the wall "trying to find first downs." I just needed to get away from the game and find myself. I started to try to figure out who the heck I was and what my purpose was. I wanted more out of life and I wanted to give something back. In some ways it was like, "Okay, what do you want to be when you grow up?" I wasn't sure, so I made a vision board and set some goals for myself. It was a very enlightening time for me. The one thing that I knew for sure was that I needed to keep my family in Raleigh. That was non-negotiable. Somehow I needed to figure out my next career move, but it had to be on those terms. I wasn't going to pack up the girls and move them around again, no way, not now. I was going to keep my promise.

I dove in head first and tried to make myself as marketable as possible. I did it all. I did my weekly radio show with Hank Goldberg; I made weekly appearances on Sirius Satellite Radio during the playoffs; I consulted with General Sports Venues, a local company in Raleigh that bought the rights to Astroturf; I consulted with a company called Scholarships for Athletes, which assists college bound athletes with information and guidance to pick the right schools; I wrote articles for Sports Illustrated's website (SI.com); I did a few guest television appearances on the NFL Network previewing the quarterbacks for the 2007 draft; I spent time mentoring law students at Elon University School of Law in Greensboro, N.C.; I taught a Coaching and GM course for an on-line company called Sports Management

Worldwide; I spoke at football clinics; and I finally began doing some motivational speaking to businesses, which is what led to me writing this book. To prepare myself I feverishly read self-help books dealing with change and leadership, as well as metaphysical books dealing with life and how to make it better. Once again, I was a student of the game.

I did such a variety of things during this period and loved every minute of it, but one of my favorites was working out and training college quarterbacks who wanted to improve their draft status. This was something that started out as a side-business, but has really grown into something that I thoroughly enjoy today. Working with these guys was amazing for me both from a personal enjoyment standpoint as well as from a financial standpoint. Initially, agents would fly prospects into Raleigh or I would fly to them to work their clients out and evaluate them. Two of my first clients I had the privilege of working out were Jay Cutler and Jason Campbell, who have both gone on to become stars in the NFL. Andre Woodson would follow, and in 2010 I was blessed to work with Jimmy Clausen and Tim Tebow, both of whom I'm sure are headed for future NFL stardom.

I also spent some time with a handful of NFL players who wanted to get an impartial evaluation of their careers and needed advice on how to get back on track. This was something I really enjoyed. From there, it grew to working with college and high school quarterbacks as well. Parents today are willing to pay a price to have their son's coached properly in hopes of them either getting a scholarship or to play professionally. I have really enjoyed spending time with these young men and am thankful that their parents would show this kind of trust towards me. Afterward I enjoy donating some of the money back to their school's athletics departments to say thanks. To be able to have fun and be able to give back at the same time is the definition of success in my book.

I eventually got to the point where I felt if I never coached again, I could still be able to support my family and live comfortably. In fact, I was busier in the six months after being fired than I had ever been at any point in my life. I was trying to reinvent myself, and that in itself was both challenging and exhilarating. It seemed like the more I had on my plate, the more opportunities kept coming my way. It was amazing.

In February of 2007, I ran into Sean Payton at the annual scouting combine in Indianapolis. I was there as a guest speaker for Sports Management Worldwide, the on-line sports training company I had been teaching for. We started talking and he asked me if I would be interested in coming in to serve as a consultant for him during training camp later that Summer. I said absolutely. Then in May, I got a call one day out of the blue from an old acquaintance by the name of Jim Popp. What a story this guy had. You see, back in the late '80s, when I was the offensive coordinator for the Browns, there was a coach on our staff by the name of Joe Popp. Joe had a son who was in his early 20s at the time, Jim, who was always hanging around our practice facility. He would occasionally ask if he could sit in our meetings and just be a fly on the wall. I told him to feel free to come by anytime and that he was always welcome. He was a nice young man, trying to learn everything he could about the game he loved. Well, Jim went on to become an assistant coach and eventually ended up in the Canadian Football League. There, after a lot of hard work and determination, he worked his way up the ladder and to become the general manager and head coach of the Montreal Alouettes.

Knowing that I was out of work, Jim called me and asked if I would be interested in coming up to spend a couple of days in Montreal with his team to do some consulting for him during training camp. We caught up for a while and eventually I said I would be very interested in seeing how things are done in the CFL. So, I flew up and checked it out, not really knowing what to expect. When I got there I was blown away. I was really impressed with the coaches as well as with the players. They had a first class organization up there. I was never that familiar with the CFL, but I left with a much different impression of it than when I arrived. Practices were organized, disciplined, and the players worked hard. At the end of my visit, Jim called me up to his office. He told me he was serving as both the general manager and the head coach, but wondered if I would ever consider coming up there in the future, possibly to take over as the team's head coach.

I told him I was flattered and that I would be open to considering anything at that point, as long as it fit with my objective of staying based in Raleigh. It didn't go much further than that, but I could tell he was getting a sense of whether or not I might be interested down the road. That night at dinner Jim asked me to speak to the team before their evening meeting. When a head coach asks you to speak in front of his team, it's a true honor. He trusts them to you, and that's huge. Jim introduced me by telling the team about how we met some 20 years earlier in Cleveland

and about how much he appreciated the respect I showed him when he was just a young guy starting out in this business. That meant a lot to me. I spoke to his guys for about a half an hour. I didn't have time to prepare a big speech, but it was well received and I very much enjoyed the opportunity.

Several weeks later I flew down to Jackson, Mississippi, to meet up with Sean Payton and the New Orleans Saints at their training camp facilities. I was really flattered by the way Sean and GM Mickey Loomis treated me. Sean even asked me to sit in on his team and staff meetings, which was quite an honor. The guys welcomed me and made me feel very much a part of the staff, which I appreciated. Then, just before the last pre-season game, Sean took me aside and asked me to stay on with the team full-time for the rest of the year. I was very appreciative, but knew it would be difficult to be away from Cindy and the girls for the next six months. Sean was persistent though and luckily we were able to come to a compromise that I felt we all could live with. I would fly into New Orleans every Monday morning and then fly out on Wednesday nights. It was a good situation and my girls were all excited that their guy was back in the game.

Working for the Saints turned out to be a tremendous opportunity. It was such a different experience for me, I mean I didn't go to single practice that entire season. Not one. I would get in on Monday and start watching tape of our upcoming opponent and then give my game planning thoughts to Sean and the guys on the staff. Then, when I was at the games, I would just stand on the sidelines just as an observer. What a trip. I remember going to the first game of the season, it was the Thursday Night NFL opener against Indianapolis. Before the game Sean had to turn in a list to the officials of which coaches were going to be on the sidelines. The Colt's GM Bill Polian saw my name on the list, one more than the league normally allowed, and forced me to sit in the stands for the game. That's how competitive Bill is. I didn't care, heck, I took it as a pretty big complement. So, I wound up sitting in the press box with Mickey. It was the first game I had ever watched a game from that perspective and I didn't like it. It felt weird. Being in a suit and tie was so uncomfortable. I wanted to be on the sidelines, back in my element. As for the season, the Saints got off to a slow start after having a playoff team in 2006. They played well down the stretch but in the end they just missed the playoffs. It was a good experience and I was appreciative of the opportunity that Sean had given me. I will never forget it.

That December the Duke University head coaching position opened up. This was it; this was the ideal situation for me. I wanted to coach and I wanted to stay in Raleigh, and I believed I was a perfect fit for an academic school like Duke. Wanting to make sure I got an interview, I had some

"I was fortunate enough to be able to work with Marc in 2007, when we brought him in to New Orleans as a consultant. I first met him when I was a lowly quarterbacks coach for the Eagles back in the late '90s. My coordinator, Jon Gruden, introduced us and we hit it off right away. Jon had a lot of respect for him and was somebody who I think he looked up to."

"I remember Marc taking the time to talk to me and help me when I would see him at the Combine, or at the Senior Bowl. He would let me pick his brain and was genuinely interested in me as a person. There aren't that many guys who would do stuff like that, but that is the type of person he is. He is very selfless and he treats people with respect. He took the time to get to know me and that always really impressed me about him. Our relationship has always been strong ever since and I think very highly of him."

"Marc is someone who I have a lot of respect for in this business. From an analytical standpoint, he has the distinct ability to think through and see what you want to do offensively through the eyes of the quarterback. He is very detail oriented, very smart, very creative and he thinks outside the box. Marc understands group dynamics. He understands personnel. He is a good delegator as well as a pretty good communicator. He has a very high IQ, and intelligent people are very valuable in our industry. He is able to look at problems and solve them."

"Marc has a tremendous understanding of what it takes to be successful at this level and has proven himself to be a winner. He brings fresh ideas to the table and I admire that about him. He may be a quiet person, but he is certainly respected amongst his peers. He is not a shouter or screamer, he is a teacher. He also has a lot of tact with regards to presenting ideas and offering his opinions, and then being a good listener. That is totally unique, but then again, so is Marc Trestman." — *Sean Payton, Head Coach, New Orleans Saints*

very influential people with Duke connections, including Tony Dungy, Sean Payton and Mickey Loomis, make some calls on my behalf. I was really excited about this potential opportunity. Sadly, however, they didn't see it the same way I did. I believed I had done everything right and had my priorities in line, but it just wasn't meant to be. At the end of the day, Duke University was NOT going to hire the recently fired offensive coordinator from neighboring and rival N.C. State. To say I was bummed out would be such an understatement.

A short while later I got an intriguing phone call from Jim Popp up in Canada. He told me he had stepped down as the team's head coach, and his owner, Bob Wetenhall, and team president, Larry Smith, were in the process of collecting head coaching candidate names for interviews. Jim wanted to know if I was interested in coming in to interview. I told him I was flattered to be considered and that I would love to talk to them about it further. It would be a helluva commute, but I was willing to discuss it, right?

With that, they flew me to Montreal, where Jim, Mr. Wetenhall, and Mr. Smith met with me in a hotel room for a little over two hours. To my understanding, I was the last of 11 interviews. It lasted nearly two hours and it really never felt like any interview I had ever been a part of before. Rather, it felt much more like a conversation. The conversation covered a spectrum of topics from backgrounds to philosophy, but it was mutual

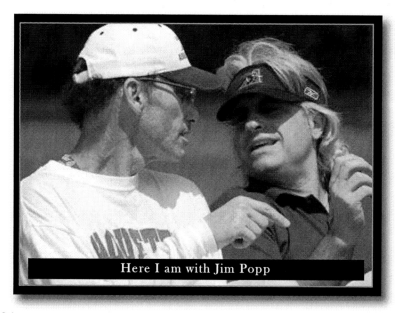

Here I am with Jim Popp

and insightful. After a while I really felt like we were four buddies sitting at a bar making conversation.

To prepare for the interview I did my homework and put together a 30 page game-plan for how I envisioned the team's success, should I be offered the job. In it, I laid out specific details about how I was going to lead the team both on and off the field. I broke it all down for them and made a real impact. It was clear and extremely detailed specifically to the situation in Montreal. The Alouettes were a team with a great winning tradition and they didn't need a major overhaul in any area. I wasn't sure how the interview went, but it must have gone well because the next day Jim called to offer me the job. How bittersweet it was. I was now being given the opportunity to be a head football coach of a professional football team, but it was in Canada. I had finally found an ownership group that took the time to get to know me and evaluated me on my merit. They did their research and came to the conclusion that they wanted me to be their next head coach. That meant a lot to me. I told Jim that I wanted to come up one more time to make sure I understood the ground rules of the job. He agreed and they flew me back up the next week.

The four of us met again and it went extremely well. Mr. Wetenhall closed the deal when he told me that once the season was over I didn't have to be in Montreal until late May, at which time the snow in Montreal was long gone. I thought he was kidding, but he wasn't. He wanted me to be with my family during the six month off-season and then to come back, reinvigorated. I was blown away. This was it. This was what I had been searching for, a head coaching job that would allow me to remain in Raleigh. Most importantly, Cindy and the girls were on board with it and were excited for me to finally get a head coaching opportunity.

The next step was to fly to Montreal for the team's introductory press conference where they were going to announce my hiring. Cindy was in Ohio visiting her family at the time, so I flew from Raleigh to Cleveland to meet her for the next leg of the trip. We got snowed in that night though and all airports were closed. That next day, as we were waiting for the blizzard to pass so we could fly out, I got a call from my mom informing me that my dad had just had a heart attack while he was flying on a plane from Minnesota to Florida. I was really unnerved. As soon as the winter storm cleared, Cindy and I got on a plane and immediately flew to Tallahassee, which was where the plane had made an emergency landing for my dad to get medical attention. Luckily, they were able to land in time for the doctors to save his life. It was an incredible turn of events and emotionally I was completely spent.

Meanwhile, as I was in the hospital with my dad, I read on-line in one of the newspapers in Montreal that I was "trying to avoid coming up there." The buzz in Montreal was that the team made a terrible mistake hiring a coach with not only zero CFL experience, but no head coaching experience. I was being portrayed as this hot-shot know-it-all NFL coach who couldn't make it to his own press conference on time. Speculation started to swirl that I had decided not to take the job after all. It was unbelievable.

Two weeks later, when my dad had improved, Cindy and I flew up to Montreal to finally do my press conference. I had explained what happened and everybody calmed down, which was a relief. It was then that I realized being the head coach in Montreal was no small matter. When Cindy and I arrived at the Molson Brewery, where many public events take place, I was floored. We don't hear a lot about Montreal in the States unless it deals with the Canadiens hockey team, and we forget that it's a

Being introduced to the media

huge city of almost four million people. They have five big newspapers and tons of local TV and radio coverage. There is also the French ESPN, called RDS, and the ESPN affiliate, TSN. I brushed up on my French so that I could say a few words to the bilingual press. I got a few chuckles and it broke the ice.

As of January 2008, I was officially back in the game. A chance meeting between me and a young Jim Popp precipitated into a relationship that enabled me to reach one of my professional goals and keep a promise to my children. How many times in this book have I talked about a coincidental moment where a relationship initiates because two people are simply being gracious and respectful? Is that not proof alone that anytime we cross paths with others we must have the insight to see how profound that moment is in time, and how important it is to make the most of it? I had to pinch myself, I really did. I mean three months earlier I knew essentially nothing about the Canadian Football League, and now I was a head coach in it. More importantly, I had finally gotten my head coaching job. I was truly excited about the new opportunity that was lying ahead of me. This was by far the biggest leap of faith I had ever taken in my career. I had been out of the game for over a year and was coming back with a new attitude and a new perspective. It was amazing. That May, with passport in hand, I kissed my girls good bye and headed north of the border to begin the "second half" of my professional life.

CH. 17) TAKING ANOTHER LEAP OF FAITH, THIS TIME NORTH OF THE BORDER

Those in new positions of leadership are most successful when they come in open minded, establish guidelines of expectation, and set a clear vision for the organization. Organizations are often made up of many members and it should be recognized that each member listens and hears each message differently. Leaders recognize "buy in" takes time and they begin by assessing what is being done well, and what areas need to be improved upon. Total overhauls often slow the process, so sometimes it is better to take what is done well and build on it rather than reinvent the wheel.

So here I was headed to my first head coaching job, almost 30 years to the day from graduating high school. It wasn't supposed to be this way. It was suppose to happen years ago, in a much different place. Eighteen months earlier I knew little or nothing about the CFL, other than what I had seen on TV as a young football fanatic in Minnesota. I handed my passport to the customs officer upon arrival at Montreal Trudeau International. She looked at it and said in her thick French Canadian accent, "You da fubal coach?" I smiled and said, "Yes." She said, "Gude luck coach, and have a nice day." I answered with, "Merci beaucoup." She smiled back, and I went to pick up my luggage.

As much as I thought I was prepared for this job, I quickly realized that I had a lot to learn. The differences between the CFL and NFL were significant. In the CFL, the field is 65 yards wide (as opposed to 53); 110 yards long (as opposed to 100); and the end zones are 20 yards deep (as opposed to 10). In addition, they play with 12 players (as opposed to 11), and offenses only get three downs (as opposed to four). There are motion rules for the offense that make coaching the defense next to impossible. There are also a ton of rules that I had to familiarize myself with, including how many Canadians (as opposed to Americans) had to be on the active roster as well as how many Canadians had to start each game. This was tricky because you may even have to bench a starter in the middle of a game to adhere to this rule. There were all sorts of rules that I had never heard of, but I just embraced it and tried to have fun with it.

A lot of Americans wouldn't believe so, but football in Canada is really a big deal. It's not as big of a deal as hockey, but it's a big part of the fabric of life up there. The Montreal Canadians are THE featured attraction in town, but we play during most of their off-season, so we don't really compete with them. Every home game is a sell-out (and has been for over 90 straight games) and every game is televised nationally throughout the country. I figured out pretty quickly that you are in a fish bowl up there. Surprisingly, late in the first season I couldn't go anywhere without being recognized. We play our regular season games in Molson Stadium at McGill College. It seats just over 20,000 but in 2010 a second deck is being constructed to increase capacity. They are passionate about their Als up there. To put it in perspective, when the Als won the Grey Cup in 2009, they had a parade with nearly a half million people in the crowd.

Beyond that, the team does a great job in the community by getting the players out in the schools teaching life lessons to the kids. This is part of the Als mission statement and a big part of Mr. Wetenhall's plan with Team President Larry Smith to be an organization that not only wins games, but also reaches out to serve the city of Montreal and Province of Quebec. I thought that was pretty good stuff. Mr. Wetenhall is known as the cornerstone of owners in the league. He is an extremely successful businessman and passionate about the Alouettes and the CFL.

There are eight teams in the CFL and the vast majority of the players are former U.S. college players who just missed making an NFL team. The pay is much less than in the NFL. In fact, the entire salary cap in 2009 was a little over $4 million, compared to roughly $80 million for the NFL. These guys play for the love of the game, and in my first year in the league, I grew to love them. I told Cindy, "If you didn't know it, going to work in Montreal is no different than going to work in any NFL city I have ever coached in. These guys love the game. Their work ethic is second to no group I have ever coached and these guys are really good players!"

Before arriving in Montreal that May, I had spent time speaking to players by phone and introducing myself, but for the most part (with the exception of meeting a few at the press conference in January) I didn't know
these guys and they had no clue who I was or what I was all about. This
was an odd experience. I mean in the NFL the coaches get to know the
players ahead of time at mini camps and at OTA's (organized team activities) during the off-season. This gives them an opportunity to develop
relationships, to get to know their personalities, and most importantly to
evaluate their ability to play the game. That was all out the window here
though, so I knew I was going to be behind the eight ball from the start.

Putting the coaching staff together was another huge challenge. I would
have never believed this would happen in my first head coaching opportunity. First of all I knew I needed to bring in some CFL coaching experience. I started with the remaining staff, but once I was hired, most
headed for the hills before I could reach them. No way were they going
to hang around to ride on this new ship. There were too many unknowns,
most notably this guy from south of the border who had no idea what he
was getting himself into. I really wanted to talk to members of the previous staff. There were some good coaches who deserved consideration,
but they didn't give me a chance. My plan wasn't to come in and just start
letting people go, not if they could bring value to our new program.

For starters, I was able to retain the prior year's quarterbacks coach Scott
Milanovich. He had a close relationship with our quarterback, Anthony
Calvillo, and I knew how important it was for our team to keep him on.
Scott was the father of two young daughters who lived in his wife's hometown in upstate New York, just six hours from Montreal by car. He was-
n't going anywhere. Scott played in the NFL and had also coached in
NFL Europe prior to coming to the CFL. He was a perfect fit so I gave
him the title of offensive coordinator/quarterbacks coach. From there, I
wound up hiring four guys with previous CFL coaching experience, with
two of them having served as head coaches along the way (one at a small
college and the other in NFL Europe). I then rounded out the staff by hiring former Seattle Seahawks lineman Mike Sinclair as my defensive line
coach, and Andy Bischoff, a former coach from Cretin High School in St.
Paul, Minn., as my running backs coach and administrative assistant.
Usually a new head coach knows the work product, reputation, or has

worked with those that come to work for him on his first job. Not the case here. I worked hard to research and it took almost three months to complete the staff. In retrospect, I hired most of the staff on feel more than reputation. The way things would ultimately turn out, I think I was luckier than good. I didn't know the rules or idiosyncrasies of the game, didn't know how good our talent was, didn't know the coaches, and found soon upon arrival that English was the second language. I watched tape; I watched television copies to get a feel for the speed of the game; and I

ON SEEING
PLAYERS AS PEOPLE

"Football brings people together from all walks of life and I think that is what ultimately drove me towards it in the first place. There is such a diverse background of people on your team from year to year, and you go through so much with them. Every player's perception of reality is completely different. I wasn't a 'people person' early on in my coaching career, and I think that hurt me. That didn't happen until I got married. My wife Cindy is the one who made a 'real man' of me, because all of a sudden people in my life became very important to me. When I first got into this business I used to look at football players as nameless, faceless chess pieces, with each player having a value that I could move around a board in order to win a game. Eventually, I began to see them as people though, and that is when I started to get smart as a coach."

"Once I realized that it wasn't about me, but about caring for others and wanting to see them be the best that they could be — it was like a light bulb went off. That is when coaching became fun for me and I started to see the game on a whole new dimension. I used to be in the football business but now I am in the people business. There is a big difference. People matter. I learned that to be successful as a coach, you have to get to know people and understand where they come from. You need to know about what is going on with their families and about their personal interests, and learn about what motivates them. You can't just sit in an empty room and watch video to understand people, that only gets you so far. You have to make it personal. This was a process for me that took years to finally figure out."

asked a lot of questions of players and coaches; but that was about the extent of my knowledge.

If that wasn't enough, the Grey Cup (the CFL's Super Bowl) was to be held that first season in the 68,000 seat Olympic Stadium in Montreal. The public pressure on the Alouettes and on their rookie head coach with no CFL experience was huge. In fact it had already begun the day I was hired in January. I was picked up at the airport by a team intern and we drove the 45 minutes to our training camp site in St. Jean, about 30 minutes south of Montreal, very close to the Vermont border. There was so much to do and in the CFL it is even tougher get it all done. The season is 18 games, unlike the 16 games in the NFL, and training camp only lasts 17 days. That's it, and you have got to have your roster of 42 set with just four reserve players. Also, once the season begins, you are limited to only four and a half hours per day with the players. That's all you get.

When I had my interview the previous December, I made it clear that my role as head coach would not include direct involvement with actual football. I was new to the game and I didn't know how quickly I could learn the science of the CFL game. "South of the border" coaches moving to the CFL were not known for their immediate success. In fact most were known for coming in, making sweeping changes, and then falling on their face. In a way it was good we didn't discuss X's and O's because I wanted to focus on what I wanted our program to be about, my vision, and how I wanted us to be perceived in the community. I was head coach now, and although on the field performance ranked high in priority, there were other things that went to the top of the list. I now had the chance to get out of my office and bring people together. Since the day I was hired, my focus has never been on my individual success. My focus has been on serving the players, coaches, support staff, and others. I am a facilitator trying to find hidden and unexposed value in each and every person. And in so doing, I have never had more fun!

I knew that in order to be successful I had to come in and establish a guideline of expectations setting forth what our team would stand for and who we would be. This started in training camp and continued through the season. Training camp was tough on the players. I watched them the year before and they worked hard, but we worked them even harder. Over the course of the first week I laid out our training camp objectives, went over what I call a "code of ethics" for the safety of our players and how we practiced, and set my vision for the 2008 season.

We opened camp with a conditioning test. I wanted to quickly assess how good of shape the guys were in as they began camp. I laid it out for them in an early spring letter and was curious to see who had taken it seriously. No matter what, I asked everyone to finish, even if they didn't make the designated time. There were a few who didn't make it in time, but everyone finished. It was a good start. The guys, who didn't make it the first time, took the test one week later, and they all made it.

The evening meetings gave me time to break down our basic philosophy that would be the foundation of all our work. I wanted our team to be humble, hard working, and disciplined on and off the field. Everything we did and everything we said would be centered on a common respect for everyone in the organization, for our opponents, and for the game of football. I wanted our players to allow our staff to be a resource to each of them and let us assist them in developing their football skills. I wanted them to understand that everyone in the organization was interconnected.

ON WORK-LIFE BALANCE...

"I feel very strongly that there has to be a balance between work and personal life, otherwise your productivity will plummet. This has been proven time and again throughout the business community. The football business, like other businesses, is highly competitive and at times demands long hours. I am always conscious in planning our work schedules of what is ahead for us during the course of the season. I look closely at future opportunities for our coaches to get rest and family time. I communicate this to our coaches as soon as I finish the plan. I want them to know I am conscious of the work load ahead and this allows them to put a plan together to get rest and have family time. There were many times during my career as an assistant coach where the head coach would come in at the last minute to tell us to get out of the office and go home. He thought he was doing a great thing from a leadership standpoint, and inherently he was, yet it wasn't enough time to get a baby sitter so I could take my wife out for a quiet dinner, or make an affordable plane reservation. These are little things that will go along way with your staff."

As the season went on, this fundamental principle became the team mantra that "Everything Matters," as we established the importance of each individual's accountability to the team. If everyone felt the weight of accountability for their role on the team, nobody would carry too much weight and they could all perform at a high level. It was important that the parameters of their accountability were tied to a clearly defined and pre-determined role.

As far as the football went, we were going to put a system in place that would not try to put a square peg in a round hole. In other words, we were going to evaluate the existing talent and personnel and then use the system to produce highly efficient play at every position in order to win games. I made it very clear that I didn't care how fast they were, how smart they were, or how tough they were; we were going to have a locker room of high character guys. I backed this up by releasing a few players early and some during the season. I wanted them to know that I was very serious about it and that I meant it.

I also invited Marv Levy, the longtime coach of the Buffalo Bills, to come up to training camp and spend a few days with the team. He had coached the Als for five years prior to going on to the NFL and had won two Grey Cups. I had also called him prior to taking the job to ask him for his ad-

ON RESPECT...

"Respect is one of the great motivators for player and team accountability. We work hard at creating three areas of respect in our program. No. 1 is respect for everyone in the organization, no matter what their position. When everyone realizes that success is a result of individual accountability to their job and that we are all interconnected, it creates a sense of urgency to fulfill their obligations to the team. No. 2 is respect for your opponent. Regardless of the business, appreciating the fact that those on competing teams or businesses have as talented a work force as you have, will create a high set of standards within the organization. No. 3 is respect for the game. Football is not only a game we love, but it allows us to make a very good living. Further, it represents a set of values which allows us to become a part of something bigger than ourselves. In football, or in any other business, the desire to respect the industry is a core value that pushes us to do our best."

vice and he couldn't have been nicer. He is very well respected throughout Canada and I was really appreciative of him coming up to give our guys his perspective. He addressed the team the week before our first preseason game and he talked about football "not building character, but revealing it."

As training camp began to wind down and the final roster started to crystallize, I told the players that I didn't think that we had to make a bunch of wholesale changes to have success, but rather we needed to get focused on redefining the overall attitude and culture around us. I trusted Jim to get our team the best personnel that was out there, and from there it was my job to take that group of individuals and motivate them to be the best that they could be.

The one unique aspect of our roster and something that was particularly appealing to me coming in, was the fact that we had a veteran quarterback by the name of Anthony Calvillo. He was the second leading passer in the history of the CFL and a really smart player. I was very impressed with him right away. He is very humble, a man of sincere faith, and an extremely hard worker. Despite the fact that he has been a CFL lifer, I would say he is as good as any quarterback who I have been around. He had taken some time off the year before to be with his wife, who was suffering from cancer. She went into remission that 2008 season, so he decided to come back and rejoin the team. I have a lot of respect for him both personally and professionally. I knew that if we were going to be successful that season, it was going to be in large part because of Anthony.

After training camp I got excited about moving into my new apartment in Old Montreal. Just outside my door were cobblestone streets made up of buildings and churches with incredible architecture. During the season my exposure was limited to the demands of the season, but in my first year I got to experience the French influence, the food, the history, and the cultural diversity. I totally immersed myself in the experience, as did the girls whenever they came up to visit. Most days I would walk across the street from my apartment and jump on the subway for the 24 minute ride right into our offices at Olympic Stadium. I would use that time to think and reflect.

As the opening game got closer and closer, the big question again in the media was how we were going to handle the pressure of having the Grey

Cup in Montreal that season. My answers were always the same, "I haven't really thought about it." That was the truth. Yes, my vision was to get to the Grey Cup and to win the championship. But, I really was more concerned with doing everything I could to help our guys win each day. My focus was with our team's development. I wanted each player to be consciously aware of their level of performance in each and every moment. I told them that no one day or one game whether won or lost would ultimately define us. At the time I would describe our team as being was what I called "fluid," and that it would only crystallize at the end of this six month journey. I believe this, pounded it at them daily, and eventually we had a buy in.

When you talk to 60 guys each day, you might as well make up your mind that the message you are giving will be perceived 60 different ways. Each day the challenge is to express the message differently. I always tell them, "Guys, some of you understand what I am saying, others of you have no clue, but eventually you will." In 2008, I was confident yet humble in saying "eventually they did."

I also told them about my expectations with regards to them having positive attitudes. I was clear with them that upon walking into the football office that they had to have at least one of three mindsets. First, everyone had to at least accept their role on the team. Acceptance is not easy because sometimes you have to be accepting when things are unfair. Mar-

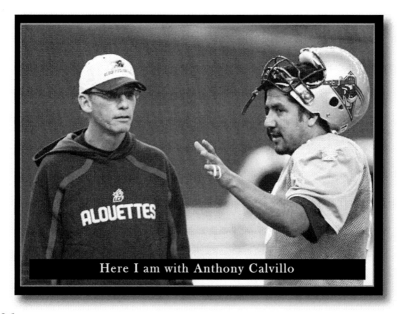

Here I am with Anthony Calvillo

cus Brady, the team's backup quarterback, never got the opportunity in 2008 to even compete for the job. This clearly was not fair to him. I made the statement in my opening press conference that Anthony would be the starter. Yet, everyday Marcus came in with a smile on his face and had an all-business attitude. By his demeanor you would have thought he was the starter. I respected him so much for that. He bought in and was rewarded that off-season when he was hired as the team's new wide receiver coach.

Second, I hoped guys would come to work with a sense of enjoyment toward their work. Football players and their coaches are creatures of habit and they need structure, but I wanted to create an environment where football was not drudgery and where a sense of humor was embraced. Football is a tough and brutal game at its core, so I worked hard to eliminate the drudgery in an attempt to create a more enjoyable work environment. Third, I wanted players to be enthusiastic. Enthusiasm is contagious. I often reminded them that as football players and coaches we were blessed with being able to live our childhood dreams on a daily basis.

I tried to make it clear that when a player comes to work without at least one of these very important attitudes, a psychological "dis-harmony" takes place in our locker room that can suck the energy right out of all of us. If I could get them to buy in, I knew it could possibly turn into something special. Then, when guys weren't doing their jobs, I called them out in meetings — but never in the press. I worked each and every day in the morning team meeting to illustrate through practice video how everything we did was interconnected. From there, I worked hard to get to know the veterans and I hoped they would help me reach the younger guys. I was fair and reasonable, but I was still hard on everybody and demanded a lot from the players and coaches.

Practices were not long but they were demanding and I set very high expectations. I wanted them running from drill to drill and I wanted their helmets buckled from the time we started until the time we stopped. I wanted every practice to be like a game, so practice was fast, frenetic and chaotic.

This job gave me a chance to step back and be mindful of all the coaches I had worked for and with over the years. I had taken everything in over the years from all of them and was now applying it to my own players and

ON MOTIVATION...

"Motivation to me isn't about making speeches. It's about creating an environment where everybody feels your passion, your preparation, your self-accountability, your attention to detail, your knowledge, your sincere desire to serve others, and your sense of accomplishment that you feel when assisting others on their journey to be the best they can be. When others feel confident in the fact that you, as their coach, have done everything in your power to put them in a position to succeed, then that is the true definition of motivation to me."

"The motivation you give your team comes from the standard of performance that you set in every phase of team development: from the locker room, to the meeting room, at practice and on game day. It even goes to the sense of responsibility everyone feels towards the team when they go their separate ways at the end of the day. Most professional athletes are self-motivated. They are motivated to be the best they can be, to win, and to maximize their economic value on the field. As a coach it is up to you to figure out how to enhance that motivation on an individual level. Figuring out which buttons to push on which individuals is the key to success in my mind. This is why I am not in the football business, I am in the people business, and so are you."

"When I speak to my team at various times during the course of a day and season, I am the first to realize that there are roughly 65 men out there who hear a message from me, yet each of them perceives it differently. My words are translated differently based on a player's worldly outlook, upbringing, education and various other ideological reasons. Once I understand this, the more it motivates me on a daily basis to find different ways to send the fundamental messages of our program in different ways. The better I get to know the individuals, the more I can customize the message to be sure that I reach them."

"The translation of these messages on a daily basis does not necessarily happen at that moment. It is a process and it often takes time. As I say to our players, 'Some of you get it while others of you don't, and that's OK, because eventually you will.' In my mind, the best way to motivate players is to create the kind of environment that makes them feel a sense of accountability and urgency to perform at their highest level, because they ultimately do not want to let their teammates down. When each player begins to feel that sense of responsibility, nobody has to carry the weight totally on their shoulders. Players can relax knowing that the man next to him 'has his back,' and at the same time he has his. You can then freely enjoy and express yourself unselfishly on the field of play. So, to be able to empower them to love each other, appreciate each other, play for each other, and succeed with each other is extremely challenging. When it happens though, it is just amazing."

staff. But the truth was, as I look back, I never thought about how "that" coach would have done it. I just did it, and it came very natural in every way. The beauty of it all is that we had the right pilot in Anthony Calvillo to lead us on the field. We all knew we were riding the wave of his brilliant play.

I am asked so often what it takes to play the quarterback position at the highest level. My answer is that there is no formula for who will get there. Heck, Tom Brady was the 199th pick in the draft, Kurt Warner was bagging groceries the year before he was MVP in the Super Bowl, and Ryan Leaf by some was a "can't miss" No. 1 pick. (Brady and Warner will wind up in the Hall of Fame, while Leaf struggled.) Breaking down the quarterback and what it takes to play is a complex and abstract equation, but there are some prerequisites that separate them from one another.

Anthony, like other greats I have crossed paths with, has those qualities. He is a gym rat and loves to prepare for games. He is so grounded, so emotionally intelligent, and he carries himself with so much humility. I watched him weekly as I did Bernie Kosar, Steve Young, Rich Gannon, Jake Plummer, and Scott Mitchell — completely focused through the week, watching tape, and taking meticulous notes. Their day started early, and they never stopped until game time. Anthony, like the rest, had a personality that transcended all the players and coaches. He was the perfect fit for a team to rally around and he gave hope not only to the players, but to the entire organization. Without Anthony flying the plane and keeping us at the right altitude and wing level, my first year coaching experiment could have blown up in my face. I know without question, when the quarterback has success, the team always follows. In 2008, the team was definitely able to ride on his successes.

I also worked hard to make our culture about the little things. I told the players that I expected them to push their chairs in after they were through eating in the dining hall. I told them that I wouldn't tolerate any hazing between the older players and the younger ones. We had two weeks to get ready for the season. I did not want players who were competing for jobs being concerned about rookie's singing their school fight songs at dinner. In the locker room, I told the players that they could play whatever music that they wanted to, but that I wasn't going to tolerate anything with the "N-word," the "B-word," or anything else that would be disrespectful to women. These words have no place in football or anywhere else. Eventually, when they didn't follow those parameters and music became a distraction, I had everybody go to I-Pods. I can't tell you how many players thanked me.

Every week was a challenge to define ourselves. That was our approach each and every day. Trust would be a foundation in the program. Early, I wanted a curfew because this is all I knew from my NFL experience, but the leadership group I had put together talked me out of it. I decided to grant their request, so we never gave them a curfew — not even on nights before games when we were staying in hotels. The veteran guys said that they would take care of things and I left it up to them. I also told them that I wasn't going to tolerate any women in the rooms. These were not our rooms. We were guests of Mr. Wetenhall, our owner, and if they needed to get a room they had to do so somewhere else. As such, we never had any major disciplinary problems. Credit is due to our great GM Jim Popp, who brought in a bunch of high character guys.

It seemed that everyday we continued to redefine ourselves. I remember being on the team bus headed to Hamilton for our first game of the year and our bus driver somehow got lost. Some of the players started chirping at the guy, razzing him, calling him "bussy," and generally disrespecting him. I just lost it. I stood up, turned around, and screamed "What are you guys doing?! You haven't ever made a mistake before, I haven't made mistakes before? This man is doing the best he can, and he happened to make a mistake. Now be quiet and show him some respect!" They shut up and that set the tone for the type of things I was and wasn't going to tolerate on our team.

We won that game, 33-10, and I even got my first Gatorade bath, which was pretty cool. Anthony played phenomenally well, as I quietly reminded myself how so few head coaches in the history of the game ever had winning records without a productive quarterback. I had waited 25 years to get my first win as a head coach and it felt really, really good.

We followed that up the next week by winning our first home game against Winnipeg, 38-24. We had gotten our season off to a fast start, which was key for the team and organization's confidence. I was feeling good about where we were at, but everything started to unravel after we lost three straight really close games to Calgary, Saskatchewan and British Columbia. One of the nuances of the CFL is clock management, which I didn't understand very well early on and it cost us. We lost all three in the final three minutes after being ahead, and that really opened my eyes to one of the key differences between the NFL and CFL. Because the clock stopped after every play under three minutes in the first and second halves, the amount of possession changes can be enormous in a three-down game. As I would soon learn, the strategy was very different. It was like there was 57 minutes of a game and then there were three more at the end. And believe me, those last three minutes can seem like a lifetime.

So, in the CFL it is a totally different dynamic. Frankly, I am still not comfortable with the last three minute rules, but I am learning. In some ways the CFL is much more of a thinking man's game than the NFL. I always loved calling the plays in the two-minute drill and handling the multitude of situations that would come up. Not the case for the last three minutes of the game in the CFL. It got my attention early in the season and it became the focus of my attention and preparation for the remainder of the season. Again, it was about adapting and changing to this new environment.

My first Gatorade bath...

When we arrived back in Montreal from Vancouver after our third loss in a row, I knew that initial meeting would be my first real defining moment as the new head coach of the Alouettes. The players would look to me to see how we would handle adversity. I told them that we were not changing our plan and that it was a long season. As I had told them in training camp, every season will be filled with both success and adversity, and that the team that developed backbone during training camp would be the one to weather the storm.

I also chose to give the players two days off after games, which was very unique and totally unheard of in the NFL. Because of the limited roster and a grueling 18 game season, I felt without the rest there would be residual effects of injury and wear on our players. I even asked them to stay off their feet, to get plenty of rest, and eat right. I felt strongly that it would pay off for us in the end and it did. As a result, the coaches were able to get in two good days of game planning without any distractions. The players then would return well rested and ready to go. It went over so well that I even decided to shorten up our practices, to give them even more rest. To make up for it, I encouraged the players to spend some time visualizing their success. They were skeptical at first, but they eventually came around. We also added longer walk-thrus and meetings, but physical activity was kept to a minimum so we could keep guys fresh. It was radical, but I went with my gut and luckily it worked out.

From there, I held team meetings where we watched the tape together as a unit, with all of the staff and all of the players. This too was radical and almost unheard of. Teams have typically always done this in small groups, like running backs or offensive linemen, or whomever. There was total transparency with the players now, and they had to be accountable for their actions in front of the entire team. Everybody could see what everybody else was doing. It gave them perspective and put things into a context that they would not have otherwise gotten.

It also had a dramatic effect on the chemistry of the team. We became a very tight group. The philosophy of everybody being interconnected became our team culture. I even tied it into the media. I told the guys that whenever they were asked questions about themselves, to please reverse it and make it about the team. We knew what was going on inside our locker room wasn't perfect, but rather it was a part of an ongoing process that would take time. Everything was about the team. Eventually I could

242

see that the guys were buying in.

Chemistry was really important to me, so I tried to get to know the players in their own spaces. For instance, even though I am Jewish I consistently went to our pre-game chapels. I would go and listen and use the time to reflect. It was fun to be around the players and to build that trust. When they see you outside of your coaching box, they let their guard down a little bit and that is when you get to know them as people. They see you as more human and approachable. I wanted to do whatever it took to get to know them so I could better relate to them.

I tried to bring my family around the team as much as I could too, to share that part of my life with the players. It wasn't easy because of their travel back and forth from Raleigh, but I wanted them to know in addition to being a tough coach, I was also a dad and a husband. I wanted to open up to them, and I wanted them to do the same to me. I asked them to call me Marc, not coach — just like we used to call Coach Grant, "Bud." He understood that in professional football the season is so long, and that the time we spent together as coaches and players was immense. He felt that there was just no time for formality, and I totally agreed.

Like most of my head coaching mentors, I wanted to treat my players like professionals and men. As such, I wanted them to work hard. I constantly reminded them that they didn't get to pick how hard they were going to work. That was my job. It was their job to trust me to do the right thing and what was ultimately best for the team.

I reminded the team almost daily that we were in the people business and I encouraged the players to branch out to get to know one another. I wanted them to sit with new people at team meetings, at team meals, on the team bus, and in the locker room. I wanted them to build team chemistry from within. I really wanted them to get to know each other and to learn as much as they could about each other along the way. Even when a new player would join the team, I purposely never introduced him in front of the rest of the team. I left it up to the guys to do that, and they did.

In keeping with my theme of "team football," I never had my players elect captains. I never wanted to isolate any one individual player either, so in 2008 I gave out just two game-balls that entire season. That is unheard of in football. Usually it is a post-game tradition after a win, to honor the game's top player. The first came after we won the Eastern Conference Finals and secured our place in the Grey Cup game. It went to a former Alouette player named Tony Proudfoot, who was a guest coach for us in training camp. He is a brilliant man in the middle stages Lou Gehrig's Disease (ALS).

The other went to an older gentleman name Jacques, who was one of the assistant equipment men, who I believed epitomized our culture of coming to work with a positive attitude. He unselfishly executed his role with pride and did everything he could to help the team. One day during the season I saw that there were a bunch of used washcloths lying on the floor in the player's shower room next to a laundry basket placed conveniently there for their disposal. It really upset me. Was it so hard to throw a used washcloth into an empty basket after you were done showering? At the next team meeting I brought Jacques into our team meeting and said "Guys, this is Jacques. He is the person who vacuums our floor, cleans our lockers, washes our helmets, puts the chairs away after meetings, cleans the bathrooms and showers, and does a lot of the dirty work that has to be done around here in order to keep our 'house' clean. He does the stuff nobody else wants to do. He takes great pride in his work and asks nothing in return, other than you please take the washcloths that you just used to wipe your butts with, and put them in the laundry basket. No, that basket is NOT a basketball hoop. So show Jacques some respect!" Needless to say, we never saw a washcloth on the floor again for the rest of the year. When Jacques was given that ball, all you saw was a bunch of grown men in tears. It was awesome!

Accountability is huge with me. I remember one time a couple of players were a few minutes late boarding the team bus, so I sent the bus off without them. I wanted to make a point about being punctual and about not letting your teammates down. We were never "white knuckled" about being late, but these were rookies who were more than late, and they were keeping a lot of the vets waiting. So they had to catch a flight home at their own expense. The younger players were saying, "Coach, wait, here they come!" I then heard some of the veteran players tell them to be quiet, inferring I had done exactly the right thing.

I remember another time trying to teach the team a lesson during our win over Toronto about how sometimes perception is reality. We were ahead 32-14 with just a few minutes to go in the game, when the camera panned over to a couple of our defensive linemen, one of whom had just gotten a big sack. They were all smiling and pointing to their wrists. You see, the MVP of the Friday Night Game received a new watch from a local Jewelry store as a marketing promotion. I saw this on video after the game and it really unnerved me. The next practice I showed the video to the defensive linemen, but not the whole team. I called them into my office and explained to them how I felt they were disrespecting the game, disrespecting their opponents, and disrespecting themselves. They were having harmless fun in their minds and had no idea of the ramifications that ensued, or how our team was perceived. They were so disappointed in themselves and were really apologetic. I was glad they got it and that it hit home with them. I was able to build a little trust too, because they appreciated me not showing it to the entire team.

We had a season defining moment in Calgary in mid-September when we lost 41–30, and got sucked into playing a style of football we hadn't seen in ourselves thus far in the season. Guys were trash talking and playing undisciplined. Afterwards I did something that I had never done before. I not only talked about the Grey Cup, I told them that we were going

ON DEALING WITH PRESSURE...

"Pressure is a huge part of football, just enormous. How you deal with it, however, is the key to success. Imagine yourself coaching a football game and you have to call a play within 40 seconds left on the clock, with 60,000 people screaming at you, all believing they can do a better job than you can. Don't forget about the countless millions more who are at home watching you on TV. It can be tough. To stay focused and to be able to think clearly, you have to believe in yourself and trust that all the hard work and preparation you have done will see you through the difficult times. You also have to trust your assistants, and the decisions that you entrusted them to make. The best way I have found to deal with pressure is by selling accountability to everyone involved, because if everyone has done their job properly then no one single person will have to carry the weight of the entire team on their shoulders. This enables me and others to fluidly work through the course of a game, knowing that everybody's work ethic will ultimately take care of the end result."

to win the Grey Cup. It was the only time I talked about the Cup or about winning the entire year. I said it very passionately too, which really resonated throughout the locker room. I told them that the reason we were all here at that moment wasn't about winning the Grey Cup, it was because each and every one of us had a desire to be a part of something that was bigger than ourselves. That was it. I don't remember why I said it, but when I heard it come out of my mouth, I realized after all the years I had been around the game, that this is why I coached, pure and simple. I am not sure if everybody bought into it, but it certainly gave them something to think about. We were a different football team from that point on.

We had big wins down the stretch over Edmonton, Saskatchewan, Hamilton, and Toronto which put us into the post-season mix. We had some ups and downs along the way, but we made it. In one of the final games of the year, I lost my focus and got very upset with a couple of players who did an orchestrated touchdown celebration. I felt strongly that they were being disrespectful to the opposition by doing what they did so I not only called them out in front of everybody right then and there, I called out their coaches too. I felt that everybody had to be accountable. It was an ugly scene and it really disrupted our rhythm and focus. For the first time during the season I lost my composure on the sideline. I thought about it a lot that night and the next day I apologized to the entire team. I didn't want to dwell on it so we quickly moved on, I had made my point.

From there we faced off against Edmonton on the road in the last game of the season. We had already gained home field advantage in the playoffs and for all intents and purposes this game meant nothing in the standings. We were essentially one win away from playing in the Grey Cup. So, I decided not to play Anthony and it proved to be a really controversial move. Not only was Anthony the MVP of the league that season, he was also just eight completions away from setting a CFL passing record. So I was torn. I knew that it was not the best message to send to our team by sitting our best player, but our backup hadn't had a single rep all season and I felt strongly that we needed to get him in there so that he would be prepared in case we had to call upon him in the playoffs.

I had expressed to the players weekly that we were going to play every game to win, yet here I was sitting Anthony because I didn't want to risk losing him to injury in what many perceived as a meaningless game. I

246

thought about playing him for the first quarter to get him his eight completions for the record, but figured that would have been disrespectful to Edmonton. At the end of the day, I made a decision I felt was in the best interests of not only our team, but the city of Montreal — I benched him. We ended up losing the game, 37-14, but it was another defining moment for our team. The result of my decision was reinforced two weeks later when we beat Edmonton again, this time in Montreal, to win the Eastern Division Championship and advance on to the Grey Cup title game.

Hosting the Grey Cup in Montreal was a major nationwide event. The game was played at Olympic Stadium, the former home of the Montreal Expos Major League Baseball team. More than 66,000 fans came out to root us on, which was really exciting for all of us. We started out very explosively on offense but had to settle for a field goal on our first drive after a Calgary defender tipped a sure touchdown pass. From there things went back and forth until they scored a late touchdown to make it 13-10 at halftime. We then came out in the second half ready to go, but we just could not get on track. Anthony had five tipped balls and two interceptions. Calgary played great down the stretch. Their quarterback, Henry Burris, broke a few key runs which were difference makers in the game and they went on to beat us in a close one, 22-14. I had to tip my hat to them, the Cup was theirs.

I was obviously disappointed for our players and coaches in the outcome, but I thought we played a very hard fought game. My post-game speech was short and my message was clear. "Guys, do not let the disappointment of the last three hours take away from what we have accomplished as a team. There will be a party at the team hotel that starts in an hour and I hope all of you will be there with your family and close friends. It's time to celebrate our season." I was very emotional, yet very upbeat and positive.

I have always said that you should never judge a player by how he takes a loss. It's not fair. Some guys can be upbeat while others take it very hard. It's a very subjective, personal thing. I just asked that everybody please respect everybody else's individual privacy in terms of how they dealt with the situation. Just about everybody showed up at the party and it turned out to be a fantastic evening. I got a chance to meet a lot of the player's parents and family members, which was great. Afterwards I even got to spend some time with my own family, unwinding and enjoying the sights and sounds of Montreal before we headed back to Raleigh

Despite coming up short in the end, I was proud of my team. What a great bunch of guys. You know, if I closed my eyes each day and didn't know any better, I could have been in any NFL city — coaching high character men who were dedicated and passionate about the game. I learned a lot about myself that season and had a chance to stretch myself to the max. Overall, I felt great about what we had accomplished. I was even named as the 2008 CFL Outstanding Coach by the CFL Players Association, which meant a lot to me because it came not from the media, but from the players. It was a dream come true to go to a new country and to be a part of so much so quickly. I will always be indebted to Mr. Wetenhall, Larry Smith, and Jim Popp for giving me an opportunity of a lifetime.

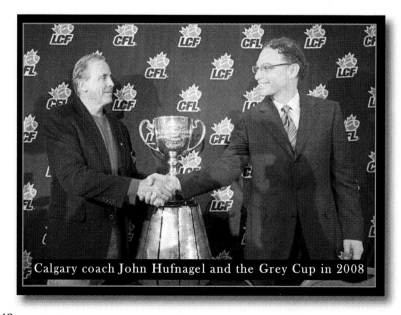

Calgary coach John Hufnagel and the Grey Cup in 2008

CH. 2)   57 + 3, PLUS ONE PLAY TO A GREY CUP VICTORY

Leaders embrace adversity, are grateful for the opportunity to lead, and follow a humble and hardworking path. It is important for them to motivate their followers for the long haul through a clearly articulated vision and steps for achieving long term goals. This is often toughest in an organization of sustained success, because complacency can easily set in and a successful team can lose the edge that got them there. Past performance is no indication of future success. Leaders find ways to focus on the good, build on the bad, and never accept failure. They focus on the now because they realize that what is going on today will affect tomorrow. They continuously assess areas that need to be improved and ask questions to make everybody around them better.

A few days after our home field defeat to Calgary in the Grey Cup, I had many thoughts running through my head about my first year as a head coach. These included how we had built a positive culture in our locker room, how well we had done to win the division, and how we handled the pressure of winning the conference to play for the championship. We had been tremendously explosive as an offense in my first year as a play caller, and Anthony Calvillo was the MVP of the League. Incredibly, I was now one of the few coaches to ever coach a League MVP both north and south of the border. Credit is also due to Scott Milanovich, our offensive coordinator and quarterbacks coach, who did a magnificent job of managing Anthony's progress throughout the year.

I originally told Bob Wetenhall, Larry Smith, and Jim Popp in my initial interview that I did not plan on calling the plays. I was simply too unfamiliar with the rules and science of football within the CFL. I just felt it would not be realistic to do so in my first year as head coach. Wally Buono, the British Columbia Lions head coach and the CFL's winningest coach, even told me that I shouldn't even try to do it. I listened closely to his advice. But after two preseason games, I decided with an open mind to call the plays. It was always my favorite part of coaching and I decided it was in the best interest of the team for me to dictate the offensive play selection. At season's end we led the league in almost every single offensive category. I can humbly say it would not have been accomplished, however, if it weren't for a brilliant veteran quarterback, a dedicated offensive line, a running back core that made pass protection a priority, an exceptional group of receivers, and a great offensive staff.

With all that being said, I was extremely bothered by the loss in the Grey Cup. I had been on a National Championship team 25 years earlier in Miami, but despite all the playoff appearances, AFC Championship games, and a Super Bowl appearance, I still hadn't been part of a true championship team. As a coordinator for four different teams in the NFL, we went to the playoffs my first year with all of them, but had no championship to show for it. Now, in my first year as head coach, we lost again. This was not good and I needed to get to the bottom of it.

I did my best to get away from football in December following the Grey Cup and kept busy working on this book as well as a new a quarterback book. The holiday season passed, and then it was time to turn on the tapes of the Grey Cup and start answering the necessary questions:

ON PERSPECTIVE...

"Football is a game that draws people together to be a part of something bigger than themselves. With that in mind, every player and every coach sees the game from his own unique perspective. It is the same in business too. As a leader I believe that no two people necessarily see the same thing the same way, because their perspectives come from different sources. As a leader I work diligently to bring all of those perspectives and ideas together responsibly in order to create one single vision for our team. That requires being open minded, being unselfish and being a good listener."

How did players play on an individual basis?

Did we have a good plan?

What were the critical mistakes that cost us the game?

If Calgary was the best team, what did we have to do to get better?

Was our scheme and talent level defensively and offensively good enough to win a championship?

If I could answer some of these basic questions, I could begin to set a plan of action necessary to return to the Grey Cup and win. So, after a complete examination by me and our staff, we came up with some objective conclusions. With all due respect to the Calgary Stampeders, we were the better team. Calgary deserved to win, no doubt about it, but if we would have played at our best, the results would have been much different. We also realized that we needed to upgrade our roster in a few areas to create more favorable matchups for our team going forward.

We had a number of players who had been in six Grey Cups and had now lost five of them. This loss stung our team more than I realized, and they came back to training camp with an edge and unyielding desire to get back to the big game. I was excited about our chances. We had a very good team, with a great quarterback and core group of veterans. The players arrived in Montreal on the first of June. Addressing the team the first evening after the conditioning test was an important event because it set the tone for training camp and the season ahead. As I looked out at the players in the auditorium, I saw a lot of new faces. Our GM Jim Popp was extremely confident that we had upgraded our football team.

Because of all that had to be covered offensively, defensively, and on special teams, I limited my address to our practice "Code of Ethics." I told the guys that at practice the next day all I expected from them was to play as fast as they could and we that would worry about assignments and fundamentals as camp proceeded. On the second night, I addressed the team on my vision of what the 2009 Alouettes would look like. This was not something that could be put together the night before; it was something that took time and focus. I told them that they had to really get quiet and think. I told them to ask themselves some questions. "What do I want this team that I am leading to be about?"

I knew that winning the championship was always the goal, but I wanted to know what they wanted their daily culture to be like so that each moment could take on true meaning. I knew this would be an ongoing process that would evolve over the 180 days of the season. I had it mapped out all the way to the parade in downtown Montreal two days after the Grey Cup in Calgary. Somewhere I once read that vision attracts challenges and unites people. The greater the vision, the more winners it will invariably attract. This vision had the chance to unite a team and an organization, as well as a city and province.

After a year as head coach, the portrait that I wanted to paint began to crystallize more clearly. I was able to articulate the vision to the team in seven steps:

1) We would be a completely unselfish team. Everyone would put the team ahead of themselves.

2) There would be a universal level of trust between coaches and players, players and players, coaches and coaches, and everyone would trust that the decisions made were only measured by what was in the best interest of the team.

3) Humility would be a measuring stick for how we handled ourselves individually and collectively. Humility, meaning that the things we accomplished were a result not just of our individual efforts, but of the collective efforts of everyone in our organization. Our humility would keep our feet firmly planted on the ground on a daily basis and keep us focused on what I began to define as "win the day."

4) With all the new players in the room, I reminded them that we were not just in the football business, but that they were in the people business. I told them that they should put together a proactive plan to get to know their teammates on a personal level. This gives more depth to relationships. My plan was to eliminate roles as much as I could. I explained to them if I was always the "head coach" and they were always "the player," then we would be playing roles that would take us away from truly having an authentic relationship. This also translated to my relationships with the assistant coaches, team medical staff, and equipment personnel.

252

5) I hoped we could all display a level of transparency and openness with each other. Being straight with the team enabled us to avoid distractions and lose focus while completing the important tasks of the day.

6) We were going to have great demeanor. There is an old saying that you either bring energy to a room or take it away. How players carried themselves would be critical to our success on a daily and seasonal basis, and would ultimately dictate our ability to enjoy the work that we do. We were all going to bring it each day and enjoy work. If a player didn't have a positive attitude, then he was a threat to team energy. Further, the team's psychological harmony would be diluted by individual selfishness.

7) The question each day, whether after a meeting, practice, or a game was going to be: "Did we win the day?"

The vision was more involved than this but the fundamental baseline of what we were trying to achieve is represented in those seven steps. During the next few days of camp, I reminded each man that he would get a legitimate opportunity to make the team. This was always a key point of discussion during our staff meetings. I reminded the players that we were looking for passionate, explosive, and violent players who would play smart, mistake free football amidst the chaos of a game, and within the rules. I also reminded them of our core values that set the tone for the culture of our football team:

1) We are a humble and hard working team with a common sense approach in victory and defeat.

2) We are disciplined on and off the field because we represent a team, a league, a city, and a province.

3) We would have common respect for each other, our opponents, and the game.

4) We are interconnected and everything "you do," "we do."

5) We would each have a job description and were all accountable to execute it.

We opened practice with an emphasis offensively on beating man-to-man coverage, and defensively on playing man-to-man. It was evident after a few practices that Jim Popp and his staff had done an excellent job of upgrading our defense, which was exactly what we needed to improve our team. Jim's additions to our personnel enabled us to get better, but during training camp some very difficult decisions were made to change the dynamic. Jim's addition of two defensive backs forced us to cut some good players who were high character guys and major contributors to our team's Grey Cup run the year before. We also moved one of our defensive backs to linebacker, which forced us to cut an all-league linebacker and team leader from that squad. Finally, we took a second year player and placed him in a starting middle linebacker role, forcing another cut of a prominent team leader from the year before.

From my position as head coach these were very difficult decisions because of my emotional attachment to those players, my loyalty to them for the job they had done the year before, the quality of people they were, and the effect these changes would have on the team's chemistry in 2009. But as a staff and organization we meticulously went through a collective process of reviewing their play. We then met as a staff to discuss the ramifications to the team, and then Jim would come in with his personnel staff and we would discuss these decisions all over again. I wanted everyone to have the opportunity to be heard and feel a sense of respect and accountability for our decisions, but I knew full well that the final call would be mine.

It was here, more than at any other time, I realized the importance of being a really good listener. I had to mindfully put my attention on what each person said, think through it, ask questions, and then make the call based on information and experience. In some cases I truly had to take a leap of faith. All the while I was constantly keeping in mind the best interests of the organization. As upcoming changes became more apparent to the team, the responses became extremely interesting. For the first time, veteran players stepped up to give opinions on certain players and about their importance to our locker room and team. Our guys were not disrespectful in any way; they just cared about the team enough to let me know how they felt about their teammates. I could have looked at this as a lack of trust of confidence by our players, but I refused to go there. I did not resent the players coming forward, in fact I embraced it. It made me take a final look at the decisions we were making. I also respected these guys for coming forward out of their love of the team.

By the end of training camp, I told the team that our defense had a chance to be great and would set the tone for our football team in the upcoming season. We were practicing hard and were focused in the evening meetings. Walk-thrus were businesslike and the guys were zoned in. Periodically, players asked me why I hadn't gone off on the team during practices or meetings like many other football coaches often do. My answer was simple, there was no reason to. They were doing what we were asking them to do.

To "win the day" transcended everything we wanted to be about as a team in 2009. I was very clear with the team that if our focus was on winning the Grey Cup, it would take away the necessary energy we needed to become better on a daily basis. Our coaches took the same approach. We would coach each day as if it was the most important day of our lives. The next day was no more important than this day, and therefore the next moment was never more important than this one. Nothing was more important than "the now."

ON COACHING & SALES...

"Coaching is sales, pure and simple. As a coach you have to sell players on your team vision and then get them to buy into it. That all starts with a solid plan, which is essential to being a good salesman. For me, demeanor (the manner in which you carry yourself) is a huge thing. I feel strongly about the impression you make when you walk into that meeting room to sell your plan. Your demeanor might be just as important as the plan itself. You have to have confidence in your ability to not only understand the plan, but in your ability to sell it as a presenter so that everybody wants to buy in. When I call a play it may be a play that every other team in the league runs. But when I install it into OUR system, I sell it as "OUR PLAY," a special play which, if executed properly, should turn into a big play. I was trained as a lawyer and by nature I believe it is important to present your case in a succinct, methodical and charismatic manner. When you do that, and you are properly prepared, good things will undoubtedly happen. The bottom line is that you have to have a passion for what you are doing. Players need to see your passion and know there is a 'science' behind it or they simply won't buy in."

One of the great challenges for a person in a leadership position is trying to eliminate the complaining and bitching that are a part of any family or organization. As training camp came to a close, with players a little worn down from practice and meetings, they began to look around to see if certain teammates were being treated differently. A few started complaining that some guys are getting more or less reps in practice, more rest, or time off. I began to refer to this as having a "fish eye," where players were looking around to compare themselves to everybody else and were not focused on their individual tasks, personal improvement, or team development. The term "fish-eyeing" became the buzzword to tell someone to keep focused on the task at hand. We all had fun with the term, but it served us well.

We even had fun with the players who were blaming, complaining and bitching. I remember the great spiritualist Eckhart Tolle once said that blaming was the ego "telling itself a story" that made you different or separate from the whole. The guys had a blast with this one. Any time a player was overheard complaining about something, one of the guys would say "there you go, telling yourself a story!" We would all laugh, but the point was that a player or coach can't separate himself from the team because they ARE the team.

During the normal course of the year in any business, especially one where there is a high level of energy and emotion expended on a daily basis, blaming and complaining becomes part of the day. Eliminating it from our work day was a major challenge, as it is with any team. The term "locker room lawyer," or the buzz of players complaining or bitching, has always been part of any organization. When this type of egotistic interaction takes place, however, the focus shifts and dilutes the effort exerted away from achieving the intended goal. This was a major focus in my second year and I knew it could not be accomplished overnight. It is a process, an evolution of sorts, and it takes time. My whole approach to handling adversity is to embrace it, be grateful for the opportunity, and to take a humble and hardworking path to resolve it.

The day before our first pre-season game is the time we teach new players how to stand for the National Anthem before each game. I first learned this in 1979 when I was in training camp as a player with the Minnesota Vikings. For years I had watched how players on other teams would look around, itch, spit, and even blow their nose, amongst other activities during the Anthem. As a player, I remember Coach Grant assigning two of the team's best players, Matt Blair and Tim Irwin, to properly stand with toes on the line, helmet under their left arm with facemask facing the field, and head up. When you looked around you saw guys being a little silly, but there was Matt and Tim, as serious as can be. Nobody in the NFL at the time detailed out the National Anthem like Bud's teams, and over the years as a fan and coach I learned to respect what he was trying to do.

ON GETTING CUT...

"I have been on both sides of this issue, having been cut by the Vikings as a player on two occasions, and then having to cut players as a head coach. I remember the patience of Bud Grant during these often life defining moments with me and other players. This has always resonated with me and I have since modeled my approach after him. As a coach, cutting players is the worst part of your job description. When you sit down and have to tell a young man that you think it is time for him to find something else to do with his life, that can be very emotional. I don't care whether the player is 25, 32 or 40 — it is a difficult thing to do. That person has been living his dream up until that point and now that dream has been shattered. You never get so callous that you don't feel for the man who you are cutting."

"Over the last two years I have had to cut a number of players. I try to be as 'transparent' as I can with them, explaining their strengths and weaknesses, and why the decision was made. I tell them that as much as it is an emotional decision, it is one that was exclusively made in the best interest of the team. Sometimes it is about economics and salary cap issues, but again, it is always a team-first decision. If I believe a player should not give up and try again I will tell him. And, if I believe it is indeed time for him to move on in his life and find a new way to make a living, I will tell them that as well. I also will tell him that I am always available for him or his agent to get back to me if I can help in any way, and I really mean it. In most cases these men have made the necessary sacrifices and given it their best to our team and with that I believe part of my job is to assist in their transition. I embrace those opportunities and will always take five minutes to make a phone call on their behalf."

When I became the head coach of the Alouettes, I looked forward to this day as a way to bring the team together. "Guys, today we are going to learn how to properly stand at attention for the National Anthem of Canada." I could feel the sarcastic energy around me but I continued on. There are a number of very good reasons why we would do this, including the fact that many players on both teams were Canadian, the fans were Canadian, and most importantly — many people died for this country to keep it a free nation. We needed to show them respect. I also reminded the U.S. players that they needed to appreciate the fact that Canada was allowing us to come there in order to make a living, and to be able to live our dream as players and coaches.

When I released the players from this informal huddle and asked them to get lined up in an organized manner, they did so very quickly and were focused. They immediately got the message. In year two, I went through the entire speech again with all the players. I could see that the veterans were taking ownership of this now and that made me proud to see them getting everybody spread out across the field in order to make sure the team was aligned properly. It was heartfelt to see these large men walking down the line, standing tall and proud. It was also great to realize that Bud Grant's legacy was alive and well in the CFL. How we presented ourselves during the Canadian National Anthem was a little thing, but a very important thing.

The 2009 Alouettes won both pre-season games and then hit the road to open the season in Calgary against the defending CFL Grey Cup champion Stampeders. The media was into us redeeming ourselves from the Grey Cup loss. For some players it might have been, and I would never take that motivation from them. But the truth is, we were not the same team and neither were they. We had different players playing and different coaches on our staff. My message to the team the night before this one had nothing to do with winning, losing, or redeeming ourselves from the last defeat. I told them when we left for Montreal tomorrow night after the game, we wanted to be known as a team that brought their collective and individual passion.

From there, I reminded them of the obvious: each player gets 20 games to express themselves; they worked nearly 180 days to prepare; we would be a smart team and not beat ourselves by falling into the trap of being selfish, undisciplined, or out of control; we would be consistent in handling adversity and success by maintaining composure, making corrections, not blaming, and not pointing fingers; when bad plays happened during the course of the game, which they always will, players always had a support group to help understand and correct the issue at hand; and finally when good things happened on the field, we were not going to make it about the individuals but about the team, because we were all interconnected and no one individual player made any one play possible by himself.

When two teams of equal ability compete like we did with Calgary in opener, there were certainly some lessons to be learned. We knew the game would go the entire 57 + 3 (minutes); we knew whichever team that scored first would generally see a methodical response; we knew when adversity hit a championship team that they would get stronger; we knew selfish penalties had to be eliminated; and we knew that special teams carried a lot of weight and their importance could not be underestimated. Our standard of performance criteria was simple for this game: "Does each player look like he is playing with the intensity of a guy who is playing his last game?" We wanted our guys playing their hearts out with passion.

We exploded out of the gate that night against Calgary in Game 1 with two quick touchdowns. Not surprisingly, the defending champions battled back, but we were able to secure the victory in the last three minutes when

ON LEADERSHIP...

"I have two primary goals as a leader. The first is to serve. When I take on this role in or out of the office, my focus is not on my personal goals or team vision, because they are already in place. Once I take myself out of the equation and concern myself with serving those around me, the energy between us flows with a unique freedom. The workplace becomes a fun and creative environment. My second goal is to squeeze out every bit of value I possibly can from every member of our team and staff. The only way to do this is by spending time with people and getting to know them — not only asking the right questions, but truly listening to the answers. Once we realize we are not in the football business or the 'widget' business, but the 'people' business, then good things begin to happen."

linebacker Chip Cox picked up a fumble and ran 70 yards for a touchdown. It was a big win for us and it felt good. After a convincing win against Edmonton in Game 2, it was time to bring our team back to Earth as we headed back west to play Saskatchewan in Game 3. Our team was playing with tremendous passion and a sense of urgency, but there were still some guys who were distracted by our early success. A year before we had started 2-0 and went on to lose three in a row. I knew it was time to talk to the guys about handling success. Part of our growth and transformation as a team was in how we handled success.

I specifically went on to talk about the media, which is everywhere in Montreal. I wanted the players to stop listening to the fairytales they were writing about us. I reminded them that these stories were designed to sell papers. I told the guys that despite all the hype that they were writing about us, building us up, we had to stay grounded. Our story needed to be focused on what was going to happen in 24 hours when we would get on a plane to go on a business trip to Regina to continue executing our plan for the week.

For three weeks we dominated our opponents, averaging 40 points a game, and outscoring them in the fourth quarter alone by a margin of 57-9. The criticism coming into the season was that the off-season would allow teams in the league to catch up with what we were doing offensively. Our coaches stayed ahead of the curve though and did a great job of executing our plan of adding on to our offensive package. We started the first month of the season at 4-0, and I reminded our guys that each and every day we got the opportunity to define ourselves.

That season we were being referred to as the "Beasts of the East," since we were the leaders in the Eastern Division. Before Game 4 against Hamilton, Anthony told the team we were not going to be the Beasts of the East that year, but the Beasts of the CFL. Upon hearing that I did a Google search and found how a beast was defined. So prior to going out in Game 4, I said, "Guys if you want to really be the beast of the CFL, you might as well know what a beast is: It is an organism that has one mission, to devour and eliminate anything in its way, no matter how much resistance!"

As we started our preparation for Game 5 on the road in Edmonton, I told the guys what I thought the definition of an Alouettes player was. He was a person who came to work to get better; had great demeanor; did anything asked of him; and whether we won or lost, he still had a humble, hard-working, and even keeled approach to work. As the media was talking about an undefeated season, we headed off to Edmonton where we lost our first game of the season. This was our team's first confrontation with adversity. We did not go into the game completely focused as a team. As much as I worked to keep our collective focus, human nature and our dominant first month of the season caused the guys to collectively lose their focus and they began to drift. As disappointed as I was in the loss, I was proud of the way they fought to the finish and didn't quit.

At our team meeting back in Montreal two days later, I told the guys it was a team loss. I was honest with them. I reminded them that we didn't play with the same edge and sense of urgency as we did in the first four games. I reminded them that our collective discipline wasn't where it needed to be. I reminded them that I had heard a few guys were not getting their rest. I reminded them that some guys had been late to meetings during the week. My consistent mantra with the team was that if one guy was doing it, then all of us were doing it.

I opened by saying this was "adversity week" and that things would not change. We would not panic, change our work week, get uptight, or lose our sense of humor. Our foundation of respect for each other, our opponent, and the game had to get kicked up a notch. I have always believed practice is not what you do on the way to the game. There has never been a player who could just turn it on and off. Rather, it is the process of respect and the emotional investment you make to be prepared to play with an emotional edge on game day.

There would be criticism in Week 6. I asked them to do the little things, cooperate, and recognize that the things they did on and off the field mattered. That week it all came together once again as our defense came out like caged animals and we defeated Toronto, 25-0. We went on to dominate in the next two games by beating Winnipeg on the road and Saskatchewan at home. As we headed into the bye week I asked the players and coaches to spend some time revisiting and renewing their vision of the 2009 Alouettes. I wanted them to get away from football for a little bit, but to still try and maintain their conditioning level. I was surprised that many of the guys stayed in Montreal to maintain their focus and get rest, it was awesome. I gave the staff time off as well so that they could go home to see our families. I went back to Raleigh to see Cindy and the girls and to get my mind right for the second half of the season.

After five days off, the team and coaches returned. I began our first meeting back by reviewing my vision of the team and having some fun by asking them if they had caught the "success flu" over the break. We had a laugh, but what I was trying to do was make a very serious point. I explained to them the symptoms of "success flu," which included contentment and a sense that "we have arrived." I explained that when a team has

MY COACHING MANTRA...

I have been very fortunate to have worked for and with some of the greatest coaches of our time. It is through their mentoring, associations, and friendship that I have been able to formulate a philosophy, or mantra, for achieving success both on and off the field:

1) To be hard working, humble, and disciplined, with a common respect for everyone in the organization, our opponents, and the game of football...

2) To be a resource to each and every player in developing their football skills and character to the highest level possible, and at the same time have them internalize that everyone associated with the team and organization is entirely interconnected with one another...

3) To communicate to everyone that they have to be accountable and that the success of the team is directly related to their individual commitment and effort...

4) To clearly define the "standard of performance" in all areas as well as the role and responsibility of each and every member of the organization...

5) To put into place a system of football that is flexible to the existing talent and personnel...

6) To produce highly efficient play at each and every position in order to win games on a weekly basis...

symptoms of the "success flu," there are different levels of effort and focus, with various degrees of discipline and teamwork. There is an inconsistent level of attention to detail. All the things that got us to where we were at 7-1 could essentially be diluted. This would cause us to lose our competitive edge. I urged the guys to keep their hunger and passion, to strive to get better, and to not take our success for granted.

Finally, I revisited one of the most important cornerstones of our program, one that goes to the core of how the great 49er teams under Bill Walsh and George Seifert operated. I defined our "Standard of Performance." Standard of Performance, or SOP, is how everything we do is measured on and off the field. It is our goal to have the highest SOP in everything we do. It is a belief system that is more than maximum effort, more than maximum sacrifice, and more than attention to detail. Our focus was to be completely present in our meetings, to keep them businesslike, and to give full attention to the coaches. SOP with the media means not drawing attention to yourself, no show boating, and being able to turn questions about YOUR success into the TEAM'S success. SOP is a value belief system, a process that allows us to improve because the bar is set so high.

During the bye week, I made a conscious decision to extend my contract with the Alouettes. It was a long process that took several months, but it was something I really wanted to do. Our owner, Bob Wetenhall, was kind enough to meet my most important request and that was to keep the extension out of the media until after the conclusion of our season. This insured that our team and organization would not be distracted by the most important goal of winning a championship. By signing that contract my most immediate goals and prayers were answered. I secured the ability to make a living while still keeping my family in Raleigh for the duration of my two daughter's high school educations. Two years after being let go at N.C. State, I was now living my dream — and more importantly, keeping my promise.

We headed to Vancouver for our first game after the bye. I found the BC Lions to be one of the more talented teams we played the previous year and I had a lot of respect for them. Both games had come down to the last minute. We split with them and lost on the road, but won at home when our defense made a goal line stand by stopping the Lions for three consecutive plays down the stretch. This game in Vancouver was no different. We were down most of the game, but in the last minute we scored an apparent touchdown that was called back when the referee said the whistle blew to stop the play. Our players were furious, but the referee's call stood and we lost the game.

Our locker room was in an uproar after the game, but I settled the team down by saying that no one play defines a game. I whole heartedly believe this to be true. You can never allow the officials to make game defining decisions like this one. Two days later the CFL made a statement that the officials were wrong and the touchdown should have counted. Our owner Bob Wetenhall put the game under protest, but to no avail. The Alouettes were 7-2 with the Lions coming to Montreal that next week for a rematch.

Instead of complaining and losing focus on something our team had no control over, our players and coaches handled this adversity in a very positive manner. We let management fight our battle so we could maintain our focus on preparing for the next game. When the media stepped in and tried to make it a game of redemption, our guys didn't take the bait. We put the loss on not doing our job in all phases of the game. We reiterated the fact that if we would have executed properly and been more detailed in our preparation, then it would have never come down to that single play. From there our players turned their focus towards the next game. At our pregame meeting the night before the game, I spoke to the team about how the emotion of redemption only lasts so long, but preparation, unselfish play, accountability and responding to adversity would enable us to succeed.

Going into that rematch game against the Lions at home that next week, I reminded the guys that our record was earned through hard work. I told them that we were a team that handled adversity collectively without complaint, and even more importantly, we had met with success in a humble and unselfish manner. I also reminded them that there was no light at the end of this tunnel and that we had a choice on this "road to greatness" that we were on. It was up to them to decide if they wanted it to be a winding road, which would cause the symptoms of the "success flu," or a straighter path that was fueled by trust, unselfishness, and a willingness to focus on winning the day. I could see that our team was evolving into something special.

We would defeat BC that night in another close game, 28-24, to get to an overall record of 9-2. Feeling energized, we went on a one month rampage and dominated our next six opponents. As we continued to win, the games took on more meaning to our team. I could see that the veterans were getting more involved and taking it upon themselves to talk to players who were drifting into a selfish or relaxed mode. Guys would periodically stop by my office to make me aware of possible letdowns that might be occurring. I listened closely during these times, and then used a team meeting to express myself passionately. I told the players that if they had a problem that it was okay to talk about it, regardless of whether or not feelings got hurt. I reminded them that a team truly is a family and that families disagree. I said that if they had a problem and didn't address it, allowing it to linger, then that could dramatically hurt the team.

That '09 season I would often refer to the CFL as the "anything can happen league," due to the fact that there were so many upsets from week to week. Every team had talented, hardworking guys. If we didn't live up to the SOP we set for ourselves each week, the opposition would win. Even if you do everything you can during the week to prepare for a team on all levels it really entitles you to nothing, but it does give you the best chance for success. If you make the mental and emotional investment during the week though, the difference will be in the execution during the games.

When I began coaching at Miami under Howard Schnellenberger, halfway through our championship season I asked him how he coped with the distractions when he was the offensive coordinator for the Dolphins' 1972 undefeated season. He didn't say anything, he just took his hand, palm flat facing the ground, and moved it horizontally in front of him. To me he was saying you had to be consistent in every way. No big ups or downs and no surprises. For the 2009 Alouettes this was my approach as well. Finding different ways to send the message each week was the challenge. One big advantage we had was that we had the right mix of veterans and younger guys, and those younger guys were buying into those veteran's model of leadership by example.

We would go on another winning streak late in the season and during this time I always tried to remind our players each day of what was important NOW. I reminded them that past performance was no indication of future success. Corrections had to be made, attention to details were of most importance, and we had to trust each other on and off the field to do the things necessary to keep our momentum going. I encouraged everyone not to be a distraction to the team in any way. I also asked them to cooperate with each other by being on time, and to spend extra time turning every page of the scouting reports that we had prepared for them.

During the week of preparation prior to the Hamilton game, I gave the team the most memorable talk of my short head coaching career. We were 12-2 at that point, a record we had clearly earned, and I wanted to remind the guys to stay focused. We were going to Hamilton to play a divisional rival and possible playoff opponent. We were getting there by train and I commented to the players about how some of them, who were out late the night before, would undoubtedly be using that time to catch up on their sleep. My comments pointed at the one or two guys left on the team who still may not have adopted our off the field level of trust that by now had prevailed on our team. I continually reminded the team throughout the season that if it was one of us, it was ALL of us.

I wanted to reinforce to them that success was very difficult to maintain on a consistent basis. Greatness in the world of professional football is so difficult to reach. I worked hard all week of practice to find a crack in our team's focus and commitment. I asked our coaches to do the same. I addressed the team the day before the game on this too. As I watched them work from meetings to walk-thrus to practices, I played a game I called "Is there any doubt?" As I went around our team meeting room I would say, "Is there any doubt that this guy is not doing what is necessary to get the job done this week?" The answer was always "there was NO DOUBT he was doing his job."

I went on to share with them some of my deeper thoughts. I said "guys, some of you may not know that the universe is said to be 15 billion years old. Although each man in here has his own set of belief systems, it would be hard to argue that all of us are in this room today because of a random act. I choose to believe this is no coincidence that we are here together today, although I certainly respect the fact that you may disagree. In a room of 75 people with multiple upbringings and various perspectives on life, this is only logical. We are in the day to day process of redefining ourselves as individuals and a team, but we are all interconnected."

I then explained, "We are not members of a team, but the team is us." I am not sure why this came out the way it did, but when I said it I stopped

266

for a moment to regain my composure. It all began to make sense to me. How could you or I ever think of ourselves as separate, because if "What you do, we do" is a fact, then how could the team exist without us? This is the only way we could exist, to find out who we were as a team and to do what I insisted all along was the ultimate goal — to be a part of something bigger than ourselves!

I further explained that night that I didn't believe that a sack just belonged to the one player who got to the quarterback and knocked him to the ground; that the touchdown run was not the running back's touchdown run alone; and that the touchdown pass didn't just belong to the quarterback and receiver. The players were beginning to see every success we had individually, belonged to all of us as a team. Conversely, the same was the case for every failure. It wasn't perfectly understood by all on that night, but we were headed in the right direction.

Once you realize it is not just about you, humility sets in. When a team is truly humble, a collective and individual sense of urgency sets in and we begin to see the true meaning of our endeavors. As I confidently said to them, "Guys, the illusion is we are 12-2, the reality is we are 0-0. The illusion is we are members of a team, the reality is the team is us!"

We beat Hamilton, 41-38, that week and I was really proud of the way the guys played. I reminded them afterward that every game was a new story and that there were a lot of different ways to win. I reminded them that although we had some things to clean up structurally in our execution, that all wins are truly to be appreciated. Again, I told them how proud I was of the players as well as the coaches. During those three hours in Hamilton, our team was stressed to the max physically and emotionally, yet and found a way to win. Winning close games benefited all of us as we started down the final road to finding out exactly who we were as a team.

At the team meeting two days later, I reminded the team we were 13-2 and breathing the "rarified air" very few teams had the privilege of breathing in the nearly 100 year history of the CFL. I reminded them that this was a very humbling position to be in. I wanted them to take the time that day to really appreciate where they were, and what they had accomplished to that point in the season. So I welcomed them to "appreciation day" as I phrased it. I wanted them to understand the nature, quality, and magnitude of the situation that existed presently.

I also spoke from my heart and told them that way down the road, at the reunion, it would not be about the wins, the hardware, or the stats; it would be about the relationships they had developed and the love in our locker room that had evolved throughout the year. I was adamant about them not drifting through the season without recognizing just what was really going on. Every year I religiously watch the NFL Hall of Fame inductions, and without exception, each inductee talks most about the friendships and relationships they had with the players and coaches on their team. I summed it up by stating, "So guys, when you feel appreciation, it not only humbles you, but it raises your level of accountability, forces you to inherently focus, brings clarity to the present, and creates a contagious positive energy that permeates your environment."

As we approached Game 16 against Winnipeg, we were going to have to do it without Anthony, who had strained his calf muscle. His backup was Adrian McPherson, who had come into the game the week before and threw the game-winning touchdown in the final minutes. We knew we were going into a playoff environment in Winnipeg, a team loaded with speed, offensive talent, and an active defense. We would have to be at our best in support of Adrian, who had gotten very little practice time throughout the season. The good news was that we had already clinched our division and secured home-field advantage for the playoffs.

We left Winnipeg that Saturday with a 41-24 loss. For the second straight week our defense was torched for over 500 yards of offense and I was not pleased. The week before, this weakness in our pass defense was covered up in a win over Hamilton, but it could not be disguised in this week's loss to a much better team. Even more problematic was the fact that we were set to play Winnipeg again eight days later. After the game I was brief. I always took time after wins and losses to take a deep breath and clear my head before speaking with the team. I never wanted to say anything to the team that I would later regret, especially relating to our effort or level of play. On this day I was no different. I did, however, tell them that I did not see a collective focus nor did I feel a high level of energy in our play. Beyond that, I told them that we had errors in our coverage scheme that needed to be addressed. That was it.

The next week was an amazing growing process for our team at every level.

Our defensive staff worked relentlessly and took complete accountability for the defensive breakdowns of the last few weeks. I knew that defensive injuries had depleted our productivity over that time, but we never used it as an excuse for our lack of success. Our defensive leadership came to the forefront as player segments spent more time outside the four and a half hour rule to make sure communication and assignments were clarified. As late as it was in the season, combined with the fact that we were playing the same team, I cut practices short in order to leave more time for our walk-thrus, to watch video, and for individual meetings.

We did not panic. I told them that our competition was locked in and focused and that we must do the same so as to not lose our edge. There is no way a team can consciously turn it on an off and win a championship, NO WAY! I reminded our team early that not everyone was hearing the message. And if they were, they were not interpreting it in the same manner. I explained to the guys that circumstances change and adversity hits amidst great success, but that our team had developed a very strong backbone due to hard work over the course of the last two years. All that mattered was for us to continue our pursuit of the highest standard of performance in everything we did from that point through the end of our season.

Then, when I heard players come into the meeting room with coffee in their hand and complaining that they were tired, I jumped down their throats. I told them that their bitching was just "themselves telling a story to separate themselves from the rest of the team." They got the message. Professional football seasons are tough and everyone is fatigued, but you don't outwardly complain about it because it serves no purpose other than to make you "special," which ultimately causes the team to lose focus.

I summarized that day's meeting with an obvious statement, around a philosophy that all our players and coaches had come to understand. I said, "After our one-sided loss in Winnipeg, do you see why we won't exactly know the team we will become until December? We have a team with Grey Cup experience, character, future Hall of Fame players, and for the second straight year we are riding the wave of one of the greatest quarterbacks north or south of the border to ever play the game!" I finished with this, "Guys, we are 60 minutes, 57+3, from going to Calgary and for a chance to ride in an unforgettable parade through downtown Montreal. It's an opportunity of a lifetime and it's your choice. Do you want it?"

We went out that Sunday and demolished the Bombers. Anthony was brilliant once again, completing 27 of 38 passes for over 300 yards with two TDs and no interceptions. Our defense was vicious and structurally sound, holding Winnipeg's quarterback to just 145 yards of passing. We never panicked, our coaches came up with great game plans, and the players executed it with undivided passion and urgency. We had gotten our swagger back after two weeks of dealing with adversity. We beat Winnipeg with the same edge that we had beaten Calgary with nearly four months earlier. The 2009 Alouettes were now 14-3, tied for the best record in franchise history, and were undefeated at home. This just strengthened my belief that we were doing things philosophically the right way. The season had flown by with a common purpose to simply "win the day."

Before that week's Winnipeg game, I heard our leaders bring the team together and make a commitment to be 4-0 in the last month. We were now 1-0 in November with what the CFL termed a "meaningless" game in Toronto the following week. I spent a lot of time on the player's day off that week speaking with our staff and some key players to try to put Game 18 against Toronto into perspective. We had the opportunity as a team to move from rarified air to sacred ground. A win in Toronto would make us 15-3 and leave us with the best record in franchise history. A year earlier we lost our last game in Edmonton because we played conservatively. We left Anthony on the bench, we left some players at home, and took our starters out early in order to make sure nobody got hurt.

With that, the team entered the meeting room to start the week of our last game against the worst team in the league that season. Everyone was aware that we were playing a team with a solid defense and an offense that had been consistently unproductive all year. They had traded an all-league receiver and were going to start a rookie quarterback who had no CFL experience. The guys would be listening closely to how we were going to handle the week and approach the game.

I began by asking our guys to completely trust our approach to the game. We wanted to win, but we would apply a forward looking approach to protect the best interests of the team and to prepare for the playoffs. We had two or three guys that were injured and it was in the team's best interest to let them heel up for two weeks before the Eastern Finals. The next issue was the ratio requirement. In the CFL you have to start seven

Canadians and have 20 on the game day roster. Because of injuries, certain guys who were season starters would not only have to play, but play the entire game. Finally, we had to use common sense. We would be lacking common sense if we played Anthony. He was our leader and the key to our chances of winning the Grey Cup. He was having an MVP season and we were not going to risk and injury by playing him against one of the league's most vicious defenses. By doing this, we would give our backup Adrian McPherson the start and more reps in case he was forced into duty during the playoffs.

I challenged the team to play all 57 + 3 of the game that was ahead. I told the players I didn't know how long we would individually play them, but that they had to play with passion and respect for our opponent and for our team. I told them that this game carried the same importance as any game we had played all year, because this was the only one we were guaranteed. I challenged them to finish the game the way we started the season in Calgary and when it was all said and done, the guys did not disappoint.

What resulted was a game I will never forget. The players completely bought into our plan. They played with a vengeance, helped out wherever they could on special teams, and let the scoreboard take care of itself. We won the game 42-7. It was our 12th game of 30 points or more, and the second year in a row our team scored 600 points. Adrian got the work necessary to continue to gain the confidence of his teammates and we came out of the game healthy. A game that had the perception of being meaningless to the world around us was played as if it was the most important game ever played. We left Toronto that night a team that had "gotten it!"

It was now Sunday morning, the day following our win in Toronto. We had earned a bye week off, which was fantastic. The calendar had let the guys know that this meeting would be short and informative, as the players would be excused for five days while the coaches began our preparation for the Eastern Finals. I reminded our guys we were 15 days from publishing our book. Our book that was going to define the team we had become, and was about to be completed. I asked them to get rest, to take care of final arrangements for family and tickets, and to get some weight lifting and conditioning in during the week. I told them I wanted to see them back the following Saturday morning ready to practice hard and ready to compete. We had a plan, and we were quietly confident.

We always had a plan. In fact, our players always had a calendar one month in advance so they could put into action their plan for weekly preparation of study and sleep, to plane reservations to off days. When I gave them the November schedule for the Grey Cup they had all of our travel and practice plan information up to the Grey Cup game, including the day of the parade. Yes, even the day of the parade. Before they left for the bye week, I wanted them to understand all of the peripheral issues that they could get done early so that they could focus on football once we returned to practice. I wanted them out of the travel and ticket business as soon as possible. One guy's lack of focus was our team's lack of focus.

On our return to practice that Saturday we had a short meeting and a terrific practice. There was no team to prepare for because the Eastern Semifinal game wasn't to be played until Sunday afternoon. So we just lined up against each other, the best offense and the best defense in the CFL, viscously competing for a 75 minute practice on Saturday and Sunday. I truly believe that our competitive periods going first team against first team have been one of the cornerstones of our team's success the last two years. The only way to get better is to pit the best against the best. When you can do so in a cooperative manner so that both sides can stay safe and injury free, you have the opportunity to get better individually and as a team. We then gave the players two days off to rest as the coaches prepared for our third game of the year against the BC Lions in the playoffs.

It was the day of the big game and I reminded our team that this was a moment we had envisioned since June 1st, the opening day of training camp. It was comforting to know that the guys next to us were prepared to hold up their end of the bargain as well. We were once again quietly confident, respectful of our opponent, and appreciative of the opportunity. And even though we had played to a tie in the four game total of points over the past two years, I said to the team, "Guys, let's be honest, it should not be close." They apparently agreed. That afternoon we exploded to beat the Lions, 56-18. In two days we would be on a plane headed to Calgary with a date to meet the Saskatchewan Roughriders for the Grey Cup and the CFL Championship.

One of the great things about being a head coach is giving out game balls after wins. As I said earlier, we never made it a common practice to do it, but after this game I wanted to honor our GM, Jim Popp. As I told the team, "There was one guy solely responsible for all of us having the opportunity to be here and that was Jim." The guys gave him a great ovation and Jim was extremely emotional and appreciative. To hear that he had never received a game ball in 14 years was astounding because was the one constant in the success of the Alouettes organization over that time.

We didn't practice the first day after arriving in Calgary. We had meetings and walk-thrus, but the plan was to allow the players to rest. The thought was that we had played an emotionally and physically exhausting game on Sunday, the travel west would take its toll, and we were used to the process throughout the season of only practicing two days. Also, the memory of the 2002 Super Bowl while I was with Oakland were still vivid in my mind. As such, we were going to be a rested football team.

That Thursday, after watching tape, the staff and I concluded that the team lacked effort and concentration, and did not meet the standard of practice performance we were accustomed to throughout the year. We had beaten the Riders handily during the season and I became concerned that after all the work and lessons learned the last two years, we were now taking this very good team too lightly. So at the morning meeting on Friday I specifically told the players they had disrespected the opponent in yesterday's practice and disrespected each other. I told them they were practicing just to save themselves for the game and that was a lack of trust of the coaching staff. I told them the football gods were watching and taking notes. I told them we were a team that had practiced like a game each day but now we had decided to change our mode of operation. I told them that we failed to trust the program and in the end we did NOT win the day.

The next day was awesome. The guys were extremely responsive. Because we compete hard in practice, the offense or defense doesn't always have consistent success and therefore our practices are measured by legitimate competition. This gives us the backbone and sense of urgency necessary to fight through all kinds of adversity — the kind of urgency and adversity we could not even imagine that would ensue two days later against the Riders.

I never really think about a pregame message until the day I have to give it. My reason is that I want to really feel the game by adding every bit of logic and emotion when necessary to reach as many players as I can. In

"Having Marc as our coach in Montreal has been fantastic. It has been wonderful getting to know him, he is really a great person. He had to learn so much coming in that first season, it was just incredible how he was able to bring himself up to speed. He practically lived in his office. He would get there at like five in the morning and stay until eight at night. It was really impressive to see him come in to an entirely new system, with new rules that were completely foreign to him, and find success the way that he did."

"The key for him that I was most impressed with was how he came in and asked questions, and then listened. Marc is a great listener. He listens to his players and respects their opinions. Even when he came in, he got together with the veteran players and really got their input as far as which plays were successful and which ones weren't. He asked them about how we should run camp; about our offensive schemes; and about the culture of our locker room. He soaked it all in and made us a part of the process."

"As a coach he is a great teacher and I am really appreciative for all that he has done for me. I have a lot of respect for him, he is such a knowledgeable guy. Marc is a great motivator too. He motivates through trust. That didn't happen overnight, but it was a process that evolved into something pretty special. There were times when a play would come up that I didn't agree with and he would listen to me. If I didn't like it, he trusted me enough to not run it. He gave me a lot of leeway with those types of things and I appreciated that. That is something that a lot of coaches wouldn't do. He treated me like a professional and that was extremely motivating to me."

"Marc took trust to a whole new level. In fact, we never really talked on game day, which was very unique. He prepared me during the week, and then let me do my thing from there. He trusted me. He might ask me how I was doing the day of a game, but that was it. I would mostly talk to the offensive coordinator during the game. He was a great manager that way, in that he would hire good people who he trusted to do their jobs."

"Each week he has new plays drawn up for us, specifically designed for that week's opponents. Talk about being able to adapt, it was amazing. He was able to take those plays and get us to take ownership of them. He would always find a way to make them interesting too, and not repetitive, so that we didn't get bored with them. He set very high expectations from the very beginning, and that was good for us. We always knew where he stood right out of the gates, and that meant a lot.

His demeanor never changed or wavered from that either. As players, we respected that."

"Marc also taught us how to be humble and how not to make it about ourselves. He brought his personality from off the field, onto the field, and that was something I had never seen before. For instance, he said that if we were going to celebrate after a big play, that we should do it as a group, rather than by ourselves. It was all about the team first, and that really resonated with the players. He wanted to make sure it was never about the individual, but rather about the entire team. It was a great message."

"Everybody continued to buy into his message, because he stressed it from Day One and reinforced it as we went. Everybody understood what he wanted from us and we all wanted to be a part of that. None of us players knew what to expect from him, but as we went along he gained our trust and confidence. We knew that he understood the Xs and Os better than anybody we had ever seen before, so we were just anxious to learn as much as we could from him."

"Throughout the season he just knows the right things to say when we are winning as well as when we are losing. I have never been around a coach who had a feel for a team that way, which was pretty special. He knows how to handle a team, from the top down. I mean on top of all of his coaching duties, he has to be an administrator too. There were so many little things that were popping up here and there, and he just rolled with the punches with all of that stuff. He handles everything and never lets it get to him, which I think is very impressive."

"All in all we had a great first year under Marc. Losing the Grey Cup was tough and we were all disappointed, but Marc helped us to keep it all in perspective. When you look back at the journey that we had, and from where we started from, we did some special things that 2008 season. Nobody expected us to compete for a championship that year but we proved them all wrong. We had a new coach, a new coaching staff, a new system and a lot of new players. So, to go from that on the opening day of training camp to the Grey Cup was a big deal up here."

"Then, to go from runner-up to champions the very next year, what can you say — amazing. It was no fluke that Marc was named as Coach of the Year, the guy is just a tremendous leader. We just hope that he will lead us to many, many more Grey Cups down the road. He showed us how great winning "unselfishly and with humility" can be and we all want to experience it again and again." — *Anthony Calvillo, Quarterback, Montreal Alouettes* most cases it just sort of comes to me and because of the work and effort throughout the week I feel there is something worthwhile to bring to the team's attention. This time I asked the guys to smile and to take a deep breath. I reminded everybody we were a team with our feet firmly planted on the ground on the same spot we started our journey almost five months earlier right here in Calgary. It was no coincidence we were in the Grey Cup. It was the result of a collective vision that was executed with passion to almost perfection. We never looked too far ahead and only looked back to learn from our mistakes. As I said to the team, "Even at 16-3, with all the praise and attention this team had, we were entitled to what?" And they responded by saying "Nothing!". We still had to go out and earn it. I told them to go out and play Alouettes football — violent, unparalleled passionate, with no man carrying more weight than the other. We all had each other's back. With that, we said our team prayer and hit the field.

Three hours later we had arguably played the most exciting Grey Cup in CFL history. We were not the Alouettes we intended to be in the first half though. We turned the ball over twice and were lucky to be down 17-3 at the half. It was a 30 minute halftime and during that time I asked the coaches to spend most of their time with our players, supporting them emotionally and getting them ready for the second half. I took the time to gather my thoughts. Then, at the five minute warning I went into the locker room. I reminded the defense that they had to go two-and-out on the Rider's first drive, and I reminded the offense that they then had to respond after the punt with a score. Amazingly, that is exactly what happened and we were back in the game.

The Riders didn't stop playing though and with 10 minutes left in this very physical game, we were down 27-11. This is when the Als really showed up and the team's backbone and collective sense of urgency came to the forefront. Our offense was executing at the highest level; from protection, to the run game, to the passing game. We were running on all cylinders. Our defense was now playing great and in a blink the score was 27-25. Then, with 1:40 left in the game we went for a two point conversion. Our receiver was clearly interfered with but there was no call. So, we lined up to kick-off and we left it up to our defense to make the stop, and they did. I had told them for five months that we had a chance to be a great defense and now was the time to prove it. Our defense did their job, forcing a two-and-out.

Our offense then took over from our own 40 yard line with just 40 seconds left in the game. Anthony stayed composed and we methodically drove down the field. We first converted on a second-and-long, followed by a third-and-three. From there we lost a challenge, followed by a second-and-10 conversion. Then, with just two seconds remaining on the clock, we lined up for a field goal. On a beautiful, late November night, with a light breeze from behind us, Damon Duval, our All-League kicker stepped up to make history. The center snapped the ball, the holder put it down and then Damon kicked it... missing the uprights wide to the right. My heart sank. But then, miraculously, the football gods intervened as penalty flags were thrown all over the field. The Alouettes had new life. Miraculously, the Riders had too many men on the field and we would get another shot for the win. With no time left on the clock, Damon kicked the ball through the uprights to give us the thrilling win. We had won the Grey Cup, the championship was ours.

The highlight of the night for me came afterward, when I was able to help Cindy, Sarahanne, and Chloe out of the stands and onto the field to celebrate the win with the team. What an amazing feeling, truly something that I will never forget. Finally, after over an hour on the field celebrating with players, coaches, and family, I spoke briefly to the team in an excited locker room. We congratulated the Riders, but for us the fairy tale had become a reality and it was time for game balls to be given out. One to our owner, Bob Wetenhall, who has done so much for the CFL and the Alouettes, and the other to our leader, Anthony Calvillo.

As for my future? I am already thinking about the repeat. No team has been a repeat winner of the Grey Cup in the last 15 years, so that would be my goal, to win it again in 2010. My biggest challenge will undoubtedly be overcoming the complacency and contentment that can permeate an organization after a championship season. I have calls to make to players and coaches, as well as gathering information from some of the great coaches who have been in the position of preparing their teams for repeats. It won't be easy, and it shouldn't be. What a new and exciting challenge. As a coach, it doesn't get any better than this!

"A great coach does more than lead others, he inspires them to lead. Marc Trestman is a great coach." — Mark Cohon, CFL Commissioner

Approximately 180 days from the start of training camp, the 2009 Montreal Alouettes completed their journey in Calgary, the same place, ironically, that they "found out exactly who they were." In the last 10 minutes of the 2009 Grey Cup game, every player and coach found a way to contribute and was instrumental in our team's success. I think about the hard work, focus, and unselfishness that existed in our locker room during that time. Over those six months there were times that individuals could have put themselves ahead of the team, but honestly, they didn't, and in the end these men got exactly what they deserved. A championship ring, a parade two days after the game in front of our amazing fans, and a life lesson that allowed them to be part of something bigger than themselves.

In the team meeting the day after the Grey Cup we said goodbye to a team that would never be together again. In 2010 there will certainly be new players and possibly new coaches. With that, chemistry will change and we will start all over again. I concluded by asking each player to do one more thing: to tell our story of collective faith that we had in each other; of our team vision, and of the day to day passion we had to execute in order to "win the day." I assured them that it would be a story worth telling, and one that would change lives forever.

Raising the Grey Cup with my girls, what a thrill!

EPILOGUE

As I sit here in Raleigh almost four months after our Grey Cup victory, so much has happened. First of all, I have been able to spend time doing what I had planned to do, and that is take the girls to school and to their cheerleading events. Second, I took Cindy on a fabulous 20th wedding anniversary trip to the Caribbean. Third, I have been able to walk the dogs, which is something I really missed while I was up in Montreal. I have also had the good fortune of working with some pretty high profile college quarterbacks in Jimmy Clausen and Tim Tebow, preparing them for the 2010 NFL Combine and Draft. In addition, I had the opportunity to work with several high school and college quarterbacks to improve their skills as well. This is an opportunity for me to keep my quarterback coaching skills sharp and do what I love, and that's to coach the quarterback. Further, I am close to finishing another book on the "essence" of the quarterback position, which I am very excited about.

Winning the Coach of the Year Award in 2009 was such an amazing honor...

Finally, with the Grey Cup win came the opportunity to speak to various business groups and associations about my thoughts on leadership. My new keynote program "Leadership Lessons on the Way to the Grey Cup" is full of content and I have thoroughly enjoyed being out on the speaking circuit. I am very passionate about leadership and I consider it to be such a blessing to be able to serve others. It has been a growing experience for me as well and has really forced me to think and grow as an individual. I love it.

In a sense, this is halftime for me in my life, both personally and professionally. I feel like I am still learning as I go and I still have a lot to offer. I am enjoying the journey, the process, and am anxious to overcome the challenges and obstacles that present themselves along the way. The bottom line for me is that I have a real passion for teaching and an immense desire to serve others in whatever capacity I can. It just feels really good to do that. I don't know what lies ahead, but I am excited to keep coaching football as long as somebody will let me. Thank you for letting me share my story of perseverance with you, I sincerely hope that you learned something along the way.

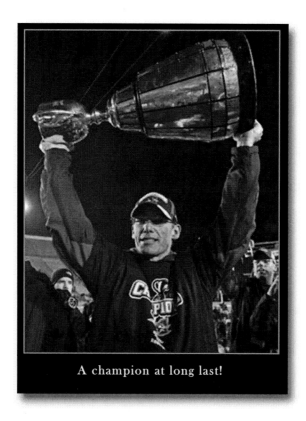

A champion at long last!